Democracy Promotion, National Security and Strategy

Robert Pee delivers a carefully crafted, nuanced, and comprehensive study of the rise of democracy promotion as a critical component of US foreign policy under the Reagan administration. The analysis is insightful and sophisticated, offering an excellent understanding of the sources of tensions that animate US democracy promotion's purpose and practices from its inception to the present days.

Dr Jeff Bridoux, *Lecturer in International Politics, Aberystwyth University, UK*

This book investigates the relationship between democracy promotion and US national security strategy through an examination of the Reagan administration's attempt to launch a global campaign for democracy in the early 1980s, which culminated in the foundation of the National Endowment for Democracy in 1983.

Through a case study of the formation and early operations of the National Endowment for Democracy under the Reagan administration, based on primary documents from both the national security bureaucracy and the private sector, this book shows that while democracy promotion provided a new tactical approach to the conduct of US political warfare operations, these operations remained tied to the achievement of traditional national security goals such as destabilising enemy regimes and building stable and legitimate friendly governments, rather than being guided by a strategy based on the universal promotion of democracy.

Analysing the relationships between state agencies and non-state actors in the field of democracy promotion, and the strategic and organisational tensions that act to limit the promotion of democracy by the US, this book will be of interest to students and scholars of US Foreign Policy, Democracy Promotion and the Reagan Administration.

Robert Pee obtained his PhD at the University of Birmingham in 2013. His research interests focus on US national security strategy, democracy promotion and the role of non-state actors in the formation and implementation of US foreign policy.

Routledge Studies in US Foreign Policy
Edited by
Inderjeet Parmar
City University
and
John Dumbrell
University of Durham

This new series sets out to publish high quality works by leading and emerging scholars critically engaging with United States Foreign Policy. The series welcomes a variety of approaches to the subject and draws on scholarship from international relations, security studies, international political economy, foreign policy analysis and contemporary international history.

Subjects covered include the role of administrations and institutions, the media, think tanks, ideologues and intellectuals, elites, transnational corporations, public opinion, and pressure groups in shaping foreign policy, US relations with individual nations, with global regions and global institutions and America's evolving strategic and military policies.

The series aims to provide a range of books – from individual research monographs and edited collections to textbooks and supplemental reading for scholars, researchers, policy analysts, and students.

United States Foreign Policy and National Identity in the 21st Century
Edited by Kenneth Christie

New Directions in US Foreign Policy
Edited by Inderjeet Parmar, Linda B. Miller and Mark Ledwidge

America's 'Special Relationships'
Foreign and domestic aspects of the politics of alliance
Edited by John Dumbrell and Axel R. Schäfer

US Foreign Policy in Context
National ideology from the founders to the Bush doctrine
Adam Quinn

The United States and NATO since 9/11
The transatlantic alliance renewed
Ellen Hallams

Soft Power and US Foreign Policy
Theoretical, historical and contemporary perspectives
Edited by Inderjeet Parmar and Michael Cox

The US Public and American Foreign Policy
Edited by Andrew Johnstone and Helen Laville

American Foreign Policy and Postwar Reconstruction
Comparing Japan and Iraq
Jeff Bridoux

Neoconservatism and American Foreign Policy
A critical analysis
Danny Cooper

US Policy Towards Cuba
Since the Cold War
Jessica F. Gibbs

Constructing US Foreign Policy
The curious case of Cuba
David Bernell

Race and US Foreign Policy
The African-American foreign affairs network
Mark Ledwidge

Gender Ideologies and Military Labor Markets in the U.S.
Saskia Stachowitsch

Prevention, Pre-Emption and the Nuclear Option
From Bush to Obama
Aiden Warren

Corporate Power and Globalization in US Foreign Policy
Edited by Ronald W. Cox

West Africa and the US War on Terror
Edited by George Klay Kieh and Kelechi Kalu

Constructing America's Freedom Agenda for the Middle East
Oz Hassan

The Origins of the US War on Terror
Lebanon, Libya and American intervention in the Middle East
Mattia Toaldo

US Foreign Policy and the Rogue State Doctrine
Alex Miles

US Foreign Policy and Democracy Promotion
From Theodore Roosevelt to Barack Obama
Edited by Michael Cox, Timothy J. Lynch and Nicolas Bouchet

Local Interests and American Foreign Policy
Why international interventions fail
Karl Sandstrom

The Obama Administration's Nuclear Weapon Strategy
The promises of Prague
Aiden James Warren

Obama's Foreign Policy
Ending the War on Terror
Michelle Bentley and Jack Holland

United States–Africa Security Relations
Terrorism, regional security and national interests
Edited by Kelechi A. Kalu and George Klay Kieh, Jr.

Obama and the World
New directions in US foreign policy
2nd edition
Edited by Inderjeet Parmar, Linda B. Miller and Mark Ledwidge

The United States, Iraq and the Kurds
Mohammed Shareef

Weapons of Mass Destruction and US Foreign Policy
The strategic use of a concept
Michelle Bentley

American Images of China
Identity, power, policy
Oliver Turner

North Korea–US Relations under Kim Jong II
The quest for normalization?
Ramon Pacheco Pardo

Congressional Policymaking in the Post-Cold War Era
Sino-U.S. relations
Joseph Gagliano

US Foreign Policy and China
Bush's first term
Guy Roberts

Presidential Rhetoric from Wilson to Obama
Constructing crises, fast and slow
Wesley Widmaier

American Exceptionalism
An idea that made a nation and remade the world
Hilde Restad

The President, the State and the Cold War
Comparing the foreign policies of Truman and Reagan
James Bilsland

Democracy Promotion, National Security and Strategy
Foreign policy under the Reagan Administration
Robert Pee

Democracy Promotion as US Foreign Policy
Bill Clinton and democratic enlargement
Nicolas Bouchet

Democracy Promotion, National Security and Strategy

Foreign policy under the Reagan Administration

Robert Pee

LONDON AND NEW YORK

First published 2016
by Routledge
2 Park Square, Milton Park, Abingdon, Oxon OX14 4RN

and by Routledge
711 Third Avenue, New York, NY 10017

Routledge is an imprint of the Taylor & Francis Group, an informa business

© 2016 Robert Pee

The right of Robert Pee to be identified as author of this work has been asserted by him in accordance with sections 77 and 78 of the Copyright, Designs and Patents Act 1988.

All rights reserved. No part of this book may be reprinted or reproduced or utilised in any form or by any electronic, mechanical, or other means, now known or hereafter invented, including photocopying and recording, or in any information storage or retrieval system, without permission in writing from the publishers.

Trademark notice: Product or corporate names may be trademarks or registered trademarks, and are used only for identification and explanation without intent to infringe.

British Library Cataloguing in Publication Data
A catalogue record for this book is available from the British Library

Library of Congress Cataloging in Publication Data
Pee, Robert.
Democracy promotion, national security and strategy : foreign policy under the Reagan administration / Robert Pee.
    pages cm. – (Routledge studies in US foreign policy)
    Includes bibliographical references.
    1. United States–Foreign relations–1981–1989. 2. Democracy–
    Government policy–United States. 3. National Endowment for
    Democracy (U.S.) I. Title.
    E876.P44 2015
    327.73009'048–dc23   2015003333

ISBN: 978-1-138-82865-0 (hbk)
ISBN: 978-1-315-73807-9 (ebk)

Typeset in Times New Roman
by Wearset Ltd, Boldon, Tyne and Wear

Printed and bound in the United States of America by Publishers Graphics, LLC on sustainably sourced paper.

Contents

Acknowledgements	viii
List of abbreviations	ix
Introduction: democracy and national security in US foreign policy	1
1 The roots of democracy promotion: from covert operations and modernisation to party-building	10
2 Democracy and national security during the early Reagan administration: no grand design	40
3 Democracy promotion and national security policy	71
4 Building a consensus for democracy promotion	97
5 The foundation of the National Endowment for Democracy	128
6 Promoting democracy	150
Conclusion: US democracy promotion during the final phase of the Cold War and beyond	187
Bibliography	200
Index	212

Acknowledgements

This book began as a PhD thesis researched at the University of Birmingham, stimulated by my interest in US democracy promotion. The writing of this book was a solitary enterprise, but it and the research it is based on could not have been completed without help from many quarters. My earnest thanks go to: Professor Scott Lucas of the University of Birmingham, who provided invaluable advice and guidance as my PhD supervisor; Professor Giles Scott-Smith and Doctor Steven Hewitt, who offered perceptive suggestions for the improvement of the work; the staff of the Ronald Reagan Presidential Library in Simi Valley, California, and the Library of Congress; and the organisers of the Transatlantic Studies Association Conference, 49th Parallel Conference and British Association for American Studies Conference, and the editorial staff of US Studies Online, for giving me the chance to present a portion of my ideas to others. Finally, thanks go to my family – Stuart, Linda, Thomas, James, Nicola and Asher – for their unstinting support. Without them, this book could not have been written.

Abbreviations

AAFLI	Asian American Free Labor Institute (US)
AALC	African American Labor Council (US)
AFL-CIO	American Federation of Labor-Congress of Industrial Organizations (US)
AID	Agency for International Development (US)
AIFLD	American Institute for Free Labor Development (US)
APF	American Political Foundation (US)
CGT	General Confederation of Labour (France)
CIA	Central Intelligence Agency (US)
CIPE	Center for International Private Enterprise (US)
COMELEC	Commission on Elections (Philippines)
CPD	Committee on the Present Danger (US)
CPSU	Communist Party of the Soviet Union (USSR)
CSIS	Center for Strategic and International Studies (US)
CTP	Confederation of Workers (Peru)
CUS	Confederation of Trade Union Unity (Nicaragua)
CUSG	Trade Union Confederation of Guatemala (Guatemala)
DIA	Defence Intelligence Agency (US)
DNC	Democratic National Committee (US)
FAO	Broad Opposition Front (Nicaragua)
FSLN	Sandinista National Liberation Front (Nicaragua)
FTUI	Free Trade Union Institute (US)
GABRIELA	Assembly Binding Women for Reforms, Integrity, Equality, Leadership, and Action (Philippines)
IPC	International Political Committee (US)
IRI	International Republican Institute (formerly NRI) (US)
KABATID	Women's Movement for the Nurturing of Democracy (Philippines)
KMU	May First Movement (Philippines)
NAMFREL	National Citizens' Movement for Free Elections (Philippines)
NDI	National Democratic Institute (US)
NED	National Endowment for Democracy (US)
NLC	National Labor Center (Nigeria)

x *Abbreviations*

NNP	New National Party (Grenada)
NPA	New People's Army (Philippines)
NRI	National Republican Institute (now International Republican Institute, US)
NSA	National Security Advisor (US)
NSC	National Security Council (US)
NSDD	National Security Decision Directive
NSSD	National Security Study Directive
OAS	Organization of American States
ORIT	Inter-American Regional Organisation of Workers (Latin America)
PSD	Socialist Democratic Party (Guatemala)
PZPR	Polish United Workers' Party (Poland)
RAM	Reform the Armed Forces Movement (Philippines)
RFE	Radio Free Europe (US)
RNC	Republican National Committee (US)
TUCP	Trade Union Congress of the Philippines (Philippines)
UCN	Nationalist Change Union (Guatemala)
UDT	Democratic Workers Union (Chile)
UNI	Inter-University Union (France)
USIA	United States Information Agency (US)
USICA	United States International Communications Agency (USIA before 1978 and after August 1982, US)
VOA	Voice of America (US)

Introduction

Democracy and national security in US foreign policy

The world must be made safe for democracy. Its peace must be planted upon the tested foundations of political liberty.

Woodrow Wilson, 1917[1]

I believe that it must be the policy of the United States to support free peoples who are resisting attempted subjugation by armed minorities or by outside pressures.

Harry S. Truman, 1947[2]

Let every nation know, whether it wishes us well or ill, that we shall pay any price, bear any burden, meet any hardship, support any friend, oppose any foe to assure the survival and the success of liberty.

John F. Kennedy, 1961[3]

... it is the policy of the United States to seek and support the growth of democratic movements and institutions in every nation and culture, with the ultimate goal of ending tyranny in our world.

George W. Bush, 2005[4]

US policymakers have consistently claimed that the US has a special mission to protect and support the spread of democracy, both to assist other countries and to create a more secure world for itself. However, the US' foreign policy record is much more ambiguous and also includes hostility to democratic governments and support for dictatorships. This ambiguity has spurred a constant and continuing debate between scholars who see the promotion of democracy as a key element of US strategy and others who argue that, in practice, democratic rhetoric has been used as a tool to legitimate the pursuit of other goals.

Liberals and neoconservatives argue that efforts to democratise foreign societies have played a key role in US national security policies. The most comprehensive statement of the this view is made by Tony Smith, who argues that 'Since Wilson's time, the most consistent tradition in American foreign policy ... has been the belief that the nation's security is best protected by the expansion of democracy worldwide'[5] and that this had been 'the greatest ambition of

2   Introduction

United States foreign policy over the past century'.[6] Smith cites the creation of democratic institutions in the Philippines during its period of American rule, the foreign policy of Woodrow Wilson, the democratisation of Germany and Japan under the Truman administration, the Alliance for Progress in Latin America under John F. Kennedy and Ronald Reagan's crusade for democracy against Soviet communism in support of his argument.[7] Similarly, Joshua Muravchik claims that the US has been 'the engine of [the] transformation'[8] of much of the world in a more democratic direction, while Henry Nau argues that by containing the Soviet Union during the Cold War, the US, 'played the key role in defending and strengthening democracy.'[9] G. John Ikenberry sees the promotion of democracy as one component of a US liberal grand strategy which also included the creation of international institutions and an open world economy after World War Two.[10] While these scholars acknowledge that the export of democracy is not the only motive for US actions abroad, and that the US has sometimes engaged in foreign policy behaviour that violates its ideals, they do argue that in US foreign policy the impulse to spread democracy and pragmatic national security goals are often conjoined and are mutually reinforcing.

In contrast, academics working within a leftist/progressive or conservative/realist framework argue that the goal of spreading democracy has not had a significant impact on US foreign policy practice except at the rhetorical level, where the use of democratic ideals 'mobilize(s) domestic forces and resources' to legitimate the pursuit of goals unconnected with democracy overseas.[11] The reality of US foreign policy practice is that democracy has been subordinated to other foreign policy considerations, and ideological declarations '[are] all too often scarcely more than public-relations exercises.'[12] William Appleman Williams, Gabriel Kolko and Noam Chomsky argue that US foreign policy has been largely driven by the need to secure foreign markets, investment opportunities and supplies of raw materials, not democracy;[13] David Ryan and David Schmitz broaden this economic argument to include security motivations. Ryan argues that democracy has often been secondary to other US interests such as stability, order and the exercise of hegemony,[14] while Schmitz contends that US rhetoric on democracy and human rights has been belied by support of authoritarian regimes as a more expedient method of containing Marxist forces, ensuring that key countries pursued a pro-US foreign policy and creating a supportive environment for US business interests abroad.[15] Stephen Kinzer goes further, noting that during the Cold War the US overthrew democratic or constitutional governments in Iran, Guatemala and Chile.[16] These actions are seen as representative of US foreign policy practice rather than as unfortunate deviations from a policy based on the extension of democracy. Thus, the goal of exporting democracy is subordinated to other motives and often in tension with them.

An important factor preventing a clear analysis of the role of democracy in US foreign policy is the tendency of both of these groups of scholars to focus on the cases that support their own theoretical frameworks. The fact that many of the studies that champion a connection between supporting democracy overseas and national security have been aimed at prescribing future policy in these terms has often led scholars such as Smith and Muravchik to highlight those cases in which they believed democracy and US national security reinforced each other in the past, while minimising discussion of counter-examples. Similarly, more critical works tend to minimise discussion of those cases in which the US has promoted democracy, or to treat democracy promotion as a rationale for policy rather than an element of it.

This problem can be approached from a different perspective by examining how the role of democracy in US foreign policy has been conceived within the US government and the wider foreign policy elite at the strategic level, rather than at the level of cases or specific regions. As efforts to spread democracy have never occupied the position of a dominant and overriding imperative in US foreign policy, a complete analysis of the role of democracy in US foreign policy would need to consider how it was meshed with other US goals such as national security in order to produce a coherent strategic approach. Decisions at this strategic level inevitably affect the choice of tactics to implement new strategies, which further translate into decisions on which organisational forms are the most effective tools to implement these approaches. Furthermore, these strategic, tactical and organisational decisions are affected and modified by struggles over the goals and control of the implementation of democratisation policies within the US government between bureaucratic departments, and between executive agencies and US private groups interested in the pursuit of democratisation overseas.

The Reagan administration and the rise of democracy promotion

The rise of democracy promotion under the Reagan administration in the early 1980s represents a case study that can be used to examine the strategic, organisational and bureaucratic factors that shape the relationship between democracy and US national security strategy. It was also a key turning point that has shaped US efforts to export democracy up until the present. The concept of democracy promotion put forward under Reagan differed from previous attempts to intervene in and shape the political development of foreign countries such as covert CIA operations, policies of nation-building informed by Modernisation theory and the Carter administration's campaign for Human Rights. Whereas these previous programmes had focussed on the projection of democratic ideology or attempts to reform foreign societies by working through sitting governments, the new concept of democracy promotion operationalised under Reagan was focussed on supporting sub-state democratic political forces overseas such as parties, unions and business groups in order to create functioning democratic systems from the bottom up. Furthermore, while former policies had often been concerned with the role of democratisation in the US approach towards a particular country or region, the effort to integrate a global campaign of democracy promotion into US foreign policy in the early 1980s led to an examination of the relationship between democracy and US national security at the strategic level. This process resulted in the creation of the first US organisation tasked solely

4 Introduction

with the promotion of democracy: the National Endowment for Democracy, a semi-private foundation run on a day-to-day basis by private citizens but funded by the US government, charged with aiding and strengthening democratic forces overseas.

This process had an important impact on future US foreign policy practice. After the Cold War democracy promotion was further institutionalised by the Clinton administration, and then made a key element of US national security policy towards the Middle East by the George W. Bush administration. Both administrations also created government agencies charged with promoting democratic reform overseas, many of which run programmes to strengthen foreign civil society groups similar to those begun and still conducted by the NED.[17] While the Obama administration has given less priority to democracy promotion rhetorically, it has continued to pursue many of these programmes, and democracy promotion has become an element of US foreign policy practice accepted by both major parties and most of the foreign policy establishment.

Despite the increasing importance of democracy promotion in US foreign policy, its formative period under the Reagan administration has been largely neglected by scholars, with only a small body of literature extant, and two book-length studies which engage with the factors underlying the rise of democracy promotion. Nicolas Guilhot discusses a variety of ideological factors that impacted on the rise of democracy promotion as a foreign policy paradigm in the 1980s, such as the rise of a Human Rights discourse, shifts in academia away from a preoccupation with Modernisation and towards democratisation as a development paradigm, and the role of neoconservative ideologues.[18] The other main study, by William Robinson, discusses the rise of democracy promotion as a strategy pursued by a transnational capitalist elite headquartered in the United States to create political structures overseas compatible with a global free market system.[19]

This study differs from these two works in seeing the rise of democracy promotion as the result of a contested decision-making process involving negotiations within a disunited US elite that was influenced by strategic and geopolitical calculations, disagreements over appropriate organisational structures, and convergence and divergences between elite factions located in the state and civil society. The generation of democracy promotion was impelled by two trends that had developed over the 1970s: the appearance of a more threatening strategic environment due to the rising power of the Soviet Union and the wave of Third World revolutions during and after the Vietnam War; and uncertainty within the US foreign policymaking elite over how to confront this due to a shattering of the ideological consensus which had previously legitimated an activist foreign policy as the defence of democracy. These trends culminated in importance during the early Reagan administration, which found its attempts to legitimate its activist Cold War national security strategy using democratic rhetoric hampered by internal divisions and domestic criticism from other factions of the elite over how support for democracy related to US interests in specific cases.

Introduction 5

It was the generation of the new vision of democracy promotion by a network of US groups and individuals outside the administration which made a resolution of these tensions possible. Rather than taking a case-by-case approach to the meshing of democratic reform overseas and US national security interests, this network presented the administration with the element which it lacked – a framework which could subsume and integrate these problematic cases into a much wider vision which meshed democracy promotion and national security at the strategic level. The process of debate and negotiation which followed constituted the first serious attempt by US policymakers and private groups to take a strategic approach to the export of democracy in the interests of national security.

This study examines this process in order to address several questions. First, it investigates the relationship between the promotion of democracy and US national security interests. The actors involved in the rise of democracy promotion championed different relationships between these two goals: some argued in favour of a narrow campaign focussed on the pursuit of democratic reform in dictatorships opposed to the US to remove threats to US national security; others advocated a more expansive campaign of democracy promotion in both enemy dictatorships, and in friendly authoritarian regimes perceived to be unstable; while yet others were focussed on a global campaign largely untied to immediate and specific security interests. The question is whether these differing views were synthesised to produce a unified strategic perspective which informed US democracy promotion.

The second area for investigation is the role of non-state actors in this process. A growing literature on the role of US civil society groups in the implementation of US Cold War foreign policy already exists, largely focussed on the 'state–private network', a series of ad hoc covert alliances the CIA developed with US civil society groups to conduct anti-communist propaganda operations in Western Europe and the Third World from the late 1940s to 1967.[20] These studies usually terminate in 1967, conceptualised as the end-point of the state–private network due to its public exposure and the Johnson administration's subsequent ban on such covert relationships between state and non-state organisations. However, the state–private network concept, minus the covert dimension, is clearly applicable to the National Endowment for Democracy. Study of the formation and early operations of the NED from a state–private network perspective extends enquiries in this field chronologically, while also allowing examination of state–private relationships that go beyond the previous state–private network's mission of opposing the ideological spread of communism to focus on interaction in the broader mission of promoting the creation of democratic political structures overseas, a goal more deeply rooted in US political culture. In addition, whereas in the 1950s and 1960s private groups were recruited on an ad hoc basis by the CIA to achieve strategic and tactical objectives already decided upon by government officials, during the late 1970s and early 1980s non-state forces actively shaped the strategy and network they were to participate in. Thus, this study examines both the influence of non-state

6   *Introduction*

groups on the strategic and organisational design of democracy promotion, and their relationship with the state in the early years of US democracy promotion.

Finally, an examination of the rise of US democracy promotion presents an opportunity to engage with the academic debate over whether the type and depth of the political reform the US promotes overseas has been limited by competing US interests. Several scholars have argued that the US democracy promotion initiatives of the previous three decades have resulted in 'low intensity democracies' in which power is exercised by elites and redistributive reforms are not pursued. However, they differ over whether this is a deliberate strategy rooted in the subordination of democracy to other US interests[21] or whether it represents an unreflective export of US models of democracy.[22] The present study examines this question by investigating what form the architects of democracy promotion expected political reform overseas to take and how far they believed it could be prosecuted in conformity with US national interests.

Overview of the book

The debates on democracy promotion in the early 1980s did not result in the creation of a unified and coherent blueprint which reconciled competing strategic perspectives. Instead, the process produced a hybrid solution in which liberal political methods and structures were to be promoted to reform problematic regimes, consistent with US national security interests, on a tactical case-by-case basis through an organisation influenced by the US government but not fully controlled by it. This line of argument is pursued through the chapters that follow.

Chapter 1 examines the origins of the new concept of democracy promotion during the 1970s as a response to the rise of a more threatening international situation linked to a perceived rise in the political-military power of Soviet communism and the erosion of the domestic legitimacy of US political intervention overseas. While the US state apparatus was unable to generate a legitimate and effective approach to promoting political reform in line with US national security interests, academics and political organisers in the private sphere generated a concept of democracy promotion to be implemented by US civil society groups in the Third World.

Chapter 2 examines the foreign policy of the early Reagan administration and attempts by democracy promoters located outside state structures to lobby it to support their blueprint for democracy promotion in its first year. Although the administration deployed democratic ideology as a tool of legitimation and as an ideological weapon, divisions between policymakers prevented the generation of a framework that integrated the pursuit of tangible democratic reforms overseas and US national security goals.

Chapters 3, 4 and 5 consider the strategic, organisational and ideological factors that affected the efforts of the administration and non-state democracy promoters to create an overt democracy promotion organisation capable of mobilising civil society groups in the national interest, as the debate on

Introduction 7

democracy promotion took on a global dimension in early 1982. The strategic and organisational dimensions of democracy promotion were interrelated, as disagreements and decisions on whether to pursue an expansive vision of democracy promotion aimed at both friendly and hostile dictatorships, a narrow campaign against Soviet communism, or even a global campaign untied to any specific and immediate US national security interest, fed into debates on whether democracy promotion should be a primarily state-led or privately-implemented activity. The organisational resolution was the hastily designed National Endowment for Democracy, which emerged as the ad hoc vehicle for the campaign. This organisational solution was able to mobilise the consensus necessary for the creation of a new, overt state–private network aimed at political operations overseas. However, this concentration on an organisational solution actively blocked the resolution of the strategic debates. The lack of strategic consensus between and within the administration, Congress and non-state actors meant that the new organisation suffered from strategic and tactical incoherence and an unclear relationship with the Executive.

Chapter 6 examines the emergence of a clearer approach to democracy promotion during the NED's first few years of operation. Influence from Congress and the administration defined the NED's purpose as the support of democratic movements and structures on a case-by-case basis in key states where US national security goals could be achieved through democracy promotion. The Endowment's interventions supported democratic groups friendly to the US, while limiting the extent of political reform in target states by blocking more radical change incompatible with US interests. While democratic ideology served to ease and rationalise state–private co-operation, national security was the key driver of these operations.

The conclusion examines the results of the process during the final years of the Cold War in terms of the strategic framework, the relationship between state and non-state actors, and the relationship between democratic reform overseas and US national security, before briefly considering the development of democracy promotion, and the persistence of tensions identified throughout the study, on post-Cold War democracy promotion. The final outcome of these debates was not a strategic approach which finally resolved the tensions in US foreign policy between the promotion of democracy and other US interests. However, the concept of democracy promotion was capable of generating a consensus sufficient to create a new structure that allowed state and non-state forces to co-operate in the promotion of political reform on a tactical basis, in line with and limited by pre-existing security interests. Thus, the final reconciliation occurred on the terrains of ideology, organisation and tactics, not at the strategic level.

The failure of this attempt to generate a strategic approach to democracy promotion indicates that the relationship between democracy and national security has been and will continue to be characterised by constant and continuing tension. The fundamental problem that animates this tension is that while the US gains a measure of strategic and ideological power from its invocation of democracy and its pursuit of some types of political reform in some states, it cannot

8 *Introduction*

be certain that democratic change overseas will always be consistent with US national security interests. Thus, the relationship between democracy promotion and US national security can only be negotiated and renegotiated in terms of policies towards specific areas or countries, but never finally resolved.

Notes

1 Woodrow Wilson, 'War Message to Congress', 2 April 1917, accessed 4 June 2010, *The World War I Document Archive*, http://wwi.lib.byuedu/index.php/Wilson%27s_War_Message_to_Congress.

2 Harry S. Truman, 'Special Message to the Congress on Greece and Turkey: The Truman Doctrine', 12 March 1947, *The American Presidency Project*, accessed 8 December 2014, www.presidency.ucsb.edu/ws/index.php?pid=12846&st=Truman+Doctrine&st1=.

3 John F. Kennedy, 'Inaugural Address,' 20 January 1961, *The American Presidency Project*, accessed 12 July 2014, www.presidency.ucsb.edu/ws/?pid=8032

4 George W. Bush, 'Second Inaugural Address,' 20 January 2005, *Project Gutenberg: Inaugural Addresses of the Presidents of the United States*, accessed 4 December 2014, www.gutenberg.org/files/925/925-h/925-h.htm#link2H_4_0056.

5 Tony Smith, *America's Mission: The United States and the Worldwide Struggle for Democracy in the Twentieth Century* Expanded Edition (Princeton, New Jersey: Princeton University Press, 2012), 9.

6 Ibid., 4.

7 Ibid., 40–54; 84–109; 146–176; 214–236; and 266–307.

8 Joshua Muravchik, *Exporting Democracy: Fulfilling America's Destiny* (Washington DC: American Enterprise Institute, 1991), 221.

9 Henry Nau, 'America's Identity, Democracy Promotion and National Interests: Beyond Realism, Beyond Idealism' in *American Democracy Promotion: Impulses, Strategies and Impacts*, ed. Michael Cox, G. John Ikenberry and Takashi Inoguchi (Oxford: Oxford University Press, 2000), 143.

10 G. John Ikenberry, 'America's Liberal Grand Strategy: Democracy and National Security in the Post-War Era,' in *American Democracy Promotion: Impulses, Strategies and Impacts*, ed. Michael Cox, G. John Ikenberry and Takashi Inoguchi (Oxford: Oxford University Press, 2000), 103.

11 Amos Perlmutter, *Making the World Safe for Democracy: a Century of Wilsonianism and its Totalitarian Challengers* (Chapel Hill: University of North Carolina Press, 1997), 8.

12 Gabriel Kolko, *Confronting the Third World: United States Foreign Policy, 1945–1980* (New York: Pantheon Books, 1988), 12.

13 William Appleman Williams, *The Tragedy of American Diplomacy* (New York and London: W.W. Norton & Company, 1959), 59 and Noam Chomsky, *Deterring Democracy* (London: Verso, 1991), 2.

14 David Ryan, *US Foreign Policy in World History* (London: Routledge, 2000), 53.

15 David F. Schmitz, *Thank God They're On Our Side: The United States and Rightwing Dictatorships 1921–1965* (Chapel Hill and London: The University of North Carolina Press, 1999), 3–5 and David F. Schmitz, *The United States and Right-wing Dictatorships, 1965–1989* (Cambridge: Cambridge University Press, 2006).

16 Stephen Kinzer, *Overthrow: America's Century of Regime Change from Hawaii to Iraq* (New York: Times Books, 2006), 111–128, 129–147 and 170–194.

17 Examples of this bureaucratic 'infrastructure of democracy' are the State Department's Bureau of Democracy, Human Right and Labor, and the United States Agency for International Development's Bureau of Democracy, Conflict and Humanitarian

Assistance,, both of which channel US government funding to political and civil society groups overseas. See Thomas O. Melia, 'The Democracy Bureaucracy: The Infrastructure of American Democracy Promotion' (Discussion paper prepared for the Princeton Project on National Security Working Group on Global Institutions and Foreign Policy Infrastructure, September, 2005), accessed 14 September 2012, www.princeton.edu/~ppns/papers/democracy_bureaucracy.pdf, 49 and USAID, 'Democracy, Human Rights and Governance,' accessed 17 December 2014, www.usaid.gov/what-we-do/democracy-human-rights-and-governance.

18 Nicolas Guilhot, *The Democracy Makers: Human Rights and International Order* (New York, Chichester: Columbia University Press, 2005.)

19 William I. Robinson, *Promoting Polyarchy: Globalization, US intervention and Hegemony* (Cambridge: Cambridge University Press, 1996).

20 See Frank Ninkovich, *The Diplomacy of Ideas: US foreign policy and cultural relations, 1938–1950* (Cambridge: Cambridge University Press, 1981); Hugh Wilford, *The Mighty Wurlitzer: How the CIA Played America* (Cambridge Mass and London: Harvard University Press, 2008); Scott Lucas, *Freedom's War: The US Crusade against the Soviet Union 1945–56* (Manchester: Manchester University Press, 1999) Anthony Carew, 'The American Labor Movement in Fizzland: The Free Trade Union Committee and the CIA,' *Labor History* 39, no. 1 (1998): 25–42, accessed 16 May 2014, DOI: 10.1080/00236679812331387276; and *The US Government, Citizen Groups and the Cold War: the State–Private Network*, ed. Helen Laville and Hugh Wilford (London: Routledge, 2006).

21 See Barry Gills, Joel Rocamora and Richard Wilson, 'Low Intensity Democracy', in *Low Intensity Democracy: Political Power in the New World Order*, ed. Barry Gills, Joel Rocamora and Richard Wilson (London: Pluto Press, 1993), 3–35; Robinson, *Promoting Polyarchy*, 4–6; Steve Smith, 'Democracy Promotion: Critical Questions', in *American Democracy Promotion: Impulses, Strategies and Impacts*, ed. Michael Cox, G. John Ikenberry and Takashi Inoguchi (Oxford: Oxford University Press, 2000), 73–75; Gerald Sussman (2010), *Branding Democracy: US Regime Change in Post-Soviet Eastern Europe* (New York: Peter Lang, 2010) and Michael J. Barker, 'Taking the risk out of civil society: harnessing social movements and regulating revolutions' (refereed paper presented to the Australasian Political Studies Association Conference, University of Newcastle, 2006).

22 Jason G. Ralph, ''High Stakes' and 'Low-Intensity Democracy'': Understanding America's Policy of Promoting Democracy,' in Cox, Ikenberry and Inoguchi, 213–215.

1 The roots of democracy promotion

From covert operations and modernisation to party-building

The blueprint for democracy promotion emerged during the 1970s from a small number of academics and political organisers working outside the US national security bureaucracy. The idea drew on previous modes of political intervention such as the state–private network of CIA-supported US civil society groups and the modernising socioeconomic reforms pursued by the Kennedy administration; however, it went beyond these in two ways. First, it abandoned the ideological and socioeconomic approaches to the export of democracy pursued through these modes of intervention to focus more narrowly on strengthening democratic political forces. Second, it tied this new tactic to a more strategic approach to the spread of democracy.

The opportunity to design and promote this new conception was created by the collapse of these previous modes of political intervention in the late 1960s and early 1970s. Before this crisis the state–private network and Modernisation policies had been deployed within an overarching framework of containment which meshed US national security and democratic ideology. However, the deep strategic, organisational and ideological clashes inherent in the attempt to use these tactics to export democracy in support of US national security interests culminated in a rupture between the state and the private civil society groups which were allied to it and a downgrading of Modernisation in the Third World as a US policy aim.

This rupture, coupled with the failure of the administrations of the 1970s to regenerate an effective US capability for the reform of political structures overseas and a rise in political instability in the Third World, provided the opportunity for non-state figures to reformulate elements of the state–private network and the Modernisation paradigm into a new conception of how democracy could be exported. In contrast to the pre-1967 situation, when private groups had been deployed on a tactical, case-by-case basis within a strategic framework generated by the national security bureaucracy, however, the rising network generated its own strategic framework that deployed these reformulated organisational and tactical concepts as elements of a program of democratisation which was far wider and more coherent than previously implemented by the US government. By 1980 these figures had coalesced into a loose network that was preparing to lobby the US government for funding to implement this new design.

Pre-existing tensions between democracy and national security in US foreign policy

The most consistently deployed US strategic framework for waging the Cold War was containment, conceived by George Kennan in 1946–47 as a method of forcing political change within the USSR or the break-up of the Soviet Empire through denying the Soviets opportunities to expand their zone of political control.[1] The decline of containment and the instruments and strategies associated with its implementation opened up space from 1967 onwards for new paradigms of US foreign policy, including democracy promotion, to rise in importance. Geopolitically containment, as it evolved, had to face three problems: the rise of Soviet power; the weakness of Western Europe in the face of this power; and, particularly after the initial phase of the Cold War in the late 1940s and early 1950s, the power vacuum in the Third World which appeared due to the decline of the European colonial empires. This final development brought greater instability in the former colonial areas and increased the threat that independent nationalist leaders would pursue foreign and domestic policies not compatible with US interests.[2] Thus, the core of the strategy was the prevention of political change outside the boundaries of the Soviet bloc which might increase the power of the USSR or harm US security and economic interests in other ways.

However, containment's strength as a framework for US foreign policy was its construction and explanation of this geopolitical and anti-communist strategy as a defence of freedom against a totalitarian slave state.[3] This public explanation of the doctrine eased its acceptance by the wider foreign policy elite and US civil society by tapping into long-standing traditions of US nationalism that conflated the fate and power of the United States with the fate and expansion of democracy, as both a political doctrine and a form of government, and saw the US as the 'the project of mankind'.[4] Democratic ideology thus consolidated containment as a framework for perceiving US foreign policy practice and goals by 'translating its objectives into an understandable and compelling reflection of the domestic society's dominant norms.'[5]

The equation of US national security with the defence and spread of democracy was not cynically deployed by US officials and national security bureaucrats to legitimate a policy shaped wholly by realist security and economic concerns, however. Rather, the US' pre-existing liberal democratic ideology functioned as a filter through which policymakers perceived the threat from the USSR in terms of ideology as well as security.[6] Thus, ideology and security concerns fused in the construction of the containment framework.[7] The practical result of this fusion was the construction of a liberal foreign policy elite which supported a US foreign policy it perceived as aimed at safeguarding both US national security and freedom. This elite consensus extended into US civil society and included the leaders and members of US civil society groups which co-operated with the CIA to project democratic ideology and the academics who advised US policymakers on designs for political reform in the Third World.

12 *The roots of democracy promotion*

However, while democracy may have meshed with national security concerns at the ideological level, support for democracy did not serve US national security goals consistently in pragmatic terms. Although the Truman and Eisenhower administrations waged a covert campaign to for the 'Liberation' of the USSR's Eastern European satellite states involving propaganda initiatives, covert action, support to anti-Soviet guerrillas and a serious attempt to destabilise the communist government of Albania,[8] this campaign was waged sporadically and inconsistently, and US policymakers were forced to recognise early in the Cold War that while it was possible to broadcast propaganda into the Soviet bloc, little could be done in practical terms to 'liberate' it due to the strong political control exercised by the governments of the USSR and the Warsaw Pact nations, and the brute fact of Soviet military power. This geopolitical fact of life constrained the US response to a workers' uprising in East Germany in 1953, and to the Hungarian Revolution of 1956.[9] In the Third World, democratic processes did not always produce leaders who were willing to de-emphasise the interests of their own countries and populations in favour of US national interests, leading the US to mount coups against a constitutional regime in Iran in 1953 and an elected government in Guatemala in 1954 to defend these interests.[10] The application of democracy to national security policy produced tensions at the strategic level which were then replicated at the organisational and tactical levels in the projection of democratic ideology by the state–private network, and in the US attitude to democratising reforms in Third World dictatorships.

The state–private network

The tension between democracy and national security at the organisational level occurred in attempts to project democratic ideology through US civil society groups funded and managed by the CIA: the state–private network. This network consisted of civil society groups such as anti-Soviet committees and radio stations staffed by Eastern European émigrés,[11] intellectuals,[12] women's groups, African-American groups,[13] students[14] and trade unions[15] receiving 'covert guidance and ... assistance from the Government'[16], usually the CIA. The network was the brainchild of George Kennan, architect of the containment policy, acting as Head of the State Department's Policy Planning Staff. It was Kennan who proposed the earliest state–private network operations in 1948, in order to implement a strategy of 'political warfare', defined as:

> the employment of all the means at a nation's command, short of war, to achieve its national objectives. Such operations are both overt and covert. They range from such overt actions as political alliances, economic measures ... and 'white' propaganda to such covert operations as clandestine support of 'friendly' foreign elements, 'black' psychological warfare and even encouragement of underground resistance in hostile states.[17]

The functions of the US private groups supported by the CIA within this conception were initially to secure Western Europe against Soviet subversion and to solidify Western European commitment to NATO by promoting a common Western democratic identity, and also to complicate control of the Soviet regime's own population, and of Eastern Europe, through the projection of democratic propaganda behind the Iron Curtain. After the abandonment of Liberation, the network continued many of its programmes within the framework of the containment policy, while broadening the scope of its operations to include key countries and regions in the Third World. These groups were focussed on the projection of democracy as a counter-ideology to communism in order to secure the loyalty of key overseas demographic sectors for the US cause in the Cold War, rather than in a consolidated effort to build democratic parties and structures overseas. This was a tactical alliance in which private groups lacking a clear strategic plan which transcended a commitment to democratic ideology or the needs of their particular section of civil society deployed their political skills within a strategic framework created by the state. State agencies thus acted as a coordinating hub for a constellation of private groups who did not function as members of a wider network independent of these agencies and did not possess a strategic framework of their own.

The role of the US state as chief coordinator and financier of the network gave rise to ideological and organisational tensions, however. The state sought to use the democratic nature of the groups to present freedom as an attractive alternative to totalitarianism through providing examples of democracy in action. As Lucas argues, 'it was the nature of American ideology that demanded a private facade'.[18] Furthermore, NSC-68, the founding planning document for the US' global containment campaign, also stated that one component of US Cold War strategy was to 'demonstrate the superiority of the idea of freedom by its constructive application'.[19] The state–private network could be seen as one way of operationalising this goal, projecting an attractive image of American democratic freedom to foreigners. Within the network, democratic ideology also performed an important function in rationalising and easing the convergence between non-state forces and national security officials; thus, the conflation of democracy and US national security at the strategic level was replicated at the organisational level and created the consensus which bound the state and private forces together. However, the covert role of state organisations as coordinators was not congruent with the democratic ideology which enabled state–private convergence, and constituted a key vulnerability.

This meshing of state organisations and civil society groups also produced an organisational tension. The private facade of the groups was the key to their operational effectiveness overseas, as their actions were 'plausibly deniable' and could be disclaimed by the US government as they were funded covertly, while the groups also possessed more credibility than the US state with their counterparts abroad, who were more likely to co-operate with an American representative of their own civil society group than a US official. However, a measure of state guidance was necessary to ensure that the groups' actions were consistent with the US' anti-communist foreign policy and constituted a coherent part of this wider strategy.[20] Without such a guidance function, the effort ran the risk of

14 *The roots of democracy promotion*

degenerating into a dispersed and incoherent series of private programmes led by private interests or democratic ideology rather than more narrow state goals, or of proceeding beyond national security policy due to ideological fervour.

The nature of the state–private relationship thus created an autonomy/control dilemma for the state. A measure of government control was necessary to manage clashes between ideology, sectional interest and national security policy; however, too much obvious government control of these groups would call into question their status as non-state entities. This, in turn, would destroy the plausible deniability and credibility with foreign governments and groups that these groups derived from their private status, and thus their usefulness to the state. This tension was never fully resolved while the state–private network existed. The state was unwilling to abandon control of the network; however, it was forced to rely on 'long strings of control' that did not risk compromising its private allies such as co-opting group officials, infiltrating its own agents into the groups and maintaining control of funding by dispensing it in small amounts or tying it directly to specific projects and demanding audits and accounts.[21] These tactics did not aim at controlling all the actions of a particular private group; rather, they produced a 'ringed autonomy'[22] in which group personnel were free to act within certain defined limits but pushing this autonomy to the point where it conflicted with US national security interests could lead to consequences such as withdrawal of funding.[23] While this control function was not obvious to casual observers, the private groups resented the limits put on their freedom of action and often clashed with covert action managers over strategy and tactics. For example, early private consultants to the CIA such as James Burnham and Sidney Hook often tried to prod the agency into more aggressive anti-communist actions,[24] while private psychological warriors directing democratic propaganda against the Soviet Union in co-operation with the state also complained that the government was not aggressive enough on occasion.[25] The clash between democratic ideology and more particular national security goals present in US foreign policy at the strategic level was thus replicated in the state's continuing efforts to guard against rogue private actions that may have been consistent ideologically but inconsistent or harmful strategically, and the efforts of private groups to obtain greater independence and levels of funding.

Support for dictatorship or democratic reform in the Third World?

Although the tensions inherent in the deployment of private civil society groups to project democratic ideology in order to achieve national security objectives were formidable, a set of more potentially damaging tensions between democracy and geopolitics were present in the Third World as decolonisation opened up a new arena of US-Soviet competition composed of new states with weak political structures. Decolonisation triggered growing demands for social, economic and political participation throughout the Third World[26], which the US saw as being at risk of capture not merely from communists but also nationalists and populists.[27] These conditions led to successive waves of revolutions

The roots of democracy promotion 15

spearheaded by radical and nationalist forces, sometimes allied to the Soviet Union, which challenged the US and its allies.[28] Successful revolutions could lead to changes in the Cold War balance of power, as the defection of a Third World country that was important strategically due to its location or resources could materially damage US national security. This situation, then, led to a contradiction between a containment policy focussed on preventing change hostile to US interests and the democratic ideological basis of the policy, as it was unclear whether support of democratic political change in the Third World would produce governments aligned to the United States.

These realities faced US policymakers with two key decisions to make. The first was to decide whether support of Third World anti-communist dictators in order to block Soviet or radical influence or the promotion of a degree of political reform in pro-US states in order to undercut demands for more radical change was most likely to guard US security interests more effectively. In situations where the US decided to follow the path of political reform, policymakers also had to decide how far such reforms could be pursued before they began to undermine the security and economic interests they sought to protect by destabilising friendly states or opening paths to power for more radical elements. This was not merely a matter of making a choice between basing policy primarily on ideology or national security; instead, the question was whether and how far supporting the construction of democratic systems would assist the US in strategic terms by containing revolutionary forces.

The US made no definite decision on these questions before 1967 and was not able to produce an overarching policy framework towards the Third World which reconciled national security objectives and the export of democracy definitively at the strategic level. Instead, it oscillated between support for dictators and support for reform, employing different tools and tactics in different regions and in different periods on a case-by-case basis. A policy of relying on friendly authoritarians to guard US strategic and economic interests by blocking political change calmed policymakers' fears that such change in the Third World would lead to the growth of communist strength.[29] The contradiction this created with the ideological justification for containment was elided through the argument that by supporting authoritarians in order to prevent totalitarians from seizing power, the US was in fact defending the space in which liberty might develop in the future.[30] However, the dictatorial governments the US often supported tended to lack legitimacy, which made their long-term stability doubtful. These dictatorships also effectively repressed liberal opposition movements which aimed at the creation of a democratic successor state, which meant that radical forces tended to gain hegemony over opposition movements. Support for dictatorships thus tended to open up a long-term strategic vulnerability, as when such regimes collapsed they were often replaced by revolutionary forces hostile to the US. President Kennedy articulated this link in 1963, commenting that 'Dictatorships are the seedbed from which communism ultimately springs up.'[31]

The alternative policy of fostering the Modernisation of Third World societies was based on the idea that gradual reform could bring developing countries into

16 *The roots of democracy promotion*

a state of political, social and economic modernity without triggering major upheavals that would disturb the geopolitical balance of power, and so provide an alternative to radical revolutions.[32] The end-point of a democratic society specified in models of Modernisation was also congruent with the desire of policymakers to demonstrate to Third World populations that 'man's unsatisfied aspiration for economic progress and social justice can best be achieved by free men working within a framework of democratic institutions',[33] and thus represented an attempt to align geopolitical and ideological frameworks.

This policy approach was derived from academic Modernisation theories that held that by emulating the stages of development followed by the US and Western Europe, Third World states could transform themselves into modern, democratic societies. These stages were set out by Walt Rostow, an influential development theorist and advisor to President Kennedy, as; traditional society, the preconditions for take-off, take-off, the drive to maturity and the age of high mass consumption, at which point a fully modern society would exist.[34] Encouraging a developing country to progress through these stages entailed supporting or engineering far-reaching social and economic transformations which could not be achieved through a state–private network model of political intervention based on projecting democratic ideology and strengthening pro-US civil society groups within the target country, although such programmes were also mounted in the Third World in this period as an adjunct to Modernisation projects by groups receiving US government funding such as the AFL-CIO.[35] Instead, the required transformation would be implemented through deploying US foreign aid and the services of US technocrats to implement socioeconomic reforms, such as land reform, tax reform, the strengthening of institutions and advanced technical training,[36] which would, in turn, lead to the emergence of a strong middle class who would inevitably press for US-style democracy.[37]

This policy of reform was never deployed consistently as a coherent framework for US policy towards the Third World. However, it was deployed in countries and areas where there was thought to be a high risk of successful radical revolution, such as Latin America after Fidel Castro's seizure of power in Cuba, and in Vietnam. The process of establishing democratic regimes or deepening democracy in the areas targeted proved to be problematic, however, due to both the paradigm of reform the US followed and clashes with short-term national security considerations. The channelling of many elements of reform programmes through existing political and social structures meant that their implementation often depended on the co-operation of indigenous ruling elites, who feared dilution of their power through large-scale socioeconomic transformations and thus resisted them.[38] This process was clearly visible in South Vietnam, where US support of Ngo Dinh Diem, who in turn relied on the landlord class as the social base of his power, translated into the dilution of programmes such as land reform.[39]

The US focus on socioeconomic structures also neglected the role of agency in the middle class-led political transformations which policymakers hoped would result. The lack of an integrated effort to strengthen the political forces the US wished to place in power meant that the reform processes and the short-term destabilisation that accompanied Modernisation could result in the rise of more independent-minded and radical reformers who did not share the US agenda for their societies. Thus, while the end-point of Modernisation was more consistent with the wider ideological framework for US foreign policy, in the short-term its pursuit created tensions with geopolitical aims. This tension was often resolved through a return to support for authoritarian governments as a barrier against further radicalism in the short term, as when the US encouraged the Brazilian army to seize power from President Goulart in 1964 due to its unease concerning his planned reforms and supposed communist sympathies.[40] The US also made little protest when the democratically elected reformist President of the Dominican Republic, Juan Bosch, was overthrown in 1963, and subsequently despatched marines to prevent his restoration during a popular rebellion in 1965.[41] The implementation of a long-term policy through a national security bureaucracy often galvanised by short-term considerations thus often led to the abandonment of reform in specific cases.

The turn away from the export of democracy

Before 1967 the imperfect coordination of democratic ideology and US national security goals within containment, both at the strategic level and at the operational level, had been underpinned by an ideological and strategic consensus among the US foreign policy elite which accepted the equation of US national security strategy with the defence of freedom from communist totalitarianism. This consensus could not be maintained from 1967 onwards due to rising disillusionment with political intervention overseas. The flash point for increasing criticism of US foreign policy was the conduct of the Vietnam War, which exposed the tensions inherent in a Cold War strategy waged in the name of democracy.[42] Although unease over US foreign policy was not limited to Vietnam and also included other factors such as US policy in Latin America and the actions of the CIA, the war acted as a focal point for these disparate concerns. The resulting lack of consensus within the elite, both in governmental institutions and in civil society, translated into damage to the two key tools of political intervention and reform: the state–private network and the pursuit of Modernisation. This process opened up a tactical and organisational gap in US national security policy which could be filled by other paradigms and actors.

The decline of the state–private network

The exposure of supposedly private US groups projecting democratic ideology as recipients of CIA funding by *Ramparts* magazine in 1967 brought the organisational contradiction between the projection of an ideology of freedom and the state's need to manipulate and direct the private proponents of this ideology in the service of defined national security goals into the open. This exposure resulted in the destruction of large parts of the state–private network due to

18   *The roots of democracy promotion*

President Johnson's subsequent ban on covert funding for US civil society groups.[43] In fact these civil society groups and the US government had been drawing apart ideologically due to the impact of Vietnam before the exposure of the network, as more liberal private groups and individuals engaged in criticism of the war. For example, the leadership of the National Students' Association, a key organisation in the network, had been quietly working to sever its CIA connection and locate alternative sources of funding.[44] This rift paralleled splits within the foreign policy establishment, as hawks and doves divided over military escalation in Vietnam after 1965.[45] The exposure itself was also a product of the loss of consensus produced by the war, as *Ramparts* magazine in its contemporary form was a product of the anti-war mood,[46] and it is unlikely that the story would have had such an impact or been featured more widely in more mainstream media if the wider consensus had still been effective.[47]

Structurally, this loss of consensus produced a political climate in which the state–private network, which depended on the existence of a cohesive civil society bound by anti-communist ideology and a cohesive elite in the state willing to fund it,[48] could not have continued in its existing form. However, the problem was deeper than a short-term lack of cohesion between elites. Rather, the outcome was a product of the inherent fragility of the covert state–private network structure, which was rooted in the fact that Americans did not see covert government subsidies to private groups engaged in promoting democratic ideology as legitimate. As Ninkovich points out, 'there was a huge gap between the needed propaganda instrumentality and the possibility of its social acceptance.'[49] Thus, the structure collapsed when it was revealed to the public.

The 1967 scandal left an organisational gap in the US state's capacity to project democratic ideology which the Executive attempted to correct initially by resurrecting a state–private network system which would still be devoted to the ideological projection of democracy, but which would function in an overt form. National security officials believed that an overt operating framework would be less vulnerable to the type of shock that had damaged the previous set of relationships. This process was already in train when *Ramparts* published its exposé, as the chief of the CIA's International Organisations Division, Cord Meyer, the highest-ranking government official with direct responsibility for the state–private network, had suggested the creation of an overt endowment to replace the CIA funding for private groups[50] several months before the scandal broke. CIA Director Richard Helms had also believed that finding an overt funding channel would make the network more stable, but 'seemingly more urgent problems took precedence.'[51] A similar suggestion was made several days after the scandal emerged by Assistant Secretary of State for Cultural and Educational Affairs Charles Frankel, who argued that placing the responsibility for such programs under a semi-autonomous foundation governed by a Board of prominent citizens would 'eliminate the cloud of suspicion' surrounding government activities in the field.[52] The Katzenbach Commission, established by the Johnson administration to provide recommendations on how to proceed after the CIA scandal erupted, also favoured such a solution, recommending the creation of a 'public-private mechanism' for funding US private organisations in its report in April 1967.[53] The common theme in these proposals was that making the state–private funding relationship overt would render it more acceptable: relationships which were already public and accepted could not be destroyed through exposure.

The deliberations of the Committee on Overseas Voluntary Activities, chaired by Secretary of State Dean Rusk and set up to devise ways of implementing the recommendations of the Katzenbach Commission, took a different turn, however. Rather than aiming merely at the resurrection of a capability to wage ideological warfare, the committee staff argued that in the future a key operational task would be 'the support of private organizations helping to build political, social and economic institutions in key areas of developing countries'.[54] These recommendations implied a transition in state–private network operations from ideological projection to a greater level of involvement in tangible projects of modernising and democratising reform than had previously been the case. The Committee argued that such state–private network-implemented reform plans could be best funded through an Executive branch body reporting directly to the President.[55] However, the poor relations between the administration and Congress that had developed due to the 1967 scandal meant the legislation was not presented during Johnson's term due to fears that it would not pass.[56]

The decline of modernisation

Although Rusk argued that it would be better to let a new administration attempt to implement such legislation,[57] the collapse of elite consensus in favour of Modernisation as a tactic for preventing revolution through socioeconomic reform which also occurred at this time made this shift to a greater focus on institution-building in the Third World difficult to implement. The influence of Modernisation theory over US national security policy was damaged by splits within the academic community which had promoted it to policymakers, and within the policymaking elite. Liberals, and those further to the left, turned against a doctrine that was coming to be associated with US interventionism and the support of unsavoury regimes rather than democratisation. In Vietnam, US aid and Modernisation programmes had not produced a 'showcase for democracy', as Eisenhower and Kennedy had argued they would;[58] rather, US policy had led to the dictatorship of Diem and then military rule. The Modernisation paradigm also suffered from its links with US military tactics as Walt Rostow, Modernisation's most visible exponent, came to be perceived as a major architect of policies such as the bombing of North Vietnam through his position as National Security Advisor to President Johnson.[59] The idea was also attacked from the political left in academia as the influence of counter-paradigms such as dependency theory grew.[60]

In contrast, more conservative scholars and policymakers turned away from the paradigm not due to its failure to secure democratic reform, but due to its failure to secure US national security goals. Influential political scientist Samuel Huntington launched a scholarly attack on it from the right in the late 60s and earlier 70s, arguing that preserving political stability in Third World societies

20 *The roots of democracy promotion*

took precedence over poorly delineated plans for schemes of too-rapid change;[61] a line of argument foreshadowed in his criticism of Modernisation policies in Vietnam under the Johnson administration.[62] In Latin America the policy suffered what Taffet refers to as a slow slide into irrelevance,[63] as the Nixon administration elevated the preservation of political stability over reform, preferring to rely on authoritarian governments to contain revolutionaries in the Third World.[64] By 1971 Nixon's National Security Council had concluded that the Modernisation effort in Latin America had been oversold as a possible method of promoting development and democracy.[65] This abandonment of reform efforts in Latin America reflected the administration's overall solution to the problem of meshing democracy with US national security strategy, which was to abandon democracy in favour of negotiating with the totalitarian Soviet regime while relying on anti-communist authoritarians in the Third World to defend American security interests. This represented a de-universalising of the US' democratic commitment, not merely in terms of cases but at the level of national security strategy.

Splits in the foreign policy elite and the severing of links between the state and liberal anti-communists in civil society provoked by Vietnam thus led to the decline of the state–private network and the Modernisation paradigm. This loss of elite cohesion, within the state and outside it, placed formidable barriers to the reconstitution of a state–private network based on a policy of ideological warfare and to the generation of a new network more devoted to Modernisation. It also prevented the resolution of the tensions involved in state deployment of private groups and in the pursuit of democratising reforms in the Third World.

The initial blueprint for democracy promotion

This turn away from attempts to shape foreign political structures on the part of the state created a space in US strategy and the US state's national security apparatus for alternative concepts to occupy. William A. Douglas, a political development academic, proposed the blueprint for a new campaign for political reform in the Third World in 1972. Douglas' ideas offered a solution to both the autonomy/control dichotomy and the tension between the US' long-term interest in exporting democracy and its short-term need to preserve relations with friendly authoritarians to contain hostile political movements. Furthermore, Douglas set a strategic goal for non-state action that transcended the tactical, case-by-case approach which had been implemented until this point.

Strategically, Douglas argued emphatically that the creation of Third World democratic regimes was more in line with Western strategic interests than support of authoritarians. In contrast to authoritarian regimes, democracies had mechanisms which could incorporate new political groups into the existing system without revolutionary upheavals and a clear succession mechanism: elections.[66] Therefore, support for the growth of democracy would create more stable and legitimate Third World governments able to contain or defuse communist movements more efficiently than authoritarian governments. This was clearly in

The roots of democracy promotion 21

the Western strategic interest, as the accession to power of communist or pro-Soviet regimes in Third World countries could lead to the West being cut off from access to supplies of vital raw materials such as oil and uranium.[67] Support for democratic forces would allow the West to 'meet the Communists on their own chosen ground of modern politics'[68] and remove the need to prop up politically weak reactionary regimes through military intervention, as had occurred in Vietnam.[69] This argument was not ideological; rather, it was based on the utility of constructing Third World democracies in strategic terms. This scheme took in the whole of the non-communist Third World and was thus more comprehensive than Modernisation policies pursued in Latin America or Vietnam in the service of containment.

To create these Third World democracies, Douglas called for a new tactic which would break decisively with former modes of Western intervention such as propaganda programmes, ideological projection of democracy by civil society groups, CIA operations and economic aid, all of which had failed to build durable political structures.[70] Instead, he conjoined state–private network methods of organisation and operation with a reformulated Modernisation approach, in which the initial objective was not nation-building, but the construction of modern, democratic political parties. In this scheme, socioeconomic change would not trigger political change; rather, political change would precede it and create the conditions for it. Traditional Third World populations would be organised and mobilised to carry out the task of socioeconomic development by regimes of 'regimented democracy'[71] led by modernised Third World elites[72] and based on strong, mass democratic parties.[73] In turn, these parties would be built through training promising foreign leaders of democratic parties in techniques of organisation and party-building while also giving them the skills necessary to cope with the political tactics of extremist and anti-democratic movements.[74]

Douglas argued that this aid would be delivered most effectively through a new private network focussed on political parties rather than civil society organisations, to ensure credibility and plausible deniability. Private implementation was necessary because the programmes would have to be carried out in areas of former Western colonialism. In this situation, private programmes would be far more credible with Third World nationalists and democrats, who would fear that programs implemented by Western governments merely aimed at the control and manipulation of indigenous democratic movements.[75] In addition implementing political reform initiatives through private groups would prevent the support of democratic opposition movements in a Third World country from damaging diplomatic relations between the US and the government in power.[76]

However, rather than defaulting to a state–private network model of organisation in which the state would provide the guidance and strategic framework for operations and private groups would supply their political skills, Douglas proposed a new organisational model that divorced such programmes from US government control. Instead of relying on coordination provided by the US national security bureaucracy, these programmes would be managed by an International League for Democracy composed of both Western democratic parties and mass

22   *The roots of democracy promotion*

democratic Third World parties.[77] This organisation would provide financial and technical support to regional and national party schools which would teach Third World party activists the democratic theory and party-building skills required to turn Douglas' vision into a reality.[78] The League would still require funding from countries such as the US to conduct its operations. However, Douglas was opposed to covert subsidies, which he feared might allow foreign governments to exert undue influence over democracy programmes in line with their short-term national security priorities, and damage the credibility of the organisation if exposed. To correct this problem, he hoped that funding could be provided by governments making a one-time contribution which could then be invested by the League for Democracy to support its activities,[79] which would have given contributors no continuing control over the League. He also hoped that specific projects could be funded by private donors such as the Ford, Carnegie or Rockefeller Foundations,[80] and that governments could pass laws making private donations to the League tax-deductible.[81] In the US these donations could be channelled through a bipartisan foundation of Democrats and Republicans, which would then transfer them to the international organisation.[82]

This organisational model would insulate Douglas' project from the type of scandal which had destroyed the previous state–private network, as there would be no covert state involvement which could delegitimise the League if exposed. It also separated the long-term and short-term goals of US foreign policy organisationally, making it possible to pursue engagement with dictators and the development of democratic successor movements simultaneously through different structures. The implementation of democratic reform programmes through a multilateral private organisation separated from the policymaking procedures and clashes of the US national security bureaucracy would thus remove the short-term counter-pressures which often motivated officials to soft-pedal long-term reform in favour of preserving current relations with dictators, as there would be no need to reconcile these two imperatives within state structures. In organisational terms, the US state would lack the leverage or control over democratic reform programmes which would allow it to de-emphasise or block them.

Douglas' ideas are of key importance in the shift to democracy promotion, as he articulated a cogent strategic rationale for the promotion of democracy. He also suggested the modification of previous modes of political intervention to implement this vision by altering the focus of his Modernisation project from a socioeconomic, government-to-government approach to an approach focussed on working with political parties inside target states. Organisationally, he proposed the creation of a new network based on political parties rather than a resurrection of the previous state–private network of unions, intellectual circles, student groups and women's organisations. Most significantly, Douglas' ideas constituted an overarching strategic framework for private action independent of the state's strategy for the first time. This independence was replicated at the organisational level, as Douglas' International League for Democracy would not rely on state agencies to provide a coordinating function for its campaign or to identify strategic priorities.

However, although these ideas had an important impact on US national security policy eventually, they had little impact at the time. Douglas published his ideas during the Nixon administration, which had staked the prevention of revolution on the support of authoritarian regimes, not on democratisation of any type. There also seems to have been little immediate interest from non-state forces or factions of the foreign policy elite, possibly due to the disillusionment with the idea of private and state involvement in attempts to influence political systems overseas which had become widespread at this time. The project would have to wait for the issue of how democracy related to US national security interests in the Third World in terms of Cold War strategy to rise in importance, and for the organisational question of how democratising reforms could be implemented and by whom, to progress.

The rise of human rights and the American political foundation

The rise of Human Rights as a new foreign policy approach in the latter half of the 1970s re-legitimised US intervention in political structures overseas by placing it once again in a moral framework. This new approach rose in the context of strategic and organisational disarray in US policy towards the Third World. From 1974–79, 13 Third World states fell to radical insurgent movements or substantially radicalised their governments,[83] including: Vietnam, Laos and Cambodia in South-east Asia; the Portuguese colonies in Africa, which fell to indigenous Marxist movements; the downfall of the monarchy in Ethiopia; the radicalisation of African states such as Benin and Madagascar; and the fall of pro-US regimes in Iran and Nicaragua at the end of the decade.[84] This new wave of instability indicated the need for US intervention in the Third World, but such intervention was difficult to engineer through the usual paradigms and tactics.

This incapacity was in part a legacy of the turn away from US involvement in projecting democratic ideology and implementing programmes aimed at the reform of overseas political structures discussed earlier. However, the US capacity to intervene politically overseas had been further reduced by the restrictions placed on the CIA in the wake of the Church Committee's investigations into the agency's covert actions, which placed sharp limits on covert political intervention.[85] This continued erosion of the US' capacity for foreign political intervention, coupled with the worsening strategic situation, resulted in an attempt by the Carter administration to deploy the promotion of Human Rights as a method of waging ideological combat against Marxism and Third World radicalism. However, the failure of the administration to reconcile the strategic and organisational tensions between long- and short-term US interests blocked the pursuit of a consistent approach and once again opened up a space for further non-state initiatives. The non-state response was the creation of a private democracy foundation: the American Political Foundation.

24   *The roots of democracy promotion*

The Carter administration: human rights versus national security

The cultural/ideological shift in US society that had led to disenchantment with previous modes of political intervention overseas also generated increased interest in Human Rights during the 1970s. The number of non-governmental groups involved in Human Rights grew to 200 by the end of the decade; while prestigious institutions such as the Ford Foundation began funding human rights work in 1973. Congress also became interested, holding hearings on the area in 1973 and passing legislation in 1975 and 1976 which made it possible to halt US economic assistance to countries which violated Human Rights.[86] This, together with the signing of the Helsinki Accords, which mandated Soviet compliance with basic Human Rights in the USSR and Eastern Europe,[87] placed the issue on the foreign policy agenda.

The Carter administration engaged with this shift and embraced the issue partly because a Human Rights policy was expected to provide domestic political benefits by uniting liberal Democrats concerned with abuses in anti-communist authoritarian states in the Third world and Cold Warriors on the right of the party who wanted to use Human Rights to criticise the Soviet Union[88] around a foreign policy concept which was universal enough to include criticism of both types of regime. However, it was also expected to provide geopolitical benefits. In the communist world, it was hoped that pressure on regimes to observe Human Rights would promote the growth of more open societies.[89] The inclusion of Human Rights in Basket III of the Helsinki Accords, signed by the USSR in 1975, gave the United States a legal mechanism to pressure the Soviet Union to undertake gradual internal reforms which would open up its society. The creation of a new US joint Executive-Legislative body, the Commission on Security and Cooperation in Europe, headed by Democratic Congressman Dante Fascell, under the Ford administration had put organisational machinery in place to pursue this goal.[90]

In the Third World, it was hoped that pressuring dictators to reduce Human Rights violations would remove popular incentives to join or support revolutionary movements and thus increase political stability.[91] The policy would be carried out on a government-to-government basis, as modernising reforms had been, but by denying US military and economic aid to regimes which abused Human Rights rather than investing in socioeconomic transformation. It would thus perform a similar function to Modernisation by instituting pre-emptive reforms, which could defuse revolutionary movements. However, the Carter administration resolved the conflict over whether to support authoritarians to block revolution or support democratising reforms by pressuring authoritarians to reform their most repressive practices rather than by seeking to alter political systems. PRM-28, the administration's principal study of Human Rights policy stated that, 'we do not seek to change governments or remake societies.'[92]

The key weakness of the administration's Human Rights policy was its failure to produce a clear strategic framework which reconciled the promotion of Human Rights with competing US interests such as economics and security. The

The roots of democracy promotion   25

tensions between Human Rights and security interests which resulted from the absence of their coordination at the strategic level was also replicated at the organisational level within the national security bureaucracy, as the administration's decision to take a case-by-case approach to the implementation of the policy produced bureaucratic turf wars. The split between Human Rights and other imperatives was institutionalised at the bureaucratic level in the vesting of responsibility for the Human Rights policy in distinct bodies such as the State Department's Bureau of Human Rights, headed by Patricia Derian, and the Interagency Group on Human Rights and Foreign Assistance, chaired by Warren Christopher, which was to review military, security and economic assistance in light of Human Rights considerations.[93] This resulted in the Departments of Commerce, Treasury and the State Department's Bureau for Security Assistance successfully lobbying to have programmes within their purview removed from the Interagency Group,[94] thus protecting their own bureaucratic turf.

The Bureau of Human Rights also found itself locked in bureaucratic battles with the State Department's regional bureaux. These conflicts arose because as a functional bureau, the Bureau of Human Rights did not often consider its policy recommendations in the light of competing security concerns, whereas the regional bureaux did. It is no coincidence that the bitterest clashes occurred with the Bureau of East Asian and Pacific Affairs, which oversaw policy towards regimes such as the Philippines which abused Human Rights but were critical to the US strategic position in the Pacific.[95] Thus, the effect of proceeding on a case-by-case basis was bureaucratic struggle which resulted in authoritarian regimes important to US security such as the Philippines, China, Pakistan and a host of others being provided with aid despite their poor Human Rights records.[96]

It is possible that the administration could have implemented more positive initiatives through developing a state–private network, which would have had more flexibility to act in support of Human Rights through non-governmental channels even in the absence of a coherent overarching framework. However, while he gave consistent support to the US division of Helsinki Watch, formed by US private citizens with government encouragement to liaise with Human Rights campaigners in the Soviet bloc,[97] Carter did not provide such support to a proposal for an independent but government-sponsored Human Rights foundation proposed by Democratic Congressmen Dante Fascell and Donald Fraser, and supported by the NSC.[98] The organisation was to be government-funded but run on a day-to-day basis by a board of Congressmen, private citizens, and ex-officio Executive officials, who would ensure consistency with government policy. It would aim to both stimulate research on Human Rights and to channel funding to Human Rights NGOs in the US and overseas.[99] However, the State Department soon raised concerns based on the autonomy/control dichotomy, fearing that the organisation would be seen as an agency of the US government, and that, therefore, any criticism it made of friendly states would damage US relations with them. The Department proposed to sharply reduce the proposed institute's mission to collecting information on Human Rights abuses and making this available rather than funding NGOs, and the plan died.[100]

26   *The roots of democracy promotion*

The American political foundation: private democracy promotion begins

While the administration debated the merits of a semi-private Human Rights foundation, Congressmen and aides supportive of Human Rights moved to fill the organisational gap in the administration's implementation machinery. As a result, they created the bipartisan political party committee that William Douglas had called for to coordinate US private democracy promotion projects in 1972. However, the idea for the creation of this committee did not derive from Douglas' work, but from observation of a real case of political foundations working to contain a revolutionary upheaval and create a democratic government. After the 1974 army coup which deposed the authoritarian dictatorship that had ruled Portugal for 50 years, the Portuguese homeland did not suffer the radical takeovers that had affected its African colonies, even though in the immediate aftermath of the fall of the dictatorship the Portuguese communists had seemed to be the best-organised political force. Instead, Western European Social Democratic parties channelled funding and political training to the Portuguese Socialist Party, which then inflicted a decisive electoral defeat on the communists.[101]

The Portuguese crisis provided an example of an instrumentality that could mobilise political parties to combat the spread of communism, thus filling the organisational gap created by the collapse of the state–private network and the restriction of the CIA's covert action capability. Much of the aid passed to non-communist Portuguese political parties was donated, and all of it coordinated, by the West German Party Foundations.[102] These four non-governmental political foundations were each connected to one of the four major German political parties and although they received funding from the West German government for their foreign activities, the foundations were legally independent from it.[103] All four foundations were active worldwide, providing a new model for political intervention which superseded both military force and covert action. US political leaders could not fail to be interested in developing a similar instrument for their own use.

The movement to create a similar US organisation was begun in February 1977 by West Democratic Congressman Donald Fraser, who proposed creating an International Department for the Democratic Party to contact other democratic parties and party internationals.[104] Fraser, a liberal from Minneapolis, had served in Congress from 1962 and had been intensely concerned with Human Rights and democratic development during his political career. In 1966 he had proposed the Title IX Amendment to the Foreign Assistance Act, which called for the United States Agency for International Development to provide assistance to democratic civil society organisations in the Third World.[105] As Chairman of the House Foreign Affairs Subcommittee on International Organisations he had also held the first Congressional hearings on Human Rights in 1973, which did much to raise the profile of the issue as a legitimate foreign policy consideration for the US.[106]

The roots of democracy promotion   27

Fraser was intrigued by the example the West German party foundations offered of how private groups could wield political influence over foreign political actors. The practical effect of the aid and political training dispensed to ideologically acceptable recipients in the Third World by each foundation, he believed, was the spread of the ideology of the West German parties to political movements in the developing world and the strengthening of the influence of the West German government overseas.[107] Fraser was also influenced by the argument that US party foundations could replace the declining CIA as conduits of US political influence[108] and proposed that one staff member of the DNC be given responsibility for international contacts in order to promote Democratic Party attendance at party international meetings and to co-operate with international political movements to fill this organisational gap.[109] The International Department would be a private instrument of political influence under the control of the parties, rather than the national security bureaucracy.

The project was pushed forward by a Democratic Party colleague of Fraser's, George Agree, a former Congressional aide to Daniel Patrick Moynihan, who also believed that transnational party networks could replace previous covert methods of political influence.[110] However, there was a crucial ideological difference in the visions of the two men. Fraser had kept his proposal within the Carter administration's foreign policy framework by proposing that the new International Department should work in support of the Human Rights policy;[111] however, Agree went beyond this policy by arguing that transnational party contacts could also help to construct democracy in non-democratic states.[112] Agree clearly aimed at deeper reform of foreign political systems than the Carter administration contemplated. Furthermore, the lack of state involvement in the project meant that he was able to articulate and pursue this goal, insulated from the bureaucratic struggles that often led to the restriction or limitation of democratisation policies and organisations.

Even without state limitation, however, there were serious problems involved in creating an organisation that would allow US political parties to conduct political programmes abroad. First, the two US parties were much more ideologically diverse than Western European parties, making it more difficult for them to take a consistent line on policy questions than parties who identified themselves as proponents of one political ideology.[113] The second obstacle was financial; Agree calculated that the annual cost of one full-time international officer would be $100,000, a significant amount of money for a party organisation with a budget in the low millions, much of which had to be earmarked for fund-raising efforts.[114] Clearly organisational changes and a massive injection of finance would be required to equip the parties as channels of political and ideological influence.

Agree's solution to the first problem was to work for the creation of a bipartisan institute staffed by Democrats and Republicans. Such a structure would subsume the factionalism within each party within the bipartisan institute,[115] with the goal of promoting democracy containing such differences within a more inclusive overarching concept. This bipartisan structure represented an

28 *The roots of democracy promotion*

adaptation of the West German model to suit the differing nature of US political parties. The institute would carry out the aims outlined by Fraser, as well, as collecting information on foreign parties and their methods of organisation.[116] Over the course of the next year Agree secured the support of the Republican National Committee Chairman, William Brock, and that of the Democratic National Chairman, Charles Manatt for his ideas. When Agree founded his institute, the American Political Foundation, both men joined the new organisation, as chairman and vice-chairman respectively. The American Political Foundation held its first board meeting on 18 July 1979,[117] with its existence being announced to the press in early November.[118] The *Wall Street Journal* was hopeful that the APF would be able to have an impact on the perceived global turn towards dictatorship and on US foreign policy, arguing that although over the previous 25 years regimes hostile to democracy had proliferated, 'the other day we heard about a new organization, the American Political Foundation, whose birth gives us hope that at least someone out there knows what's wrong and is trying to help us recover our bearings.'[119]

However, the financial problem remained unresolved. Although Agree applied to the German Marshall Fund for $100,000 in seed money for the APF in September 1979,[120] this did not materialise due to the fund's perception of the general weakness of the US party organisations.[121] Given that at the first board meeting, an annual budget of $220,000 was called for in the organisation's early set-up stage alone, this left a substantial financial deficit.[122] Agree remained optimistic about securing funding from US businesses and foundations from 1979–81; however, although a small number of corporations donated low four-figure amounts, securing a stable source of funding was a perennial problem. Difficulties with obtaining funds were a key topic during the organisation's annual board meetings of 1980 and 1981.[123]

These funding difficulties were also a consequence of the APF's poor links with the Executive, as the organisation did not receive any funding from the NSC or the White House despite initial interest from Samuel Huntington, then working as an NSC staff member.[124] The organisation did receive $74,632 from the United States Information and Communications Agency, the government organisation tasked with improving perceptions of the USA in the outside world and thus waging the ideological struggle against communism overtly, to carry out exchanges with Western European parties in 1980.[125] However, there is no evidence that the APF was any more or less important than other US private groups which received project money from USICA for their activities. Therefore, the capabilities of the nascent private network were limited to small-scale programmes due to the continuing the split between private elites interested in democracy promotion and the state. The organisation was also hampered by the lack of a clear strategy which meshed its aim with a tangible national security goal: while Agree wished to promote democracy and felt that in the long-term this would be positive for the US and the world, he did not lay out a coherent plan for doing so or a list of target countries where operations could have an impact on these goals.

Democracy promotion and national security strategy

In the early 1980s a further intervention from outside the Executive restated and narrowed the strategic focus of the emerging paradigm of democracy promotion and opened up the possibility of a renewed relationship between state and non-state actors over political intervention overseas. This partial re-strategising of democracy promotion was spurred by the failure of the Carter administration's Human Rights campaign to prevent revolution in Third World states allied to the US. The administration's strategic failure was most evident in Iran and in Nicaragua, where the replacement of the Somoza dictatorship by the Sandinistas in July 1979 led to the creation of the first Marxist-Leninist government on the mainland of the Americas. The collapse of the Somoza dictatorship had implications for US foreign policy, which extended beyond Nicaragua, as the downfall of the regime represented an episode in a wave of Third World revolutions which had begun in 1974 and showed no sign of petering out. The fall of Nicaragua thus re-opened the strategic question of whether US security could be better guarded through the implementation of reforms in order to defuse revolutions or increased support for friendly authoritarians. The crisis spurred the evolution of democracy promotion by pointing to the existence of a strategic problem that could be filled by the creation of a new state–private network devoted to party-building. This addition of a more immediate national security dimension to democracy promotion also opened up the possibility of a renewed convergence between non-state actors and the state.

The fall of the Somoza regime

The Carter administration's policy failure in Nicaragua clearly showed the limitations of the Human Rights approach to the pursuit of political reform overseas. The Central American country had been under the authoritarian rule of the Somoza family since 1936, with the current dictator, Anastasio Somoza, being the son of the dynasty's founder. Under the Somozas, Nicaragua had acted as a staunch ally of the US, even providing bases to assist in the CIA-led overthrow of Guatemala's democratic government in 1954.[126] However, early in Carter's presidential term, a power struggle erupted in Nicaragua with three main actors: the Somoza dictatorship, a Marxist guerrilla force, the Sandinistas, and a middle-class democratic opposition movement. Initially, the administration attempted to pressure the dictatorship to improve its Human Rights performance through government-to-government measures such as vetoing loans and curbing arms transfers[127] to de-escalate the situation. When Somoza proved uncooperative and the Marxist FSLN insurgency which threatened the regime continued to grow in strength, the administration began to fear that 'the longer Somoza stayed in power, the higher the chances were of a radical takeover'.[128] Administration officials were split between those who believed that the US should attempt to leverage a 'moderate Third Force' composed of democratic opposition leaders acceptable to the United States into power to replace Somoza and contain the

30 *The roots of democracy promotion*

FSLN, and others who argued that the democratic opposition was too weak to take power.[129] Those who supported the Third Force option hoped that a transfer of power to the FAO, the liberal opposition coalition, would result in the preservation of the dictatorship's National Guard and the creation of a non-revolutionary government of national unity, which would block the approaching Sandinista victory.[130] However, opponents of the policy had valid reasons to be cautious, as decades of dictatorial rule, supported by the United States, had weakened the liberal groups, which were factionalised and lacked a strong organisational base. The result was that this weak opposition group instead forged an alliance with the FSLN, ensuring the failure of the US' eleventh hour attempt to engineer a transfer of power to a centrist coalition government to preserve the National Guard and create a politically stable and legitimate regime capable of combatting the Sandinistas both militarily and politically.[131]

The failure of the Carter administration's policy was a result of a tension that it did not possess the instruments to resolve. The administration's top-down pressure on Somoza to encourage reform did not address the problem of creating a strong and cohesive middle force to succeed him, leaving the FSLN as Somoza's strongest competitor. However, an attempt to bypass the dictator by channelling aid to middle forces through US government agencies could have led to a much earlier break between the US and Somoza, ending a security relationship which was necessary to block a more rapid Sandinista takeover. The administration had been caught between its immediate need to support Somoza against the FSLN and its long-term need to midwife a more stable democratic government capable of defeating them.

Pre-emptive democracy promotion in allied dictatorships

Michael Samuels, a former State Department political appointee and a current Director of the Centre for Strategic International Studies conceived a solution to this problem. Samuels' government experience clearly informed his analysis of the problem: while at the State Department he had dealt with relations between the Executive and Congress over Radio Free Europe and Radio Liberty, formerly funded covertly through the state–private network and then overtly since the exposure of this relationship in 1971.[132] He had also been part of a US government team sent to Portugal to assess the political situation after the collapse of the Caetano dictatorship in 1974.[133] In February 1980 Samuels contacted George Agree, then President of the American Political Foundation, to outline his proposals and enlist the APF's support for them.

Samuels offered a solution to the trade-off between current support of authoritarian regimes and the promotion of democratising reforms in the interest of long-term stability by arguing for the pre-emptive creation of democratic movements in dictatorships vulnerable to instability. Rather than pressuring dictatorships to reform in order to ward off revolution and then expecting a weak and unorganised liberal movement to take power in order to head off a revolutionary victory when the regime fell, as Carter had done in Nicaragua, the US should

The roots of democracy promotion 31

begin organising democratic movements in vulnerable dictatorships immediately, in order to prepare for regime collapse. Samuels made this point by contrasting the success of transnational party work in Portugal with the failure of the Human Rights policy in Nicaragua and Iran in terms of US national security. His argument was that in the aftermath of the fall of an authoritarian dictatorship, elements 'committed to political dictatorship, monolithic politics and monolithic economies' could assume power.[134] These elements, such as Nicaragua's 'Sandinista guerrillas' and Iran's 'non-democratic, obscurantist religious forces', posed a danger to US foreign policy interests.[135] However, in Portugal 'democratic pluralistic elements emerged victorious' and Portugal remained an ally of the United States.[136]

It was clear that the mechanism used in Portugal was far superior to the US' poorly thought-out eleventh hour efforts elsewhere. This success showed that the establishment of democratic movements in unstable dictatorships could serve US interests by creating political forces which could take power in the event of a political collapse.[137] The accession of liberal forces to power in strategically important countries would maintain the US' geopolitical position in such countries, even after the fall of allied dictatorships. This reasoning paralleled that of Douglas in the early 1970s, given added urgency by the fall of Nicaragua and the overall decline of the US' ability to project its political influence through instrumentalities such as the CIA. Samuels also believed that support for democratic forces overseas should be channelled through a non-state institution so as to avoid the 'political contamination' of direct contact with the US government, which could lead to the rejection of such a programme 'in many Third World contexts.'[138] Thus, he argued for the establishment of an overt 'American Political Development Foundation', 'an autonomous, quasi-private, but government funded, foundation' to fill the gap caused by the fact that '[a]t present the US has insufficient foreign policy machinery for promoting the development of democratic-pluralist forces abroad, despite the national security need for such a capability.'[139]

This new strategic and organisational conception of democracy promotion was clearly focussed on US needs rather than the needs of democracy or of Third World populations. Samuels advanced no concept similar to Douglas' 'regimented democracy', which described a type of democracy specifically tailored for the economic development needs of Third World states, and his version of democracy promotion was focussed more narrowly on countries where the US had the greatest strategic interest, not those where democratic movements were most needed or had the greatest chance of success. Furthermore, in contrast to Douglas' proposed multilateral party league, Samuels' organisation was limited to American parties acting in American interests. Thus, Samuels' proposal pointed towards the formation of a new state–private network centred on a democracy foundation funded wholly by the US state and targeted on sub-state political organisations. Such a relationship was now more possible than it had been previously, as Samuels had linked democracy promotion to a tangible strategic goal which could be carried out only by private groups. This new concept

32 *The roots of democracy promotion*

created the conditions for the forging of a state–private network by positing a programme of action in support of a national security goal that could only be achieved by private groups provided with government funding.

However, non-state democracy promoters would clearly need to mount a focussed attempt to engage the state in their project to obtain the necessary funding. In order to accomplish this, it would be necessary to generate a new foreign policy consensus among state elites that equated democracy promotion with US national security and would tie this new consensus to the specific organisation proposed by Samuels. Generating a consensus within the Executive would not be sufficient, as the creation of an overt organisation, as opposed to a covert structure, would need to be agreed by Congress in order to secure appropriations. Thus, Samuels proposed launching a lobbying campaign aimed at both Executive branch officials and Congress to counter the 'tremendous residual reluctance to think about active American contributions to the evolution of various political cultures around the world'[140], that is, the reduced willingness of the US to intervene in the political structures of other countries. The vehicle for this campaign would be a study on how a political development foundation could be created, targeted at legislators and members of the executive connected with Third World affairs.[141]

Samuels' motivation for contacting Agree with these proposals was clear; he required assistance to convince the US government to fund his project, and Agree was the President of a credible private organisation already involved in outreach to political groups overseas. However, Agree's initial response to these ideas highlights the differences that existed between the two men in terms of their conception of democracy promotion. Whereas Samuels' proposal was aimed at convincing the US government to finance the project, Agree continued to see the activity as a purely private initiative and responded to this proposal by suggesting 'a real search for workable private sector alternatives', rather than the creation of a democracy institution funded by the state.[142] Although Agree had previously asked the White House and USICA for project money, he was clearly uneasy about making government funding the main or only source of support for democracy promotion. However, he did agree to attend a follow-up meeting.[143] After this meeting the APF as a whole seems to have supported Samuels' strategy; possibly because it promised to provide a stable source of funding from the Executive and Congress. This marked the beginning of an attempt to generate a new campaign and a new organisational structure for the export of democracy.

Conclusion

The development of democracy promotion was a product of the discrediting of previous modes of political intervention in the late 1960s and early 1970s. The failure of the state to generate an effective method of supporting political reform overseas in the national interest after this crisis, together with the perception of growing instability in the Third World, spurred private actors to generate the concept of democracy promotion in order to compensate for this state incapacity.

The roots of democracy promotion 33

In doing so, these non-state actors reformulated the pre-existing paradigms of political intervention that had been deployed by the US before the crisis of the late 1960s and early 1970s to make the pursuit of political reform more effective. The new democracy promotion organisation proposed by these actors was to function overtly, and so would not be vulnerable to the loss of credibility which had occurred after the exposure of the covert state–private network relationships after the 1967 crisis. In common with Modernisation theory, the new concept of democracy promotion focussed on the creation of democratic systems overseas; however, its focus on strengthening sub-state political actors meant that unco-operative authoritarian governments that were not open to reform could be bypassed. Most crucially, the blueprint for democracy promotion developed over the 1970s provided a strategic approach to the problem of reconciling democracy and national security that could replace the previous case-by-case approach taken by the US government.

By 1980, the growing need for a method of blocking or pre-empting Third World revolutions and the recognition that democracy promotion required financial resources that only the state could provide had opened up the possibility of a state–private accommodation which could lead to the creation of a new, overt state–private network dedicated to democratisation. However this renewed turn towards the state threatened to re-open the strategic and organisational tensions that had previously damaged the pursuit of political reform in the US national interest. The question of whether and how sub-state democracy promotion efforts would have any connection with the state's more short-term foreign policy would need to be resolved, and decisions at this strategic level could influence the contours of the relationship between the state and private groups, threatening a resurgence of the autonomy/control dilemma. These problems flowed from the decision to accept state funding, which could give the national security bureaucracy leverage over any new democracy promotion effort in a way which Douglas' multilateral model and Agree's private sector solution had guarded against.

These questions rose in importance after Ronald Reagan came to power. While Reagan was more ideologically committed to an identification of the US with the cause of democracy than the administrations of the 1970s, making a state–private convergence more possible, he was also far more committed to confrontation with the Soviet Union, something the democracy promoters had not yet factored into their blueprint, and to strong support for the US' authoritarian allies. Thus, it was possible that the private effort to re-engage the state could result in the replication of the strategic and organisational tensions that had been a structural feature of US attempts to deploy democracy in the service of national security before the 1967 crisis. The question of how much autonomy the new administration would be willing to grant a state-funded organisation whose long-term strategy might clash with its own national security priorities would need to be resolved.

34   *The roots of democracy promotion*

Notes

1 George F. Kennan, 'The Sources of Soviet Conduct,' *Foreign Affairs* 25 no. 4 (1947), reprinted in *Foreign Affairs* 65, no. 4 (1987): 868, accessed 23 November 2014, EBSCO Host.

2 James M. Carter, *Inventing Vietnam: the United States and State Building in Southeast Asia 1954–1968* (Cambridge: Cambridge University Press, 2008), 2.

3 NSC, *NSC-68: United States Objectives and Programs for National Security*, 14 April 1950, *Wilson Center Digital Archive*, accessed 6 August 2014, http://legacy. wilsoncenter.org/coldwarfiles/files/Documents/nsc68.pdf, 7–9.

4 David Ryan, *US Foreign Policy in World History* (London: Routledge, 2000), 28. See also Jonathan Monten, 'The Roots of the Bush Doctrine: Power, Nationalism and Democracy Promotion in US Strategy,' *International Security* 29, No. 4 (2005): 119–123, accessed 8 November 2014, doi:10.1162/isec.2005.29.4.112.

5 Richard Melanson, *American Foreign Policy since the Vietnam War: the Search for Consensus from Nixon to Clinton* (Armonk, New York: M.E. Sharpe, 2000), 32.

6 Michael H. Hunt, *Ideology and US Foreign Policy* (New Haven and London: Yale University Press, 2009), 153; Adam Quinn, *US Foreign Policy in Context: National Ideology from the Founders to the Bush Doctrine* (London and New York: Routledge, 2010), 114–139 and 119–136; and Colin Dueck, *Reluctant Crusaders: Power, Culture, and Change in American Grand Strategy* (Princeton and Oxford: Princeton University Press, 2006), 89–90 and 98–100.

7 Douglas J. Macdonald, 'Formal Ideologies in the Cold War: Toward a Framework for Empirical Analysis' in *Reviewing the Cold War: Approaches, Interpretations, Theory* ed. Odd Arne Westad, 180–207 (London: Frank Cass, 2000), particularly 185–186.

8 Bennett Kovrig, *Of Walls and Bridges: The United States and Eastern Europe* (New York and London: New York University Press, 1991), 43–45.

9 Laszlo Borhi, 'Rollback, Liberation, Containment, or Inaction?: US Policy and Eastern Europe in the 1950s,' *Journal of Cold War Studies* 1, no. 3 (1999): 89, 106–107, accessed 9 September 2014, EBSCO Host.

10 Ervand Abrahamian, *The Coup: 1953, the CIA and the Roots of Modern US-Iranian Relations* (New York and London: The New Press, 2013) and Stephen Schlesinger and Stephen Kinzer, *Bitter Fruit: The Story of the American Coup in Guatemala* (Cambridge, Massachusetts and London, England: Harvard University Press, 1999).

11 Sig Mickelson, *America's Other Voice: the story of Radio Free Europe and Radio Liberty* (New York: Praeger, 1983) and Arch Puddington, *Broadcasting Freedom: the Cold War triumph of Radio Free Europe and Radio Liberty* (Lexington, Kentucky: University Press of Kentucky, 2000).

12 Frances Stonor Saunders, *Who Paid the Piper?: The CIA and the Cultural Cold War* (London: Granta Books, 1999).

13 Hugh Wilford, *The Mighty Wurlitzer: How the CIA Played America* (Cambridge, Massachusetts: Harvard University Press, 2008), 149–167 and 197–225.

14 Karen M. Paget, 'From Stockholm to Leiden: The CIA's role in the formation of the International Student Conference' in *The Cultural Cold War in Western Europe 1945–60*, ed. Hans Krabbendam and Giles Scott-Smith, 138–159 (London: Frank Cass, 2003) and Paget, 'From co-operation to covert action: the United States Government and students, 1940–52,' in *The US Government, Citizen Groups and the Cold War: the State–Private Network*, ed. Helen Laville and Hugh Wilford, 66–83 (London: Routledge, 2006).

15 Wilford, 51–69

16 George F. Kennan, 'Document 269: The Inauguration of Organised Political Warfare', 4 May 1948, *Foreign Relations of the United States 1945–50: Retrospective Volume,*

The roots of democracy promotion 35

Emergence of the Intelligence Establishment, accessed 19 December 2014, http://history.state.gov/historicaldocuments/frus1945–50Intel/d269.

17 Ibid.

18 Lucas, *Freedom's War*, 3,

19 NSC-68, 11–12.

20 W. Lucas, 'Beyond freedom, beyond control, beyond the Cold War: approaches to American culture and the state–private network,' *Intelligence and National Security* 18, no. 2 (2003), 60, accessed 15 January 2010, http://dx.doi.org/10.1080/02684520 412331306740.

21 Wilford, *The Mighty Wurlitzer*; and Anthony Carew, 'The American Labor Movement in Fizzland: The Free Trade Union Committee and the CIA,' *Labor History* 39, no. 1 (1998): 25–42, accessed 16 May 2014, DOI: 10.1080/0023667981233138 7276.

22 W.S. Lucas, 'Revealing the Parameters of Opinion: An interview with Frances Stonor Saunders' in *The Cultural Cold War in Western Europe 1945–60*, ed. Hans Krabbendam and Giles Scott-Smith (London: Frank Cass, 2003), 25.

23 Ibid., 16.

24 Wilford, 75–79.

25 Lucas, *Freedom's War*, 152–154.

26 Paul Cammack, *Capitalism and Democracy in the Third World: The Doctrine for Political Development* (London, Leicester University Press, 1997), 10.

27 Irene L. Gendzier, 'Play it Again Sam: The Practice and Apology of Development' in *Universities and Empire: Money and Politics in the Social Sciences during the Cold War*, ed. Christopher Simpson (New York: The New Press, 1998), 69.

28 Richard Saull, 'Locating the Global South in the Theorisation of the Cold War: Capitalist Development, Social Revolution and Geopolitical Conflict', *Third World Quarterly* 26, No. 2 (2005): 256, accessed 16 May 2014, DOI: 10.1080/0143659042 000339119.

29 Quoted from Tony Smith, *America's Mission: The United States and the Worldwide Struggle for Democracy in the Twentieth Century* (Princeton, New Jersey: Princeton University Press, 1993), 192.

30 State Department, 'Political Implications of Afro-Asian Military Takeovers,' 1959, and NSC, 'Discussion at the 410th meeting of the National Security Council, Thursday June 18, 1959', 1959, Declassified Documents Reference System, hereafter DDRS, accessed 17 June 2013, 1.

31 Quoted in David F. Schmitz, *The United States and Right-wing Dictatorships, 1965–1989* (Cambridge: Cambridge University Press, 2006), 261.

32 Nicolas Guilhot, *The Democracy Makers: Human Rights and International Order* (New York, Chichester: Columbia University Press, 2005), 105, 112; Gendzier, 69.

33 Quoted in Stephen G. Rabe, *The Killing Zone: The United States Wages Cold War in Latin America* (Oxford: Oxford University Press, 2012), 87.

34 W.W. Rostow, *The Stages of Economic Growth: A Non-communist Manifesto* Third Edition (Cambridge: Cambridge University Press, 1990), 4–11.

35 Jeffrey E. Taffet, *Foreign Aid as Foreign Policy: the Alliance for Progress in Latin America* (New York; London: Routledge, 2007), 49.

36 Ibid., 22–23.

37 Piki Ish-Shalom, 'Theory Gets Real, and the Case for a Normative Ethic: Rostow, Modernization Theory, and the Alliance for Progress,' *International Studies Quarterly* 50, no. 2 (2006): 295–297, accessed 13 February 2013, www.jstor.org/stable/3693612.

38 Taffet, *Foreign Aid as Foreign Policy*, 48.

39 Richard Saull, *The Cold War and After: Capitalism, Revolution and Superpower Politics* (London, Pluto Press, 2007), 122–123.

40 Schmitz, *Thank God They're on Our Side* 268–282 and Rabe, *Killing Zone* 105–108.

41 Schmitz, 258 and 282–285 and Rabe, 98–103.

36 *The roots of democracy promotion*

42 Guilhot, 73.
43 Tity de Vries, 'The 1967 Central Intelligence Agency Scandal: Catalyst in a Transforming Relationship between State and People,' *Journal of American History* 98, no. 4 (2012): 1086, accessed 16 May 2014, doi: 10.1093/jahist/jar563.
44 Wilford, 246, 238–239.
45 H.W. Brands, *The Wages of Globalism: Lyndon Johnson and the Limits of American Power* (Oxford: Oxford University Press, 1995), 262.
46 Wilford, 232–234.
47 De Vries, 1076, 1083–1084.
48 Guilhot, 50.
49 Frank Ninkovich, *The Diplomacy of Ideas: US Foreign Policy and Cultural Relations, 1938–1950* (Cambridge: Cambridge University Press, 1981), 178.
50 Peter Jessup, 'Memorandum for the Record: Minutes of the Meeting of the 303 Committee,' 8 July 1966, *Foreign Relations of the United States 1964–1968, Volume X, National Security Policy*, accessed 19 December 2014. http://history.state.gov/historicaldocuments/frus1964–68v10/d134.
51 Richard Helms with William Hood, *A look over my shoulder: a life in the Central Intelligence Agency* (New York: Random House, 2003), 345–346.
52 Charles Frankel, 'The Reorganization of International Educational and Cultural Activities', 23 February 1967, DDRS, accessed 24 April 2006, 1.
53 Helms with Hood, 369
54 Anonymous, 'Staff Paper: Alternatives for Supporting US private Voluntary Activities Overseas', 3 May 1967, DDRS, accessed 28 June 2013, 6, 7.
55 Memo, Dean Rusk to the President, 4 June 1968, DDRS, accessed 28 June 2013, 2.
56 Ibid.
57 Ibid.
58 Mark T. Berger, 'From Nation-Building to State-Building: The Geopolitics of Development, the Nation-State System and the Changing Global Order,' *Third World Quarterly* 27, no. 1 (2006): 18, accessed 12 March 2012, www.jstor.org/stable/4017656.
59 Nils Gilman, 'Modernization Theory, the Highest Stage of American Intellectual History' in *Staging Growth: Modernization, Development and the Cold War*, ed. David C. Engerman, Nils Gilman, Mark H. Haefele and Michael E. Latham (US: University of Massachusetts Press, 2003), 66–67.
60 Gilman, Ibid.; Gendzier, 'Play it Again Sam', 88.
61 Gilman, 64; Gendzier, 67.
62 Christopher T. Fisher, 'The Illusion of Progress: CORDS and the Crisis of Modernization in South Vietnam, 1965–1968,' *Pacific Historical Review* 75, no. 1 (2006): 4, accessed 12 March 2012, www.jstor.org/stable/10.1525/phr.2006.75.1.25.
63 Taffet, *Foreign Aid as Foreign Policy*, 175.
64 Schmitz, *The United States and Right-wing Dictatorships*, 74–75 and 87–92.
65 Ibid., 93.
66 William A. Douglas, *Developing Democracy* (Washington DC: Heldref Publications, 1972), 6 and 98.
67 Ibid., 131.
68 Quoted from ibid., 133.
69 Ibid., 137.
70 Ibid., 150–152.
71 Ibid., 119–121.
72 Ibid., 98–99.
73 Ibid., 118–127.
74 Ibid., 189.
75 Ibid., 157–158.
76 Ibid., 161.

The roots of democracy promotion 37

77 Ibid., 178–179.
78 Ibid., 184.
79 Ibid., 188.
80 Ibid., 188–189.
81 Ibid., 187–188.
82 Ibid., 188.
83 Saull, *The Cold War and After*, 139.
84 Fred Halliday, *The Making of the Second Cold War* (London: Verso, 1984), 86–89.
85 Loch K. Johnson, *A Season of Inquiry: The Senate Intelligence Investigation*, (Lexington, Kentucky: The University Press of Kentucky, 1985), 258–261, quote from 261.
86 Kenneth Cmiel, 'The Emergence of Human Rights Politics in the United States,' *The Journal of American History* 86, no. 3 (1999): 1233–1235, accessed 10 April 2013, www.jstor.org/stable/2568613.
87 Dante Fascell, 'The Helsinki Accord: A Case Study', *Annals of the American Academy of Political and Social Science* 442 (March 1979): 71–72, accessed 15 April 2013, www.jstor.org/stable/1043482.
88 John Dumbrell, *The Carter Presidency: A Re-evaluation* (Manchester: Manchester University Press, 1995), 116–117.
89 David F. Schmitz and Vanessa Walker, 'Jimmy Carter and the Foreign Policy of Human Rights: The Development of a Post-Cold War Foreign Policy,' *Diplomatic History* 28, no. 1 (2004): 125, accessed 10 April 2013, DOI: 10.1111/j.1467–7709.2004.00400.x.
90 Sarah B. Snyder, *Human Rights Activism and the End of the Cold War: A Transnational History of the Helsinki Network* (Cambridge: Cambridge University Press, 2011), 38–44.
91 James Earl Carter, *Keeping Faith: Memoirs of a President* (Fayetteville, Arkansas: University of Arkansas Press, 1982), 143; White House, 'Presidential Review Memorandum 28: Human Rights,' 8 July 1977, *Jimmy Carter Library*, accessed 20 March 2009. www.jimmycarterlibrary.gov/documents/prmemorandums/prm28.pdf, 78.
92 PRM-28, 4.
93 Victor Kaufman, 'The Bureau of Human Rights during the Carter Administration,' *The Historian 61*, no. 1 (1998): 54, accessed 16 May 2014, DOI: 10.1111/j.1540–6563.1998.tb01423.x.
94 Burton I. Kaufman and Scott Kaufman, *The Presidency of James Earl Carter*, Second Edition, Revised (Lawrence, Kansas: University Press of Kansas, 2006), 47; Victor Kaufman, 'The Bureau of Human Rights': 58.
95 Kaufman, 'The Bureau of Human Rights': 57.
96 Dumbrell, 186.
97 Snyder, 116; 122–126.
98 Hauke Hartmann, 'US Human Rights Policy under Carter and Reagan, 1977–1981,' *Human Rights Quarterly* 23, no. 2 (2001): 414 and associated footnotes, accessed 5 April 2012, www.jstor.org/stable/4489339.
99 Zbigniew Brzezinski, 'Document 114: Memorandum From the President's Assistant for National Security Affairs (Brzezinski) to President Carter,' undated, *Foreign Relations of the United States 1977–1980, Volume II: Human Rights and Humanitarian Affairs* (Washington DC: United States Government Printing Office, 2013), accessed 27 November 2014, http://static.history.state.gov/frus/frus1977–80v02/pdf/frus1977–80v02.pdf, 394–398.
100 See *Foreign Relations of the United States 1977–1980, Volume II: Human Rights and Humanitarian Affairs* (Washington DC: United States Government Printing Office, 2013), accessed 27 November 2014, http://static.history.state.gov/frus/frus1977–80v02/pdf/frus1977–80v02.pdf, particularly: 'Document 126. Action Memorandum From the Assistant Secretary of State for Human Rights and Humanitarian Affairs

38 *The roots of democracy promotion*

(Derian), the Assistant Secretary of State for Congressional Relations (Bennet), and the Director of the Policy Planning Staff (Lake) to Secretary of State Vance,' Washington, 20 March 1978, 423–427; 'Document 128. Memorandum From the Deputy Assistant Secretary of State for European Affairs (Luers) to the Deputy Secretary of State (Christopher),' Washington, 23 March 1978, 429–430; 'Document 130. Action Memorandum from the Assistant Secretary of State for East Asian and Pacific Affairs (Holbrooke) to the Deputy Secretary of State (Christopher),' Washington, 24 March 1978, 432–434; 'Document 131. Memorandum from the Director of the Policy Planning Staff (Lake) to Secretary of State Vance,' Washington, 27 March 1978, 434–435; 'Document 133. Briefing Memorandum from the Assistant Secretary of State for African Affairs (Moose) to the Deputy Secretary of State (Christopher),' Washington, 6 April 1978, 438–439.

101 Michael Pinto-Duschinsky, 'Foreign Political Aid: The German Foundations and their US Counterparts,' *International Affairs* 67, no. 1 (1991): 55–56, accessed 16 May 2014, www.jstor.org/stable/2621218. See also Cord Meyer, *Facing Reality: From World Federalism to the CIA* (Lanham: University Press of America, 1980), 107–108.

102 Pinto-Duschinsky, 'Foreign Political Aid': 55–56.

103 Ibid., 33–34.

104 Donald M. Fraser, 'A Proposal that the Democratic National Committee employ at least one staff member assigned to follow and work with political movements abroad,' 1977, Folder 6: Reports and Proposals, Box 1, George E. Agree Papers, Library of Congress, Washington DC, hereafter LOC.

105 Robert A. Packenham, *Liberal America and the Third World: Political Development Ideas in Foreign Aid and Political Science*, (Princeton, New Jersey: Princeton University Press, 1973), 99–109.

106 Cmiel, 1235; Tony Evans, *US Hegemony and the Project of Universal Human Rights* (Basingstoke: Macmillan Press, 1996), 164.

107 Donald M. Fraser, 'A Proposal', 4.

108 Donald M. Fraser, 'A Proposal', attachment 3, Abstract of 'The Emerging Transnational Party System and the Future of American Parties' by Ralph M. Goldman, 1977 and Ralph M. Goldman 'The Emerging Transnational Party System and the Future of American Parties,' in *Political Parties: Development and Decay*, ed. Joseph Cooper and Louis Maisel (Beverley Hills and London: Sage Publications, 1978).

109 See Donald M. Fraser, 'A Proposal'.

110 George Agree, 'Proposal for a pilot study of international cooperation between democratic political parties,' 9 May 1977, Folder 6: Reports and Proposals, Box 1, George E. Agree Papers, LOC.

111 Fraser, 'A Proposal'.

112 Agree, 'Proposal for a pilot study'.

113 George Agree, 'This is a plan, consistent with political realities, for the major American parties to establish a joint tax-deductible institute for communication with foreign parties', 1977, Folder 6: Reports and Proposals, Box 1, George E. Agree Papers, LOC.

114 Ibid., 2.

115 Ibid.

116 Ibid., 4–5.

117 APF 'Minutes of Organization meeting of Board of Directors of the American Political Foundation', 18 July 1979, Folder 3: APF Minutes, Box 1, George E. Agree Papers, LOC.

118 *Wall Street Journal*, 'Democracy International', *Wall Street Journal*, 27 November 1979, Folder: Press, 1979–1984, Box 1, George E. Agree Papers, LOC.

119 Ibid.

The roots of democracy promotion 39

120 Letter, George Agree to Robert Gerald Livingston, 17 September 1979, Folder 1: APF Correspondence, Box 1, George E. Agree Papers, LOC.

121 Letter, Robert Gerald Livingston to Dr. Henning Wegener, 8 August 1980, Folder 1: APF Correspondence, Box 1, George E. Agree Papers, LOC.

122 APF, Minutes of Organization meeting of Board of Directors of the American Political Foundation, 18 July 1979, Folder 3: APF Minutes, Box 1, George E. Agree Papers, LOC.

123 APF, 'Minutes of 1980 Annual Meeting, Board of Directors of American Political Foundation', 19 March 1980, Folder 3: APF Minutes, Box 1, George E. Agree Papers, LOC, APF, 'Minutes of 1981 Annual Meeting, Board of Directors of American Political Foundation,' 7 July 1981, Folder 3: APF Minutes, Box 1, George E. Agree Papers, LOC, and APF, 'Financial Report', attached to Minutes of 1981 Annual Meeting, Board of Directors of American Political Foundation.

124 Letter, George Agree to Dr Samuel P. Huntington, 3 February 1978, Folder 1: APF Correspondence, Box 1, George E. Agree Papers, LOC.

125 'APF Financial Report'.

126 Stephen Schlesinger and Stephen Kinzer, *Bitter Fruit: The Story of the American Coup in Guatemala*, Expanded Edition (Cambridge, Massachusetts: Harvard University Press, 199), 113–114,

127 Martha L. Cottam, 'The Carter Administration's Policy towards Nicaragua: Images, Goals and Tactics,' *Political Science Quarterly* 107, no. 1 (1992): 138, accessed 10 December 2010, www.jstor.org/stable/2152137.

128 Robert A. Pastor, *Not Condemned to Repetition: the United States and Nicaragua*, (Boulder, Colorado: Westview, 2002), 94.

129 Morris H. Morley, *Washington, Somoza and the Sandinistas: State and Regime in US Policy towards Nicaragua 1969–1981* (Cambridge, Cambridge University Press, 1994), 131, and 168; and Pastor, *Not Condemned*, 84.

130 Ibid., 181–184.

131 Ibid., 195.

132 See Michael A. Samuels, interviewed by Charles Stuart Kennedy for *The Foreign Affairs Oral History Collection of the Association for Diplomatic Studies and Training*, 22 October 1991, accessed 2 July 2013, www.adst.org/OH%20TOCs/Samuels,%20Michael%20A.toc.pdf, 2.

133 Ibid., 14, 16–17.

134 Michael A. Samuels, 'Project Proposal: A Comprehensive Policy Response to Expanding U.S. Interests in the Third World,' 1980, 1, attached to letter, George Agree to Mr Michael A. Samuels, 15 February 1980, Folder 1: APF Correspondence, Box 1, George E. Agree Papers, LOC.

135 Ibid., 1.

136 Ibid.

137 Michael A. Samuels, 'Project Proposal,' 1.

138 Ibid.

139 Ibid., 2.

140 Ibid., 3.

141 Ibid.

142 Letter, George Agree to Mr Michael A. Samuels, 15 February 1980, Folder 1: APF Correspondence, Box 1, George E. Agree Papers, LOC.

143 See ibid.

2 Democracy and national security during the early Reagan administration

No grand design

The inauguration of Ronald Reagan in 1981 brought to power a chief executive with a very different view of the world, and America's role in it, to that of Richard Nixon or Jimmy Carter; one whose rhetoric identified the United States unambiguously with the cause of democracy and counterposed this to Soviet totalitarianism. This rhetoric seemed to offer non-state democracy promoters an opportunity to press their case for the creation of a government-funded democracy foundation to a more sympathetic group of policymakers. In addition, the APF had a foothold within the administration as its Chairman, William Brock, was appointed United States Trade Representative. However, the Reagan administration did not initially connect its rhetorical stance to a coherent foreign policy design incorporating the spread of democratic structures as a national security priority, for two reasons.

First, the Reagan administration did not possess a coherent grand strategy to which a coherent strategy of democratisation could be attached. Instead, it was divided into opposing factions advocating contradictory strategies for the prosecution of the Cold War. The pursuit of a 'centred' Cold War strategy of combatting communism directly at its source by pressing economic, ideological and political warfare measures directly against the Soviet bloc in order to weaken Soviet power internally was championed by a hard-line Reaganite group, which contained many key officials such as National Security Advisor Richard Allen, Reagan's newly-appointed Director of Central Intelligence, William J. Casey, and the Secretary of Defence, Caspar Weinberger. In some ways, this group's ideas harked back to the Liberation operations conducted by the US at the beginning of the Cold War. This group's proposals often appealed to President Reagan's more hard-line and ideological instincts. In contrast, a more pragmatic group located primarily in the State Department favoured a 'de-centred' Cold War strategy of building up the strength of the 'Free World', including the allied dictatorships the democracy promoters were interested in reforming, to enable it to resist perceived Soviet pressure and to strengthen containment, rather than in attempting to weaken the Soviet zone. Bureaucratic warfare between these factions, coupled with the President's often-disengaged approach to foreign policy, made the formulation of a coherent national security strategy problematic.

The second difficulty was that the administration had no blueprint explaining how practical policies aimed at the democratisation of other states could be compatible with US national security interests comparable to the Carter administration's understanding of Human Rights or the Kennedy administration's focus on Modernisation. Rather, it conceived of democracy as an abstract aspiration informing US policy as a whole, and as a tool for waging a propaganda war against the Soviet Union and shoring up domestic support for its foreign policy, much as the Cold War administrations the late 1940s and the 1950s had deployed it, rather than as a system which could be strengthened or created overseas to achieve US national security goals.

Due to this strategic and conceptual incoherence, the projection of democratic ideology and efforts to support democratic groups or the growth of democratic structures abroad tended to be attached to pre-existing geopolitical problems on a case-by-case basis, giving rise to three tracks of policy: the projection of democratic ideology in friendly democratic states; support for political movements compatible with US interests in hostile states; and support for democratic reform in allied authoritarian states. In cases where there was general agreement on the geopolitical goals to be pursued within the administration and the deployment of democracy was limited to a propaganda function aimed at legitimating US policy or waging ideological warfare, there were few problems. However, attempts to move beyond propaganda and institute programmes aimed at supporting political forces in hostile states or the growth of democratic structures in allied dictatorships, without an overarching strategic concept of how such programmes could be used to further American interests globally, gave rise to strategic and organisational tensions, as differing groups of policymakers attached democratisation to the geopolitical crises each faction saw as central to its own strategy. In contrast, the non-state democracy promoters clustered around the APF and Michael Samuels offered a far more coherent strategic and organisational blueprint for the implementation of democratic reform as a concrete element of US foreign policy than the Reagan administration had been able to conceive up to this point. The question facing the administration was whether it would examine this approach further or default back to an approach of deploying democracy largely in the ideological sphere.

The projection of democratic ideology: the case of Western Europe

In its first year, the Reagan administration embarked on an effort to reactivate the projection of democratic ideology as a tool of US soft power in Western Europe. This effort was generated by a growing crisis in relations between the US and Western Europe that led officials to support the idea of a renewed campaign to project an abstract concept of democracy to legitimate US policy in this region. The Reagan administration experienced few problems in implementing this policy, as the use of democratic ideology and US national security interests clearly supported one another and it was carried out in support of a geopolitical

42   *Democracy and national security*

goal essential to both 'centred' and 'de-centred' Cold War strategies, the preservation of a strong Western alliance.

The geopolitical reasoning behind US policy towards Western Europe

Strategic consensus over US policy towards Western Europe was organised around a core US geopolitical objective; the preservation of US hegemony over the region. Throughout the Cold War the strategic denial of Soviet access to the industrialised economies of Western Europe had been of key importance to prevent their integration into a Soviet-led Eurasian bloc possessing the military and industrial resources to successfully challenge US global hegemony.[1] This calculation was still current in the early 1980s and had been rearticulated several years before Reagan's inauguration by the Committee on the Present Danger, a private organisation consisting of conservative and neoconservative former policymakers, intellectuals and labour leaders which had argued for tougher anti-Soviet policies under the Nixon and Carter administrations.[2] The CPD had argued that driving a wedge between the US and its Western European allies through an arms build-up on the European continent to intimidate European public opinion was a key Soviet priority, as such a build-up could 'bring Europe to its knees without any shots necessarily being fired'.[3] According to a CPD analysis

> The centrepiece of the Soviet strategic view of world politics has always been that if Russia could control Western Europe and bring it under its dominion ... that it would thereby control the world.[4]

The Committee's philosophy was extremely influential in the early Reagan administration. The President had received regular briefings from the Committee before being elected and had used some of its ideas in his radio broadcasts.[5] In addition, key administration policymakers such as DCI William Casey, National Security Advisor Richard Allen and Richard Pipes, the NSC's Director of Soviet and Eastern European Affairs, were former members of the Committee.[6]

The administration saw the Soviet replacement of their SS-4 and SS-5 intermediate range nuclear missiles targeted on Western Europe with more potent SS-20s as just such an intimidating military build-up, one that could alter the balance of power in Europe in favour of the Soviet Union and facilitate Soviet diplomatic pressure on the US' NATO allies. However, the US response to this problem created a transatlantic rift. The Carter administration's original decision to remedy the perceived imbalance in European Theatre Nuclear Forces by sending new Cruise and Pershing II missiles to bases in Western Europe had been made more palatable to European public opinion by casting it as two-track process; NATO would simultaneously prepare to deploy the missiles while seeking negotiations with the Soviets to reduce the nuclear weapons deployed by both sides.[7] However, substantial sections of Western European public opinion were opposed to the US deployment, fearing that the US and the USSR might engage in a limited nuclear exchange that would devastate Europe but leave the American and Soviet homelands untouched.[8] This fear was aggravated by hard-line statements from administration officials in early 1981, including the President himself. In an interview published in the French newspaper *Le Figaro* in February 1981 Reagan stated that he would not hesitate to use US nuclear weapons in Europe.[9] The President's much-publicised opposition to arms control negotiations also indicated that one of the two tracks of policy was in danger of disappearing.[10]

Disquiet over Reagan's aggressive anti-Soviet stance led to protests against the nuclear upgrades by European publics and elites. In April 15,000 people participated in an anti-nuclear demonstration in Bonn; by October/November the numbers had swelled to 250,000 in Bonn, 150,000 in London and 200,000 in Florence.[11] In Holland government supporters of the deployment were defeated and in Britain the Labour Party stated that it would be opposed to deployment if it regained power. In West Germany the ruling Social Democratic Party voted for a review of the deployment decision, and a USIA survey indicated that 60 per cent of West Germans were opposed to Cruise and Pershing II deployments.[12] The immediate nuclear issue, however, was a symptom of a deeper strategic and ideological cleavage; while the US under the Reagan administration was moving towards a policy of confrontation with the USSR, the countries of Western Europe remained in a state of détente, mainly due to the substantial trade that some of these nations had developed with the Soviet bloc.[13] The level of economic exchange was disquieting to the Reaganites, who were considering imposing new sanctions on trade and the transfer of advanced technologies to the USSR and tightening existing ones.[14] The Western Europeans had also shown themselves less enthusiastic at backing anti-communist foreign policy positions championed by the US; for example, the European reaction to the Soviet invasion of Afghanistan had been much less intense than that of the US, even under President Carter.[15] The transatlantic alliance appeared to be decaying: a development which could alter the geopolitical balance in the Cold War.

Democratic propaganda in Western Europe

Over the course of 1981 the Reagan administration generated to a solution to its geopolitical problems in Western Europe through the deployment of democratic ideology. A clear response to the narrow and immediate problem of Western European public opposition to US missile deployments was proposed in August by USIA's Reaganite Director, Charles Z. Wick: Project Truth, a propaganda campaign aimed at portraying the Soviets as ruthless militaristic totalitarians. Wick attributed the anti-nuclear demonstrations taking place in Europe to the influence of Soviet propaganda[16] and a dangerous 'crisis of democracy' in the West.[17] According to the USIA Director, the Soviet disinformation campaign which was to blame for this was reaching a pivotal stage and the US needed to intervene, as the loss of Western Europe would represent a 'strategic Dunkirk'.[18]

44 *Democracy and national security*

After presenting the situation in such apocalyptic terms, Wick received the green light for Project Truth at an NSC meeting on 17 August 1981.[19] Project Truth first focussed on explaining the threat posed by Soviet totalitarianism to Europeans by making use of sanitised, declassified material from the CIA and Department of Defence, and visual evidence of the Soviet military build-up targeted at Western Europe.[20] The practical outcome of this was a plan for a series 'Soviet Disinformation Alerts', which would provide embassy and information personnel with information on the latest Soviet disinformation campaigns and the knowledge and arguments necessary to rebut them.[21] The plan received full support from the Secretary of State, Alexander Haig, who ordered State Department personnel posted overseas to co-operate.[22]

However, while this focus on criticising the USSR may have been a necessary first step in preserving the NATO alliance, the administration turned to a more positive approach to manage the wider geopolitical and ideological stresses on it. A solution to the problem that focussed more on the positive projection of democratic ideology than simple anti-Soviet propaganda had been proposed by officials in Haig's State Department before the USIA took over overall guidance of US ideological campaigns with the Project Truth proposal. Following a meeting between Haig and West German Foreign Minister Hans Dietrich Genscher in the first half of 1981 the State Department's Bureau of European and Eurasian Affairs proposed a major propaganda campaign to involve co-operation with Britain, France and West Germany.[23] The parameters of the campaign went beyond the initial blueprint for Project Truth in proposing not only to 'counter Soviet propaganda' but also 'sell our own policies'.[24] Haig stressed this idea again in a letter to the British Foreign Secretary at the end of August. Haig argued that '... to take the initiative we need to both educate and inspire. We must be candid about the Soviet threat, and go on the political offensive with positive Western proposals.'[25] To accomplish this, Haig suggested a greater focus on 'Western values' such as individual freedom which could be translated into positive programmes.[26] By November the scope of Project Truth was being broadened beyond a negative propaganda campaign to include these ideas, with John Hughes, head of the executive implementing committee, arguing that 'It is just as important for Project Truth to underline the common values – moral, spiritual, cultural – that bind us to our allies.'[27]

US policy in Western Europe was dictated by the geopolitical situation, with the projection of democratic ideology being added as a tool to legitimate this policy and mobilise support for it. The meshing of democratic ideology and national security policy which this situation generated was aimed at solidifying the US' leadership of its allies by conflating the US' geopolitical interests with the fortunes of democracy and stressing the collective ideological identity of the US and the NATO states as democracies. This was a relatively low-risk strategy as there was no fundamental conflict between US foreign policy interests and backing for democracy in the Western European context, especially in the wake of Iberia's transition to democracy. The fact that the geopolitical objectives that underpinned the policy were widely accepted within the administration, coupled with the fact that the US envisaged a purely rhetorical campaign rather than attempts to influence or modify political structures on the ground, resulted in a solid consensus in support of it.

Democracy as a tool of political warfare: the case of the Soviet bloc

The administration also deployed the projection of democratic ideology as an element of its policy towards the Soviet bloc, in this case as a tool of political warfare aimed at weakening Soviet power. However, unlike the case of Western Europe, the generation of a coherent strategy in this case was complicated by the fact that the administration was divided over whether to pursue a defensive approach aimed at preserving the status quo or an offensive one aimed at transforming or undermining the enemy state. While attempts to project democratic propaganda into the bloc were relatively uncontentious, the question of whether to provide American support for dissident movements on the ground behind the Iron Curtain was complicated by the geopolitical situation and the organisational gap in the national security apparatus caused by the state–private split of 1967.

Competing frameworks for US–Soviet policy

Although the whole administration agreed that the Carter administration's approach to the Soviet Union had been too soft, high-level officials were divided over whether the US should pursue a 'centred' Cold War strategy aimed at weakening or undermining the Soviet Union directly, or a 'de-centred' strategy which aimed at the containment of further Soviet external expansion. This division was, in part, spurred by differing perceptions of the Soviet Union's motives for its expansionist behaviour and differing calculations of its internal political stability and economic health. Reaganite officials tended to hold a double-sided view of the Soviet Union as being at once militarily strong enough to pose a severe threat to the United States and yet weakening internally. For these officials, Soviet behaviour sprang from either the ideological imperative to create a global Marxist empire, as Reagan often argued,[28] or from the structural imperatives of the totalitarian system, which required expansion to legitimate itself internally by convincing the population that it represented the wave of the future. This tracing of the USSR's expansionist impulses to the ideological and political system itself, together with its seemingly limitless capacity to expand its power into the Third World indicated that, as Richard Pipes' argued, 'it was a hopeless undertaking to try to prevent [Communism's] further spread at the periphery: one had to strike at the very heart of Soviet imperialism, its system.'[29]

While Reaganites saw the USSR as powerful externally, their belief that the Soviet system was decaying internally made such a policy of 'striking at the heart of Soviet imperialism' seem feasible. CIA Director William Casey, a convinced hard-liner, argued that the economy of the USSR was 'showing increasing weakness'[30] and that there was 'increasing internal discontent' in the Soviet

46 *Democracy and national security*

Union,[31] with the clear implication that this should be exploited[32] through pressure on the USSR. These views were shared by the President, who perceived the Soviet Union's growing economic weakness and signs of popular and nationalist discontent within the bloc as 'the beginning of the end'[33] and wondered how these cracks in the Soviet edifice could be exploited to accelerate the USSR's collapse.[34]

The Reaganite faction proposed to exploit these perceived weaknesses through an anti-Soviet offensive embracing both economic and political warfare. This faction believed that discouraging Western trade with and investment in the Soviet Union would cut off the foreign currency earnings which the Soviets used to manage domestic economic problems. At the same time, a Western strategy of psychological warfare that aimed to encourage opposition elements behind the Iron Curtain could also help to weaken the USSR and vulnerable Soviet satellites. While the original design for containment proposed by George Kennan had called for US actions aimed at placing the maximum external strain on the Soviet system in order to foster its mellowing or gradual break-up,[35] the actions proposed by these hard-liners went further by supplementing US external pressure on the Soviet Union with programmes designed to target internal economic and political variables in order to weaken the Soviet system.[36] This policy tendency represented a tough stance towards the USSR informing a set of disparate measures, rather than an integrated and coherent strategy for causing the collapse of the Soviet Union.

This hard-line policy stance was opposed by a faction of more pragmatic State Department career officials led by Alexander Haig who favoured a 'decentred' approach to the Cold War based on halting further Soviet expansionism while negotiating tough but realistic agreements with the USSR. These officials differed from the Reaganites in basing their policy on the geopolitical threat posed by the USSR rather than ideological anti-Sovietism, and in their argument that, while the Soviet system was experiencing problems, these problems did not indicate that it was becoming more vulnerable to Western action. The geopolitical, as opposed to ideological, basis of Haig's policies is clear from his comment that 'A major focus of American policy must be the Soviet Union ... not because of ideological preoccupation but simply because Moscow is the greatest source of international insecurity today'.[37] Haig also felt that although it might be possible to use economic and political warfare as tools to contain Soviet expansionism, they could not feasibly lead to the transformation or collapse of the Soviet state. His views on this had continuity, as he had argued at the Republican National Convention in 1979 that the key task for the US in the 1980s would be 'the management of global Soviet power'.[38] If the Soviet Union was not about to collapse, then, it was better to concentrate US resources on safeguarding the US position in the 'Free World' rather than jeopardising this for uncertain gains from economic and political warfare.[39] Rather than focussing on an attempt to weaken Soviet control within the bloc, Haig's foreign policy called for a tough version of containment, coupled with negotiations, which he dubbed 'Restraint and Reciprocity'.[40] The gap between the Reaganite conception of a tough

Democracy and national security 47

campaign against the USSR and Haig's strategy surfaced in the Reagan administration's first National Security Planning Group meeting on 30 January 1981[41] and the split continued until the Secretary of State left the administration in June 1982, and beyond.

Democratic propaganda and political operations against the Soviet bloc

Despite this division over end goals, the administration was able to reach a degree of consensus over the broadcasting of democratic propaganda into the USSR. The administration's hard-liners had begun pushing for a stepped-up propaganda campaign against the USSR based on democratic ideology in March 1981, when NSC officials Carnes Lord and Richard Pipes argued for an increase in the budget and transmission capacity of Radio Free Europe and for Radio Liberty.[42] Hard-liners at the Voice of America wanted to go even further than Lord, Pipes or Wick, urging that US propaganda aim at the destabilisation of the Soviet bloc through the exposure of corruption and Human Rights abuses.[43] This negative theme was to be complemented by a positive US broadcasting campaign to foreground the benefits of the US' democratic system and the prosperity created by free enterprise.[44] It was possible to forge an administration consensus on this policy, as such a propaganda campaign did not aim at direct support for democratic political forces on the ground; therefore the strategic and organisational problems associated with such an effort did not arise. In addition, while the Reaganites believed that broadcasting democratic propaganda into the USSR could erode the regime's internal control, in reality it was a comparatively safe tactic to deploy. The only real consequence would have been poor diplomatic relations with the Soviet Union; and relations were already poor.

This consensus was harder to maintain when the administration attempted to engage in operations that involved funding and backing opposition movements in Eastern Europe. Debates on political intervention in the Soviet bloc focussed on Poland, which was then convulsed by the political conflict between the Polish communist government and Solidarity. Discontented with falling living standards and the authoritarianism of the regime, Polish workers had created Solidarity as a trade union independent of communist party and state structures in August 1980 after a wave of wildcat strikes. Unlike previous expressions of dissent within Soviet-dominated Eastern Europe such as the Hungarian Uprising of 1956, the Prague Spring of 1968 and the dissident organisations active in the 1970s and early 1980s, which had begun or existed as small circles of reformers or intellectuals, Solidarity was a mass movement which soon had 10 million members, including one-third of the Polish United Workers' Party, Poland's governing communist party.[45] The existence of Solidarity as a mass movement posed a serious threat both to the communist government of Poland, and to the Soviet bloc. The fact that the new organisation was based on the Polish working class posed an ideological threat to the PZPR's claim to represent the interests of this class, while geopolitically, Solidarity's increasing power also posed a threat

48   *Democracy and national security*

to the stability of the second largest member of the Warsaw Pact after the Soviet Union.[46] The Soviet leadership immediately recognised the danger and adopted a dual course of pressuring the Polish government to launch a crackdown and threatening to launch an invasion of the country to restore the political dominance of the Communist Party over Polish society if necessary.[47] This threat of military intervention hung over both Solidarity and Poland, limiting the union's room for manoeuvre.

The Reagan administration, in common with the Soviet leadership, clearly recognised the geopolitical importance of Solidarity. DCI Casey and the President himself saw Poland as the weakest link in the chain of Soviet satellites in Eastern Europe[48] and Solidarity as a key anti-Soviet political movement based in the heart of the Soviet zone of control in Eastern Europe. It was hoped that US support of Solidarity could lead to the destabilisation of communist Poland, with demonstration effects that would be felt throughout the bloc. Thus, support for democracy was to be used to weaken the Soviet Union's geopolitical position. However, there was disagreement within the administration over how far the US was capable of influencing events on the ground in Eastern Europe, and thus how far the US should press its support of Solidarity. The fact that the USSR dominated the region militarily made political operations on the ground extremely problematic, as the Soviets had shown themselves to be quite willing to crush uprisings and political movements with military force. While the Reaganites pushed for greater US involvement in the Polish situation, this course of action was opposed by the State Department and Haig, who argued that US ability to affect the balance of political forces on the ground was limited in view of the geopolitical circumstances, and that US support for the Polish union could provoke a Soviet crackdown.[49] Haig's explanation of his Polish policy to the Soviet ambassador in 1981 was that 'We will stay out and we want [the Soviets] to do the same.'[50]

Implementation of the policy was also limited by the organisational gap left by the collapse of the state–private network and its aftermath. Clearly supplying US support through a private group to make the operation plausibly deniable could lessen the chance of a hostile Soviet response, a function the state–private network would have performed before the 1967 crisis. To accomplish this, the CIA attempted to re-forge the relationship it had had with AFL-CIO before the collapse of the network. The prospects for convergence between the administration and the union seemed good, as the AFL-CIO was already acting in support of Solidarity. By the end of 1980 it had provided the Polish union with $150,000, collected through the union's Polish Workers Aid Fund, and also typewriters and printing presses, to allow the organisation to disseminate its message more widely.[51] The union confederation had also provided public support by organising and financially supporting a Solidarity Information Office in New York.[52]

However, when Casey attempted to re-forge an operational relationship with the AFL-CIO targeted at Poland, his proposal was rejected[53] due to the legacy of mistrust which the 1967 exposure of the state–private network had left in the US civil society groups damaged by it. Although Irving Brown, the AFL-CIO's foreign policy chief, agreed to share information on the situation in Poland with the CIA he wanted no direct operational links between the Agency, the AFL-CIO and Solidarity, as he feared such links would taint both trade unions as puppets of the CIA, providing an excuse for a crackdown on Solidarity.[54] Brown clearly wanted to take no risks in the wake of the crisis of 1967, in which a large number of CIA operations had been revealed to the world and the private groups associated with them tainted as collaborators of the US government. This attitude is understandable, as both the Soviet and the official Polish media were at that time denouncing Solidarity as part of a 'CIA-inspired plot to alter the balance of forces in Europe'.[55] The problem was that the administration simply lacked an acceptable and effective organisational framework that could channel US funds to private groups for use abroad to match the pre-1967 state–private network as of 1981. This organisational problem and the geopolitical disagreement within the administration were inter-related, as organisational problems with delivering US aid through a plausibly deniable channel reinforced the State Department's argument that no feasible way of supporting Polish political forces compatible with US interests without provoking a Soviet crackdown existed.

While the promotion of democracy in the Soviet bloc was ideologically congruent with US values and supported US interests, tangible support for political movements on the ground in Eastern Europe was far more problematic than broadcasting propaganda, as it was limited by the problems of operating in an area under the military domination of a hostile state and the lack of a plausibly deniable organisational structure to deliver such support. In the absence of this structure, opposition to the policy crystallised on the pragmatic grounds that the US might obtain very little return for running the risk of triggering bloodshed in Eastern Europe.

Democracy as containment in allied authoritarian states: the case of El Salvador

One of the key issues facing the Reagan administration when it came into office was the development of a framework for US relations with anti-communist authoritarian regimes in the Third World. The administration initially abandoned Carter's Human Rights policy and provided support for friendly tyrannies in order to attempt to contain the perceived growth of Soviet power. However, the failure of this approach to effectively contain the Marxist insurgency in El Salvador provoked a policy switch to support for a democratic transition in that country. Indeed, it was in relation to El Salvador that the Reagan administration first came to see democratic reform as a feasible and effective method of containing the growth of Marxist movements. Although this change represented a response to the particular problems of legitimacy and stability which the Salvadoran case presented, rather than the implementation of a new approach to undemocratic pro-US governments, it did open up the possibility of convergence between the administration and non-state democracy promoters over the goal of defending strategic positions in the Third World through the promotion of democracy.

50   *Democracy and national security*

The Reagan administration and Third World dictatorships

The Reagan administration's initial rejection of the policy of political reform contained in the Carter administration's Human Rights agenda in favour of largely uncritical support for allied authoritarian regimes was based on Cold War considerations and was influenced by the arguments made by neoconservative critics of the Carter administration's Human Rights policy before and after the fall of pro-US regimes in Iran and Nicaragua in 1979. During the first two years of the Carter administration, neoconservative critics of the President's agenda such as Daniel P. Moynihan and Norman Podhoretz co-opted the language of Human Rights to argue for a narrow campaign for their enforcement directed at the Soviet Union and its clients rather than the right-wing regimes which the US was allied with.[56] To legitimise this approach, these critics articulated the same distinction between totalitarian communist regimes and authoritarian dictatorships which US policymakers had often drawn during the 1950s, arguing that authoritarian dictatorships were more likely to evolve towards democracy in the future than totalitarian communist states.[57]

The rationale for the support of pro-US authoritarians was stated in its clearest form, however, after the fall of Iran and Nicaragua by Jeane Kirkpatrick, a conservative Democrat and Professor of Government at Georgetown University. In 'Dictatorship and Double Standards', an article published in *Commentary* several months after the collapse of the two regimes, Kirkpatrick placed the question of US policy towards pro-US authoritarian regimes squarely in an East–West context marked by rising Soviet military power and influence in the Third World[58] and argued that Carter's pressure on the Shah, and particularly on Somoza, to liberalise had amounted to 'active collaborat[ion] in the replacement of moderate autocrats friendly to American interests with less friendly autocrats of extremist persuasion.'[59] Pressure on these strategically important regimes to reform had 'actually facilitate[d] the job of the insurgents',[60] resulting in the weakening and then collapse of friendly regimes and damaging US interests. Kirkpatrick's critique of US support for political reform overseas went beyond these two specific cases to set out a doctrine for future policy towards pro-US authoritarian regimes, as her argument that democratic systems were complex and took many decades to build[61] implied that the US should abandon misguided attempts to democratise authoritarian regimes under pressure from insurgents in a bid to defuse revolutionary movements. Kirkpatrick squared this policy recommendation with Human Rights concerns by duplicating the familiar argument that right-wing authoritarian regimes were capable of evolving into democracies over the long term, whereas totalitarian communist regimes could never do so.[62]

The argument made by these neoconservative intellectuals that authoritarian regimes were more susceptible to gradual democratic transformation at some point in the future than communist states provided a moral justification for the support of such regimes in the here-and-now, which they believed that US strategic interests dictated. These ideas thus largely represented a return to the argument for the support of friendly authoritarian regimes which had held sway in the 1950s, before the Kennedy administration's push for reform in Latin America and the Carter administration's Human Rights policy. However, these critics laid out no concrete plan for facilitating such transitions, and so failed to deal with the long-term strategic problem which the democracy promoters had identified: the rise of anti-US revolutionary forces which such regimes often provoked, and their poor record in defeating these forces.

This combined strategic and moral argument – the Kirkpatrick Doctrine – was extremely influential on the foreign policy of the early Reagan administration. The Cold War prism through which Kirkpatrick and other neoconservative critics of Human Rights framed their policy recommendations appealed to a President who tended to see unrest and revolution in the Third World as a product of Soviet conspiracies rather than indigenous political, social or economic factors. The President's comment in 1980 that 'the Soviet Union underlies all the unrest that is going on' left little doubt about where he attributed responsibility for the recent wave of Third World revolutions.[63] In fact, Reagan was so impressed with Kirkpatrick's article that he appointed her UN Ambassador, with Cabinet rank, and made 'Dictatorships and Double Standards' required reading for high-level foreign policymakers in his administration.[64] The President's use of Kirkpatrick's ideas is clearly shown in his comments, delivered at a press conference in 1981, that under the Carter administration

> we took countries that were pro-Western that were maybe authoritarian in government, but not totalitarian, more authoritarian than we would like, did not meet all of our principles of what constitutes Human Rights, and we punished them at the same time we were claiming détente with countries where there were no Human Rights. The Soviet Union is the greatest violator today of Human Rights in all the world.[65]

Based on this logic the administration swiftly rolled back Carter's Human Rights approach, urging Congress to restore military aid which the previous administration had removed from dictatorships with poor Human Rights records such as Chile and Argentina.[66]

In Latin America, this drive for stability was augmented by regional geopolitical fears. Kirkpatrick's follow-up article in early 1981, which was more narrowly focussed on the region, sounded alarm over what she argued was a serious deterioration of the US security position which could confront America with 'the unprecedented need to defend itself against a ring of Soviet bases on and around our southern and eastern borders.[67] A similar analysis emerged from the hard-line Committee of Santa Fe, which concluded that the Human Rights policy in Latin America had resulted in a decrease of US influence and should be replaced by a 'non-interventionist policy of political and ethical realism.'[68] While in Eastern Europe and the Soviet bloc, efforts to spread democratic ideas were thought to be in the national interest, the goal for policy towards pro-US authoritarians was to maintain political stability through support for existing regimes in order to remove opportunities for Soviet gains, not to push for reforms.

52 *Democracy and national security*

The Reagan administration's initial policy towards El Salvador

These considerations heavily influenced the Reagan administration's initial approach to the Marxist insurgency in El Salvador, which it had inherited from the Carter Administration. In 1979 Anastasio Somoza Debayle, the authoritarian leader of Nicaragua, had been overthrown by a multi-class revolutionary uprising and been replaced by the Marxist-Leninist Sandinistas. In October 1979, several months after the Somoza regime's collapse, reformist Salvadoran army officers toppled the military dictatorship of General Carlos Humberto Romero, fearing that continued repression would only lead to the growth of the insurgency and, eventually, a rebel victory.[69] The officers formed a civil-military junta and promised reform, but this more moderate government proved unable to reduce the repression carried out by the army and security forces, and subsequently resigned in 1979.[70] A second junta was then formed consisting of Christian Democrat politicians and the military. Real power continued to reside with conservatives in the army and security forces, who continued, and even expanded, the repression of the population, while the insurgency continued.[71]

The Reagan administration's policy towards El Salvador was generated by a combination of the fear of the possible consequences for US national security emphasised by the Kirkpatrick Doctrine, global and regional geopolitical fears, and concerns revolving around US credibility, rather than an appraisal of political and military conditions in El Salvador. Policymakers did not see the Salvadoran insurgency as a result of inequalities and authoritarianism within El Salvador itself, but as the product of a wave of Soviet interventionism in the Third World that included the triumph of Marxist movements in South-east Asia, Angola and Ethiopia during the 1970s. These global geopolitical concerns were bolstered by fear on the part of Reagan administration policymakers that in the fall of El Salvador would touch off a 'domino' effect in the rest of Central America that would be damaging to US strategic interests. According to Alexander Haig, the war in El Salvador was part of a Soviet plan which had begun with the takeover of Nicaragua and aimed ultimately at the control of all of Central America,[72] while Thomas Enders, the new Assistant Secretary of State for Inter-American Affairs, argued that if El Salvador fell to Marxists then key US interests such as the Panama Canal, sea lanes and oil supplies would be threatened.[73]

The final factor underlying the administration's approach to El Salvador was the question of credibility. El Salvador was seen as the US' 'front yard' and it was believed that the United States needed to react to the situation there in such a way as to demonstrate its renewed toughness and 'determination to control world events'.[74] The conflict was also thought to be winnable, leading to an easy victory for the US which would re-establish US credibility without a great deal of sacrifice.[75] In this way the situation was 'fortuitous' as 'a specific crisis already was under way in which Reagan could demonstrate his resolve'; by defeating the supposed Soviet-Cuban attempts to take over El Salvador, Reagan would be 'send[ing] a message to Moscow'[76] that further intervention in the Third World would not be tolerated. This combination of an overarching fear of the geopolitical consequences of pressuring friendly authoritarians to reform, a perceived erosion of US dominance in Latin America, the fear of a Central American domino effect and the question of US credibility created a situation in which maintaining a non-Marxist government in El Salvador was perceived as vital; there was no margin for error. El Salvador came rapidly to be seen as a test case for a US policy of confronting Marxist revolutions in the Third World.

This attitude produced an atmosphere of crisis in which the strategy of the Reagan administration differed sharply from that of the Carter administration, which had tied military aid to the Salvadoran government to calls for increased respect for Human Rights and land reform measures[77] 'as a means of alleviating the underlying causes of leftist revolutionary pressures'.[78] In contrast, in the first half of 1981 the Reagan administration argued that reforms in El Salvador should be pursued at some unspecified future time after US national security objectives had been fulfilled, in order to avoid weakening the pro-US regime and avoid a repeat of what policymakers believed had happened in Nicaragua under Carter.[79]

To avoid such an outcome, the administration substantially increased military aid to El Salvador. In March 1981 the administration granted $25 million in emergency military aid to the junta, an amount larger than the previous military aid for 1946–1980 combined.[80] Although the State Department gave rhetorical support for free elections and condemned the terror wielded by the army and rightist death squads in February 1981,[81] at the same time the administration removed the conditions which had been placed on military aid by the Carter administration to encourage reform,[82] arguing that defeating the insurgency should take first priority.[83] This approach removed the leverage that would have allowed the US to pressure the Salvadoran army to support these objectives. US support for democracy was thus reduced to negative anti-communism, as the administration and its supporters argued that a Marxist victory would be more damaging to the cause of democracy over the long-term than the status quo and pursued a purely military approach.

The shift to democracy promotion in El Salvador

This policy of supporting authoritarianism proved to be unsustainable in its initial form due to ideological and political pressures within the United States and military stalemate in El Salvador. Domestically, problems arose from the fact that in attempting to pursue a more supportive policy towards pro-US authoritarians threatened by revolutionaries, the administration had failed to factor in the cultural changes that had occurred in US society as a result of the Vietnam War and the rise of Human Rights.[84] Due to these changes the administration experienced a low level of support for its policy among the US population, with many Americans rejecting greater US involvement in El Salvador due to fears that US aid would inevitably lead to the introduction of US combat troops, as it had in Vietnam, and greater concern over Human Rights abuses by allied governments.[85]

54 *Democracy and national security*

This lack of support from the general population was exacerbated by a strategic disagreement with Congress. The Legislature argued that rather than being damaging to US national security objectives, pressuring the junta to enact reforms could help to achieve these objectives by drawing the people of El Salvador away from support for the guerrillas. Congressional pressure on the administration to change course began in the House, where Democrats on the Foreign Affairs Committee restored the conditions that the Carter administration had attached to aid to El Salvador. In May the Senate Foreign Relations Committee called for Reagan to certify, every six months, that the government of El Salvador was committed to controlling the army, curbing Human Rights abuses, moving forward on land reform and free elections, and had shown willingness to negotiate a political solution to the war.[86] If these conditions were being met, further aid would be released. While Congress may have been influenced in this stance by Human Rights considerations, the disagreement was primarily over tactics, with the debate being over 'how best to isolate and deal with these terrorists [the Salvadoran left], through military assistance or through reforms that eliminate the grievances upon which they depend for sustenance.'[87]

In contrast, the hard-line faction of the Reagan administration continued to believe that such reforms could result in the collapse of the Salvadoran junta, thus worsening the US strategic position in Central America. Several Reaganite policymakers, such as Richard Allen, William Clark, the Deputy Secretary of State, and Fred Ikle, the Undersecretary of Defence for Policy, argued that the administration should maintain its original policy to provoke a confrontation with Congress over the management of US foreign policy. If the administration won it would be able to make foreign policy in Central America, and other areas of the world, without Congressional interference; however, if Congress won it would then have to take the blame for losing El Salvador to communism.[88] Winning the war had to take priority over the promotion of democracy, which might turn out to be unachievable and lead to another US defeat.[89]

It was clear that unless the policy was changed, the Executive and Legislature were moving towards a serious confrontation over El Salvador, sparked by disagreements over whether pursuing a policy of democratisation would enhance or detract from the achievement of US national security objectives. However, the possibility of an accommodation developed as officials in the State Department began to reassess current policy. These officials concluded that there was no prospect of a military victory in the near future; instead, the situation had evolved into 'a war of attrition.'[90] With no immediate government military victory in sight, detaching the population from the guerrillas assumed more importance. The government needed to broaden its 'narrow base of support'[91] and end the political fragmentation which gripped the country.

As a result of these domestic political pressures and strategic calculations Assistant Secretary Enders publicly called for US support for elections in El Salvador in mid-1981. In part, this change was motivated by 'a growing feeling within the administration that that its policy in El Salvador had gained little popular support'.[92] To secure such support from Congress and the population,

Enders' speech stressed US support for concrete measures of democratisation, a position which was likely to resonate ideologically with Americans. Enders also tied democratisation to the need for military aid, stating that 'the search for a political solution will not succeed unless the United States sustains its assistance to El Salvador'[93] and that '[w]e can help by ... [s]tanding by our friends while they work out a democratic solution.'[94] A renewed push for democracy in El Salvador could thus legitimate continued US military aid. However, the key reason for the change of course was that, according to the Assistant Secretary, the best way to produce a stable government with popular legitimacy was through elections, which would act to dampen down the insurgency:

> We believe that the solution must be democratic because only a genuinely pluralist approach can enable a profoundly divided society to live with itself without violent convulsions.[95]

Democracy would contribute to the future stability of El Salvador, rather than undermining it, by producing a government that was seen as legitimate by the population and removing the conflict from the battlefield, where the US and its client government were just about holding the line, into the political arena.

The Department had not changed the objective of US policy towards El Salvador, which still remained the containment of the insurgency through maintaining a stable pro-US government in power in San Salvador. However, State Department officials had come to believe that in the case of El Salvador a democratic regime would be a more efficient tool of containment, as it would be more stable and more legitimate with both the Salvadoran population and with Congress, and thus a stronger barrier a Marxist takeover than the current ruling junta. This was a pragmatic decision, not an ideological one, aimed at resolving the political problems the policy was facing in Washington and securing a more stable and legitimate regime capable of facing a protracted guerrilla war on the ground. However, it is important to stress the novelty of the State Department's strategy; rather than deploying democratic rhetoric to legitimate US tactics which had little or no connection to democracy as a functioning political system, the Department was calling for the creation of functioning democratic processes in a friendly state threatened by an anti-US insurgency. Furthermore, it saw this action as a way of protecting US national security interests, not as sacrificing them to ideology or the need for legitimation. This new policy contrasted with the administration's default position of providing support to authoritarians as long as they were reliably anti-communist.

As in the case of Poland, though, the administration lacked a key organisational capability necessary to implement the policy in line with US national security objectives. Enders had had a great deal of difficulty in building a consensus for the support of elections in El Salvador in the administration due to the fear of other policymakers that the outcome of such elections would not necessarily be in line with US interests.[96] The problem was that there was no guarantee that Salvadoran political forces dedicated to the reforms the Department

56 *Democracy and national security*

believed to be necessary to win the war would win an election, and the US lacked the capability to strengthen such pro-US political forces in a credible and plausibly deniable manner.

A coherent vision for democracy promotion in the Third World: beyond the Kirkpatrick Doctrine

The State Department's pragmatic change of course to supporting democratic processes in El Salvador in July 1981 opened up an opportunity for the growing non-state democracy promotion network to present its own concepts to the administration. In contrast to the Executive's case-by-case approach, this network offered a framework which went beyond the State Department's focus on El Salvador as an isolated case where the support of democracy was possible and permissible, putting forward instead a generalised strategy aimed at the whole Third World, which was to be implemented through a new organisation aimed at the creation of democratic systems through democratic political tactics. This more coherent design was set out in the first few months of 1981 by William Douglas and Michael Samuels. In spring 1981 they amalgamated their ideas in a paper that was given at the International Studies Association[97] and then published as an article in August 1981 in order 'to further focus policy-makers' attention on the need for a political development program.'[98]

Douglas and Samuels set out a clear strategic need for the US government to support democracy promotion by arguing that 'US security is jeopardized when dictatorial leftist movements are likely to succeed in overthrowing conservative authoritarian regimes that have been pro-West.'[99] The remedy for this was to be US support for democratic parties, interest groups and coalitions who could act as 'bulwarks against Marxist revolutionaries or militarists',[100] thus averting successful Marxist revolutions and replacing unpopular dictatorships with more stable and legitimate democracies. This agenda was clearly compatible with the evolving administration priorities in Central America; indeed, Samuels and Douglas cited El Salvador and Guatemala as countries 'where the presiding regimes are shaky, the democratic center is miniscule, and dictatorial leftists lead the opposition',[101] indicating that these countries would benefit from a democracy promotion approach. They also suggested that democracy promotion would be useful in Nicaragua, where 'democratic pluralist elements have been fighting a rear-guard action to try to prevent the installation of a totalitarian dictatorship' and argued that Nicaragua's independent newspaper, *La Prensa*, labour and business organisations and 'a private sector Commission on Human Rights' should be given assistance to coordinate their efforts and make them more effective political opponents of the Sandinistas.[102] This proposal moved democracy promotion beyond being a strategy of containing revolutionary forces in friendly states to include efforts to roll back the control of existing radical governments. This recommendation again created common ground between non-state democracy promoters and the administration, which was shifting rapidly towards a more confrontational posture towards the Sandinista regime.[103] Such a

Democracy and national security 57

framework could also have been applicable to Poland, although Douglas and Samuels did not consider operations within the Soviet bloc in their article.

However, whereas the administration was beginning to develop an approach more focussed on democratisation in response to particular crises, Samuels and Douglas began from an expansive strategy focussed on the Third World as a whole, and then showed how it could be applied to the current crises that the Reagan administration was prioritising. This approach went beyond immediate national security priorities in Central America, as Douglas and Samuels argued that the US should begin to build democratic groups in pro-US authoritarian regimes such as 'Zaire, Indonesia, South Korea, the Philippines and Honduras'[104] as 'countries in which there is an apparent danger of imminent political collapse'[105], since 'US interests would be furthered by strengthening democratic pluralist forces of countries facing political collapse before such a collapse occurs.'[106] Beyond this, the authors aimed at fostering political change over the long-term, cautioning that initial 'activities [should] not be limited to purely short-term targets of opportunity' and arguing that '[m]any of the program's activities should focus on the longer range development of political institutions'.[107] The ultimate aim was to create programmes which could support the growth of democracy over the whole Third World.[108] This represented an amalgamation of Samuels' proposal for support for democrats in key authoritarian states threatened with regime collapse with Douglas' policy of fostering democratisation in the Third World as a whole, and provided the coherent approach to Third World political systems which had been missing from US foreign policy throughout the Cold War.

In addition to setting out a more specific strategic vision, these new proposals contained more concrete blueprints for an organisational structure that could implement this ambitious programme in a manner that was tactically sound and credible to foreign democrats. Douglas and Samuels argued for a 'new semi-private foundation specifically for political work abroad'[109] which would provide training rather than financial support to political parties overseas, as they felt that purely financial support could attract opportunists who wanted to benefit financially from the programme rather than committed democrats.[110] Instead of merely disbursing funding, a US democracy foundation would offer training to leaders and activists of democratic parties and seek to strengthen the organisation of political parties.[111]

Rather than being limited to the coordination of action by US political parties, as in previous designs, the new organisation would act as an umbrella for US private groups that had previously participated in political operations overseas, such as the AFL-CIO and the US business community. As noted previously, the AFL-CIO had been a key member of the CIA's state–private network in the 1950s and 1960s. It had also taken part in the Kennedy Administration's Modernisation effort in Latin America after 1962, offering training to Latin American trade unionists through the American Institute for Free Labor Development (AIFLD), a union training centre dedicated to combatting the spread of Castroism and funded by AID. At times, this role had extended to supporting unions

58   *Democracy and national security*

hostile to sitting governments, such as AFL-CIO support for a general strike against the leftist government of Cheddi Jagan in Guyana, and opposition to leftist governments in Brazil during the 1960s and Chile during the 1970s.[112] After the creation of AIFLD to attend to Latin American labour matters, the AFL-CIO had subsequently founded two other regional organisations; the African-American Labor Centre (AALC), founded in 1964 with Irving Brown as its first director, and the Asian American Free Labor Institute (AAFLI), founded shortly after the Tet Offensive in 1968 to coordinate relief supplies to South Vietnam. The AAFLI played a key role, through its influence over the Vietnamese Confederation of Labor, in keeping docks open in South Vietnam so that military supplies could be unloaded to bolster the Thieu government's war effort. Both of these foundations were also funded through AID.[113]

US businesses had also previously attempted to alter political structures overseas. Such actions included involvement in and agitation for covert operations by individual companies such as United Fruit, which agitated for the overthrow of the Arbenz government in Guatemala by the CIA in 1954 and IT&T, which had pushed the CIA to take a strong stance against the Allende government in Chile.[114] In addition to this, representatives from important US companies such as Anaconda, Pan American Airways and Standard Fruit had sat on the board of AIFLD, while others, such as United Fruit, IBM and IT&T had contributed funding to the organisation.[115]

However, the political effectiveness of both of these sectors overseas had been declining. AID restrictions on the activities its grants could be used for hobbled the AFL-CIO, while business had lost a degree of its political influence on overseas political operations when Lane Kirkland, the AFL-CIO's President, had asked corporate representatives to step down from the AIFLD board, as he reportedly felt the business connection had become too embarrassing for the union.[116] Samuels and Douglas sought to incorporate these sectors into their own democratisation project by arguing that US labour and business groups needed to expand their focus from spreading capitalist economic practices to spreading the political model which they claimed supported this economic framework. They pointed out that although the US Chamber of Commerce was active in advocating the economic value of free enterprise in its publications

> little is said about the fact that free enterprise can flourish best only under democratic pluralist conditions. Free enterprise is part and parcel of pluralism, but dictators of all kinds prefer centralization, regimentation, and hierarchy.[117]

In a similar way the authors acknowledged the work done abroad by the AFL-CIO's institutes but argued that these organisations' training programmes for foreign unionists tended to focus too heavily on the economic role of unions rather than their political role and did not provide sufficient ideological guidance.[118] 'In contrast,' the authors claimed, 'their labor colleagues who graduate from communist labor training courses have no such doubts about where they stand ideologically.'[119] Thus, the two authors called simultaneously for a re-politicisation of foreign activities by these key sectors and their reorientation towards promoting democracy, subsuming their sectional interests into the wider project Douglas and Samuels advocated. The new democracy promotion foundation would function as an umbrella organisation incorporating key US domestic groups who could wield political influence overseas.

At first glance, this model of US private groups carrying out programmes overseas to strengthen foreign civil society and political actors seems to parallel the state–private network structure of the 1950s and 1960s. However, while the authors refer to these operations in their article,[120] several key differences between this previous model of political intervention and the new network being proposed opened up issues of autonomy and credibility which would have to be solved if the foundation the authors had proposed were to function effectively to promote democracy. The first key difference was the gap between the administration's short-term foreign policy goals and the long-term strategy of democracy promotion being advocated. Whereas the state–private network groups that had functioned with covert government support before 1967 had been deployed on a tactical basis within a strategic framework set by the state, the strategy proposed in the article was based on priorities set by intellectuals working outside the Executive. Although there was some convergence between the immediate target countries for democracy promotion in Central America, such as El Salvador, Guatemala and Nicaragua,[121] and the current geopolitical concerns of the Reagan administration, the programme of democratisation advocated by the democracy promoters was wider than the administration's sphere of concern in the Third World. The aim of democratising pro-US authoritarian regimes was also out of step with the fact that most administration policymakers, even those who saw El Salvador as a special case, accepted the Kirkpatrick Doctrine's contention that support of political reform and the achievement of US national security objectives were often mutually contradictory, especially in pro-US authoritarian states. Furthermore, the authors' focus on the Third World provided little reason for Reaganites focussed on the support of political movements behind the Iron Curtain to support the project.

The fact that democracy promotion would function within a strategic framework, which did not exactly correspond to the immediate national security concerns of the state indicated the need for more autonomy for the democracy promotion instrumentalities than the previous state–private network had enjoyed. Significantly, while Douglas and Samuels accepted the need for 'a government policy input' into democracy promotion, they specified that the new democracy promotion foundation would be 'free from government control',[122] indicating that the foundation, rather than a government agency such as the CIA, would serve as the coordinating centre for democracy promotion. This meant that the relationship between non-state democracy promoters and the government would need to be carefully negotiated to avoid clashes between long-term and short-term foreign policy priorities.

The second key difference was that the new instrumentality would operate openly. This overt mode of operation, coupled with the fact that the new

60 Democracy and national security

democracy foundation would be funded almost entirely, if not completely, by the US government,[123] created a potential problem for the credibility of democracy promotion programmes. The authors argued that overt aid provided through private groups, as opposed to covert aid provided by the government, was operationally necessary, as foreign political movements could refuse to co-operate with a covert governmental programme due to fears that their independence would be compromised by direct contacts.[124] Exposure of such funding could also damage the credibility of these groups as authentic domestic political movements.[125] However, the authors did not set out a convincing argument for why overt assistance from a private group disbursing government money and with a policy input from US government officials would be seen as any more credible than the pre-1967 organisational model. Douglas and Samuels did argue by analogy that such an organisation could be successful by citing examples of other organisations which combined private management and government funding and were already operating effectively, such as the Asia Foundation, the Inter-American Foundation and the West German party foundations.[126] However, there does not seem to have been any systematic thinking on the possible credibility problem created by dependence on government funding. When the two authors did raise this question, they disposed of it rapidly by asserting that 'Political development abroad is a legitimate function for the US government.'[127]

Douglas and Samuels' blueprint was far more comprehensive than the emerging new thinking in the State Department, both in terms of the tactical and organisational blueprint offered, and in terms of their strategic approach of going beyond immediate national security crises to develop a preventative approach to democracy in the Third World by building democratic movements in dictatorships before revolutionary seizures of power materialised, and beyond this to focus on the democratisation of the Third World as a whole. They also went beyond the Reagan administration's concepts by arguing for a concrete attempt to build functioning democratic movements abroad[128] rather than seeing the promotion of democracy as a rhetorical tool for the legitimation of policy or as an ideological weapon. Finally, their vision was more internally coherent in that it envisaged the promotion of democracy through non-violent political methods rather than contradictory policies such as support for an authoritarian government or armed groups such as the Nicaraguan Contras. If accepted by the administration, the attempt to operationalise this blueprint would re-open the question of how attempts to promote political reform overseas could be meshed with US national security objectives at the strategic and organisational levels.

Democracy, human rights and ideological rearmament

By the second half of 1981 it was clear that the Reagan administration was moving towards incorporating the promotion of democracy as an element of its national security approach. Support for democracy was being deployed as an instrument in three separate tracks of policy: as an ideological tool to bind the Western alliance more closely together through propaganda programmes; as a

Democracy and national security 61

tool of political warfare to undermine Soviet rule in Eastern Europe; and as a method of strengthening containment in El Salvador. What was lacking was a coherent approach which tied these cases together into a strategic framework and a capability to implement democratic reform overseas effectively. The strategic and organisational ideas offered by the non-state democracy promoters, if developed further, could possibly form the basis of such an approach. However, the administration failed to examine this option and continued to see democracy largely as an ideological tool for the legitimation of its policy in its own zone and for launching ideological attacks on the Soviet bloc.

The Reagan administration and human rights

This continuing focus on legitimation rather than serious programmes of political reform was apparent in the administration's new Human Rights policy, produced in late October 1981, which sought to tie together the various threads of its foreign policy under a concept that could provide it with a moral basis which extended beyond anti-communism. The Reagan administration had not been greatly interested in Human Rights in its first few months, as it blamed the strategy for the perceived erosion of US power in the Third World under the Carter administration.[129] Moreover, it had experienced problems in staffing the State Department's Bureau of Human Rights and Humanitarian Affairs. Its first nominee for head of the Bureau, Ernest Lefever, had not been confirmed due to Congressional belief that he was not interested in promoting Human Rights,[130] which meant that the Bureau did little, and had little clout within the administration. This began to change when the Reagan administration's second choice, a young neoconservative called Elliott Abrams, was confirmed.[131] Abrams subsequently played a role in managing support for the Nicaraguan Contras after his appointment as Assistant Secretary for Inter-American Affairs in 1985[132] and later returned to government in the George W. Bush administrations as an NSC official with responsibility for the Middle East and then democracy promotion.[133] The transfer of the Bureau into friendly hands after this hiatus provided an opportunity to codify a Human Rights policy compatible with the Reagan administration's foreign policy.

This new doctrine, outlined in a memo produced within the State Department on 27 October by the Reaganite Deputy Secretary of State William Clark and Under Secretary of State for Management Richard T. Kennedy, showed some signs of bringing Human Rights closer to democracy promotion by narrowing the Human Rights agenda that had been advocated by the Carter administration. Whereas the previous administration had conceptualised Human Rights as containing economic and social dimensions[134] and as not exclusively aimed at exporting democracy, the authors of the memo favoured a narrower concept, which limited Human Rights to political rights and civil liberties. The new policy outline reflected this, recommending that 'we should move away from "human rights" as a term, and begin to speak of "individual rights," "political rights" and "civil liberties"'. The memo even gave consideration to changing the

62   *Democracy and national security*

name of the Bureau of Human Rights and Humanitarian Affairs to reflect this.[135] This narrower concept, shorn of the social and economic rights that the Carter administration's conception had included,[136] allowed a closer identification between Human Rights and the traditional ideological identification of US power with the cause of democracy. However, the memo put forward no programme to advance Human Rights or to spread 'political liberty' in the world on a practical basis and did not engage with the issue of promoting democracy. Instead, it was a continuation and systemisation of the administration's practice of using democratic ideology to legitimate its own foreign policy, both domestically and in Western Europe, while criticising the Soviet Union.

The new doctrine had been prompted first and foremost by attacks on the administration's foreign policy, rather than a concrete plan to push for global political reform. This is made clear in the document, which states that:

> Congressional belief that we have no consistent human rights policy threatens to disrupt important foreign policy initiatives.... *Human rights has been one of the main avenues for domestic attack on the Administration's foreign policy.*[137]

The administration also planned to use Human Rights as a propaganda concept to maintain the bonds between the US and its democratic allies, as it had been using democracy in Project Truth, arguing that 'draw[ing] the central distinction in international politics between free nations and those that are not free' was essential to combat neutralism in the West and to appeal to electorate in Western Europe, Japan and other countries.[138] To restore the US' moral and political leadership of the Western bloc, the Bureau of Human Rights and Humanitarian Affairs was given the role of providing policy guidance on Human Rights to USIA, highlighting how US ideological power and the concept of Human Rights were becoming ever more tied together.[139] Thus, the new Human Rights doctrine would support propaganda initiatives already under way, such as Project Truth.

The concept of Human rights was also to be used as an ideological weapon against the USSR, as ' "Human rights" – meaning political rights and civil liberties – conveys what is ultimately at issue in our contest with the Soviet bloc',[140] making the concept a tool in a 'battle of ideas' which the Bureau of Human Rights and Humanitarian Affairs was expected to wage.[141] In practical terms this meant '[e]xpounding our beliefs and affirmatively opposing the U.S.S.R. in the U.N., C.S.C.E. (Conference on Security and Cooperation in Europe) and other bodies.'[142] Essentially, what was being proposed was a public diplomacy campaign, which would legitimate the administration's foreign policy to the American public, Congress and US allies, while also being a useful propaganda weapon against the USSR. In these areas there was little tension between the pursuit of Human Rights and US national security objectives.

The integration of Human Rights or support for democracy into policy towards pro-US dictatorships was more problematic, as the administration had to balance its fear that the promotion of Human Rights could weaken existing governments and lead to communist advances with measures to placate its domestic critics. The administration's solution was to allow more room for criticism of the US' authoritarian allies, while essentially preserving the policy of working through and with existing regimes to safeguard US national security interests. A measure of criticism of authoritarian allies was thought to be necessary due to the fear that failing to do this would delegitimise US foreign policy, with policymakers arguing that: 'There is no escaping this [need to criticise authoritarian allies] without destroying the credibility of our policy, for otherwise we would be simply coddling friends and criticizing foes.'[143] However, rather than proposing a policy of supporting reform, the memo concentrated on how the US could rationalise its further support of such allies, arguing that:

> our response or retaliatory actions should result from a balancing of all pertinent interests. Human rights is not advanced by replacing a bad regime with a worse one, or a corrupt dictator with a zealous Communist politburo.[144]

The positive measures put forward for improving Human Rights in dictatorial allied states, such as limited embargoes of riot control equipment, amounted to little more than cosmetic actions to reassure Congress and did not constitute a strategy of political transformation.

The new Human Rights doctrine represented an attempt to systemise the administration's justification of its foreign policy initiatives in Western Europe, the USSR and Central America in terms of abstract democratic ideology into one rhetorical framework for the legitimation of its existing policy, not a genuine attempt to connect the promotion of political liberty in the world to US foreign policy aims. While the State Department, and the administration as a whole, might be prepared to deploy democracy promotion in the particular case of El Salvador, it remained uninterested in a wider campaign for democratic reform.

An institute for democracy in Central America

The Department's subsequent policy initiative on democracy promotion bears out this assessment, as it was limited to Latin America in its widest interpretation, and confined to El Salvador in its most restricted reading. In a speech to a meeting of OAS foreign ministers on 4 December on the island of St Lucia, Haig called for the creation of a democracy promotion organisation but tied it clearly to the need for credible elections in El Salvador. In his address, Haig laid out a three-point 'agenda for co-operation':

> First, to reaffirm and promote democracy; second, to create new economic opportunity, and third, most urgently, to oppose interventionism by strengthening the principles of nonintervention and collective security.[145]

Opposing 'interventionism', by which the administration meant Soviet/Cuban/Sandinista support of revolutionary movements, was the key objective, with the

64   *Democracy and national security*

other two points being methods to achieve this. Haig tied this support for democracy specifically to support for elections in El Salvador, hoping that Latin American countries would support the Salvadoran government 'as it leads its people through the electoral process toward a political solution of the conflict there.'[146]

Haig gave his proposals concrete form by calling for 'an institute for the study of democracy in the Americas' to provide a 'regular exchange of ideas and experiences among democratic leaders'[147]. It is unclear from Haig's speech what the exact duties and parameters of the new institute would be; however, the Secretary of State seemed to have had in mind some sort of central focal point for the political training of Central American democrats, which might be combined with the technical assistance and observer missions to Latin American elections which he also called on the OAS to carry out.[148] This programme represented a specific response to the crisis in El Salvador, and it is uncertain how far its operations would have extended beyond this.

Organisationally, the proposal did not include participation by the US private groups which the democracy promoters wanted to mobilise under a semi-autonomous umbrella foundation. While Douglas and Samuels had argued that this organisational form would make democracy promotion more credible to foreign democrats and serve to clearly separate it from previous covert operations, Haig's proposal resolved these concerns by casting the effort as a multilateral one involving all Latin American countries. To this end the Secretary of State began his speech by invoking Simon Bolivar, the nineteenth century Venezuelan revolutionary who had played a key role in the Latin American struggle for independence against Spain, and stated that 'by making the [OAS] secretary-general [the Institute's] director, we would insure a cooperative effort.'[149] Haig also proposed that the Institute should be named 'The Betancourt Institute' in honour of the famous and respected Venezuelan democratic leader Romulo Betancourt,[150] a further attempt to give it a Latin American image. Although the proposed Betancourt Institute represented a more concrete vision of democracy promotion than had been achieved thus far, it represented a response to a specific case rather than an attempt to implement a more expansive strategy, and the proposed organisational framework was too limited to accommodate a strategy of democracy promotion that embraced the wider transformative project urged by the democracy promoters outside the Western Hemisphere. Thus, of as December 1981, the promotion of democracy was limited both geopolitically and organisationally to Latin America at best, and at worst to El Salvador.

Conclusion

The Reagan administration's initial rhetorical support for democracy had seemed to open up the possibility that a strategy of fostering the growth of democratic parties and institutions overseas could be attached to US national security policy, as non-state democracy promoters had advocated in the final year of the Carter

Democracy and national security 65

administration. However, the administration lacked a conception of democracy promotion that extended beyond the rhetorical use of democracy as an abstract concept to build support for its foreign initiatives and criticise enemy states. Furthermore, it was divided into factions emphasising different national security strategies, such as the Reaganite focus on weakening the Soviet Union and the State Department's preoccupation with strengthening containment. While policymakers were able to agree on the tactical use of democracy in cases where both sides prioritised the same short-term geopolitical goal and the use of democratic ideology was limited to propaganda, the question of whether attempts to alter political structures on the ground were congruent with US national security interests and how this could be achieved was more divisive. In addition, the administration found itself subjected to criticism from Congress for dropping the Human Rights agenda and supporting pro-US authoritarians.

The ideas proposed by non-state democracy promoters were far more coherent. In contrast to the existing piecemeal deployment of democracy as a legitimating concept or in relation to specific cases, the democracy promoters generated an overarching strategic framework based on a long-term transformative project aimed at the whole of the Third World and then attempted to use specific cases such as El Salvador and Nicaragua to convince the administration of the value of their own pre-existing strategy. They also proposed a new organisational framework to implement new democracy promotion programmes in an effective and plausibly deniable manner.

However, these proposals did not impel a shift in the way the Reagan administration viewed the interconnection between democracy promotion and national security strategy. In general, the administration as a whole and the factions within it continued to mobilise democratic ideology as a tool of legitimation domestically and in Western Europe, and as a weapon of ideological warfare to be used against the Soviet bloc, while reproducing Kirkpatrick's justifications for support of authoritarianism in its policy towards the Third World. This policy of projecting democracy as an ideology rather than promoting or constructing it as a functioning political system did not resolve the underlying strategic difficulties caused for US policy by unstable dictatorships in the Third World or provide a mechanism for the channelling of aid and assistance to dissident forces within the Soviet bloc. The only exception to this was the State Department's policy towards El Salvador. A decisive shift in US policy produced by a further catalytic event would be needed to enable democracy promotion to transcend the limitation of the concept to Central America.

Notes

1 Barry R. Posen and Stephen W. Van Evera, 'Reagan Administration Defense Policy: Departure from Containment', in *Eagle Defiant: United States Foreign Policy in the 1980s*, ed. Kenneth A. Oye, Robert J. Lieber and Donald Rothschild (Boston and Toronto: Little, Brown and Company Limited, 1983), 70–71.
2 Jerry W. Sanders, *Peddlers of Crisis: The Committee on the Present Danger and the Politics of Containment* (Boston, MA: South End Press, Boston, 1983).

66 *Democracy and national security*

3 Richard Pipes, 'Peace with Freedom', in *Alerting America: The Papers of the Committee on the Present Danger*, ed. Charles Tyroler (Washington DC: Pergamon-Brassey's International Defence Publishers, 1984), 26.

4 Ibid., 33.

5 Robert Scheer, *With Enough Shovels: Reagan, Bush and Nuclear War* (New York: Random House, 1982), 40.

6 Ibid., 39.

7 James A. Thomson, 'The LRTNF Decision: Evolution of US Theatre Nuclear Policy, 1975–9', *International Affairs* 60, no. 4 (1984): 610–612, accessed 7 February 2008, www.jstor.org/stable/2620044; Raymond L. Garthoff, *Détente and Confrontation: American-Soviet Relations from Nixon to Reagan* (Washington DC: The Brookings Institute, 1985), 860.

8 Sanders, *Peddlers of Crisis*, 256.

9 Ibid., 324.

10 Ibid.

11 Miles Kahler, 'The United States and Western Europe: the Diplomatic Consequences of Mr Reagan', in *Eagle Resurgent? The Reagan Era in American Foreign Policy*, ed. Kenneth A. Oye, Robert J. Lieber and Donald Rothschild (Boston and Toronto: Little, Brown and Company Limited, 1987), 309.

12 Sanders, 325.

13 Kahler, 310–311.

14 Ibid., 288–290.

15 Garthoff, *Détente and Confrontation*, 1029.

16 Charles Z. Wick, 'Countering Soviet Disinformation', 7 August 1981, DDRS, accessed 11 December 2006, 8.

17 Ibid.

18 Ibid., 4.

19 *Washington Post*, 'Memo outlining "Project Truth" campaign', *Washington Post*, No. 10, 1981, Nexis UK, www.lexisnexis.com/uk/nexis.

20 Wick, 11–12.

21 Melinda Beck and Jane Whitmore, 'A Hot New Cold War at ICA', *Newsweek*, 16 November 1981, Nexis UK, www.lexisnexis.com/uk/nexis.

22 Cable, Alexander Haig to all diplomatic and consular posts, DDRS, accessed 4 January 2007.

23 Memo, Thomas M. Niles to Alexander Haig, 6 August 1981, DDRS, accessed 19 June 2008, 4.

24 Niles, 1.

25 Cable, Alexander Haig to Lord Carrington, 31 August 1981, DDRS, accessed 19 June 2008, 2.

26 Ibid., 3.

27 *Washington Post*, 'Memo Outlining "Project Truth" Campaign'.

28 Keith L. Shimko, 'Reagan on the Soviet Union and the Nature of International Conflict,' *Political Psychology* 13, no. 3 (1992): 361–362, accessed 15 September 2014, www.jstor.org/stable/3791603.

29 Richard Pipes, *Vixi: Memoirs of a Non-Belonger* (New Haven and London: Yale University Press, 2003), 198.

30 'Haig asserts Soviet wanes spiritually but rises as a threat', *New York Times*, 10 May 1981, Nexis UK, www.lexisnexis.com/uk/nexis.

31 'Haig asserts Soviet wanes spiritually'.

32 Peter Schweizer, *Victory: The Reagan Administration's Secret Strategy that Hastened the Collapse of the Soviet Union* (New York: The Atlantic Monthly Press, 1994), 41.

33 Remark made by Reagan at a June 1981 press conference, quoted in John Dumbrell, *American Foreign Policy: Carter to Clinton* (Basingstoke: Macmillan, 1997), 69.

34 Ronald Reagan, *An American Life* (London: Hutchinson, 1990), 237–238.

Democracy and national security 67

35 George F. Kennan, 'The Sources of Soviet Conduct', *Foreign Affairs* 25 no. 4 (1947), reprinted in *Foreign Affairs* 65, no. 4 (1987): 868.

36 John Lewis Gaddis, *Strategies of Containment: A Critical Appraisal of American National Security Policy during the Cold War* Revised and Expanded Edition (New York: Oxford University Press, 2005), 352–353.

37 'Haig calls Moscow the primary source of danger to the world', *New York Times*, 24 April 1981, Nexis UK, www.lexisnexis.com/uk/nexis.

38 Quoted from Don Oberdorfer, 'Haig: Soviets Focus of His Global View; 'The Task Ahead.... Will Be the Management of Global Soviet Power', *Washington Post*, 23 December 1980, LexisNexis, http://web.lexis-nexis.com/executive, 1.

39 Raymond L. Garthoff, *The Great Transition: American–Soviet relations and the end of the Cold War* (Washington: The Brookings Institute, 1994), 30.

40 *New York Times*, 'Haig calls Moscow'.

41 Schweizer, 6–7.

42 John Goshko, 'Stepped-Up Radio Propaganda Campaign Planned against Soviets', *Washington Post*, March 12, 1981, LexisNexis, http://web.lexis-nexis.com/executive.

43 Philip Nicolaides, quoted in William J. Lanquette, 'Should it be the Voice of America or the Voice of the Administration?' *The National Journal*, 23 January 1982, LexisNexis, http://web.lexis-nexis.com/executive, 3.

44 Philip Nicolaides, quoted in Ibid.

45 Arthur Rachwald, *In Search of Poland: The Superpowers' Response to Solidarity, 1980–1989* (Stanford, California: Hoover Press, 1990), 3, 19, 49.

46 Ibid., 4.

47 Ibid., 53.

48 Alan P. Dobson, 'The Reagan Administration, Economic Warfare, and Starting to Close Down the Cold War', *Diplomatic History* 29, no. 3 (2005): 542, accessed 3 August 2012, doi: 10.1111/j.1467–7709.2005.00502.x.

49 Alexander M. Haig, Jr, *Caveat: Realism, Reagan and Foreign Policy* (New York: Macmillan Publishing Company, 1984), 238–242.

50 Quoted from Haig, Caveat, 242.

51 Schweizer, 61.

52 John F. Rhodes (1981) 'untitled', United Press International, 29 September 1981, LexisNexis http://web.lexis-nexis.com/executive.

53 Schweizer, 60.

54 Ibid., 61.

55 Rachwald, 54–55.

56 Daniel Patrick Moynihan, 'The Politics of Human Rights', *Commentary* 64, no. 2 (1977): 23–24; Norman Podhoretz, 'Making the World Safe for Communism', *Commentary* 61, no. 4 (1976): 40.

57 Nathan Glazer, 'American Values and American Foreign Policy', *Commentary* 62:1 (1976): 33–34; Walter Laqueur, 'The Issue of Human Rights', Commentary 63, no. 5 (1977): 32; and Podhoretz: 40.

58 Jeane J. Kirkpatrick, 'Dictatorships and Double Standards', *Commentary* 68, no. 5 (1979): 34.

59 Ibid.

60 Ibid., 38.

61 Ibid., 37.

62 Kirkpatrick, 'Dictatorships and Double Standards', 37, 44.

63 Quoted from Garthoff, *Détente and Confrontation*, 1050.

64 Mark Gerson, *The Neoconservative Vision: From the Cold War to the Culture Wars* (Oxford: Madison Books, 1997), 176.

65 Quoted in David F. Schmitz, *The United States and Right-wing Dictatorships* (Cambridge: Cambridge University Press, 2006), 201.

68 *Democracy and national security*

66 Tamar Jacoby, 'The Reagan Turnaround on Human Rights', *Foreign Affairs* 64, no. 5 (1986): 1069, accessed 7 March 2014, EBSCO Host.

67 Jeane J. Kirkpatrick, 'US security and Latin America', *Commentary* 71, no. 1 (1981): 29.

68 Quoted from Robert A. Pastor 'The Reagan Administration and Latin America: Eagle Insurgent', in *Eagle Resurgent? The Reagan Era in American Foreign Policy*, ed. Kenneth A. Oye, Robert J. Lieber and Donald Rothschild, (Boston and Toronto: Little, Brown and Company Limited, 1987), 362.

69 Tommie Sue Montgomery, *Revolution in El Salvador: From Civil Strife to Civil Peace* (Boulder, San Francisco and Oxford: Westview Press, 1995), 74.

70 Walter LaFeber, *Inevitable Revolutions: The United States in Central America* (New York and London: W.W. Norton & Company, 1984), 247–250.

71 Mark Peceny and William D. Stanley, 'Counterinsurgency in El Salvador', *Politics & Society* 38, no. 67 (2010): 78, accessed 26 November 2014, DOI: 10.1177/0032329209357884.

72 Quoted from Morris J. Blachman and Kenneth Sharpe, 'De-Democratising American Foreign Policy: Dismantling the Post-Vietnam Formula', *Third World Quarterly* 8, no. 4 (1986): 1283, accessed 7 August 2009, www.jstor.org/stable/3991715.

73 Ibid.

74 Karen DeYoung 'El Salvador: A Symbol of World Crisis; How Tiny El Salvador Became U.S. Policy Symbol', *Washington Post*, 8 March 1981, Nexis UK, www.lexisnexis.com/uk/nexis.

75 William M. LeoGrande, 'A Splendid Little War: Drawing the Line in El Salvador', *International Security* 6, no. 1 (1981): 27, accessed 12 February 2009, www.jstor.org/stable/2538528; Garthoff, *Détente and Confrontation*, 1053.

76 Karen DeYoung, 'El Salvador: Where Reagan draws the line; Reagan "sends a message to Moscow" via El Salvador', *Washington Post*, 9 March 1981, Nexis UK, www.lexisnexis.com/uk/nexis

77 Robert Pastor, 'Continuity and Change in US Foreign Policy: Carter and Reagan on El Salvador', *Journal of Policy Analysis and Management* 3, no. 2 (1984): 179, accessed 10 February 2010, EBSCO Host.

78 Thomas Carothers, *In the Name of Democracy: US policy towards Latin America in the Reagan Years* (Berkeley and Los Angeles, California: University of California Press, 1991), 15.

79 Ibid., 16.

80 Carothers, *In the Name of Democracy*, 17.

81 John M. Goshko, 'White House stresses support for Salvador Democracy, Human Rights,' *Washington Post*, 19 February 1981, Nexis UK, www.lexisnexis.com/uk/nexis.

82 John A. Soares Jr., 'Strategy, Ideology, and Human Rights: Jimmy Carter Confronts the Left in Central America, 1979–1981', *Journal of Cold War Studies* 8, no. 4 (2006): 81, accessed 16 May 2014, EBSCO Host.

83 Goshko, 'White House stresses'.

84 David F. Schmitz, *The United States and Right-wing Dictatorships, 1965–1989* (Cambridge: Cambridge University Press, 2006), 240.

85 Schmitz, *The United States and Right-wing Dictatorships*, 208; Laurence Whitehead, 'Explaining Washington's Central American Policies', *Journal of Latin American Studies* 15, no. 2. (1983): 334–341, accessed 12 February 2009, DOI: http://dx.doi.org/10.1017/S0022216X00000742.

86 Jim Adams, 'Senate Panel examines El Salvador Aid', The Associated Press, 11 May 1981, Nexis UK, www.lexisnexis.com/uk/nexis.

87 Quoted from Schmitz, *The United States and Right-wing Dictatorships*, p.209.

88 Roy Gutman, *Banana Diplomacy: The Making of American Policy in Nicaragua 1981–1987* (New York: Simon and Schuster, 1988), 60–61.

Democracy and national security 69

89 Ibid.
90 State Department, 'El Salvador: an Assessment', 10 July 1981, DDRS, accessed 24 July 2012, 1.
91 Ibid., 4.
92 George Gedda, 'U.S. Backs Salvadoran Elections, Pledges Continued Aid', The Associated Press, 17 July 1981, Nexis UK, www.lexisnexis.com/uk/nexis.
93 Quoted from John M. Goshko, 'U.S. Calls for Elections in El Salvador', *Washington Post*, 17 July 1981, Nexis UK, www.lexisnexis.com/uk/nexis.
94 Quoted from 'Excerpts from El Salvador Speech', *New York Times*, 16 July 1981, Nexis UK, www.lexisnexis.com/uk/nexis.
95 Carothers, 20.
96 Gutman, 60.
97 Michael A. Samuels and William A. Douglas, 'Promoting Democracy', *The Washington Quarterly* 4, no. 3 (1981): 52, footnote, accessed 30 May 2012, http://dx.doi.org/10.1080/01636608109451791.
98 Quoted from Michael A. Samuels and John D. Sullivan, 'Democratic Development: A new role for US business', *The Washington Quarterly*, 9, no. 3 (1986): 170, accessed 10 June 2012, DOI: 10.1080/01636608609450839.
99 Samuels and Douglas, 'Promoting Democracy', 52
100 Ibid., 60.
101 Ibid., 52.
102 Ibid., 60–61.
103 James M. Scott, *Deciding to Intervene: The Reagan Doctrine and American Foreign Policy* (Durham and London: Duke University Press, 1996), 157–158.
104 Samuels and Douglas, 'Promoting Democracy': 52.
105 Ibid., 64.
106 Ibid.
107 Ibid.
108 Ibid., 52.
109 Ibid., 65.
110 Ibid., 61–62.
111 Ibid., 62.
112 Laxmikant Manroop and Parbudyal Singh, 'The Role of the AFL-CIO in Regime Change: The Case of Guyana', *British Journal of Industrial Relations* 50, no. 2 (2012): 308–328, accessed 30 November 2014, doi: 10.1111/j.1467–8543.2011.00854.x; Robert Waters and Gordon Daniels, 'The World's Longest General Strike: The AFL-CIO, the CIA, and British Guiana', *Diplomatic History* 29, no. 2 (2005): 279–307, accessed 30 November 2014, DOI: 10.1111/j.1467–7709.2005.00474.x; Kim Scipes, 'Why Labor Imperialism? AFL-CIO's leaders and the developing world', *WorkingUSA: The Journal of Labor and Society* 13 (2010): 471–472, accessed 10 November 2014, DOI: 10.1111/j.1743–4580.2010.00306.x.
113 Beth Sims, *Workers of the World Undermined: American Labor's Role in US Foreign Policy* (Boston, MA: South End Press, 1992), 55–59.
114 Stephen Schlesinger and Stephen Kinzer, *Bitter Fruit: The Story of the American Coup in Guatemala* (Cambridge, Massachusetts and London, England: Harvard University Press, 1999), 89–95 and Church Committee, *Covert Action in Chile 1963–1973*, 18 December 1975, accessed 24 April 2006, http://foia.state.gov/Reports/ChurchReport.asp#C. Covert Action and Multinational Corporations.
115 Tom Barry and Deb Preusch, *AIFLD in Central America: Agents as Organizers* (Albuquerque: The Inter-Hemispheric Education Resource Centre, 1990), 7.
116 Lane Kirkland, interviewed by James F. Shea and Don R. Kienzle for *The Association for Diplomatic Studies and Training Foreign Affairs Oral History Project: Labor Series*, 13th November 1996, accessed May 17, 2012, www.adst.org/OH%20TOCs/Kirkland,%20Lane.toc.pdf, 13.

70 *Democracy and national security*

117 Samuels and Douglas, 'Promoting Democracy', 56.
118 Ibid., 55.
119 Ibid.
120 Ibid., 54.
121 Ibid., 52, 60–61.
122 Ibid., 63.
123 Ibid., 62.
124 Ibid., 54.
125 Ibid., 61–62.
126 Ibid., 63.
127 Ibid.,
128 Ibid., 52.
129 Jacoby., 1067–1070.
130 Ibid., 1066.
131 Edwin S. Maynard, 'The Bureaucracy and Implementation of US Human Rights Policy', *Human Rights Quarterly* 11, no. 2 (1989): 182–184, accessed 28 November 2009, www.jstor.org/stable/761957.
132 Murray Friedman, *The Neoconservative Revolution: Jewish Intellectuals and the Shaping of Public Policy* (Cambridge: Cambridge University Press, 2005), 168–172.
133 Jim Lobe, 'The Bush Team Reloaded', *Middle East Report* no. 234 (2005): 14–15, accessed 10 June 2012, DOI: 10.2307/1559363.
134 White House, 'Presidential Review Memorandum 28: Human Rights', 8 July 1977. *Jimmy Carter Library*, accessed 20 March 2009. www.jimmycarterlibrary.gov/documents/prmemorandums/prm28.pdf, 1–2.
135 'Extracts from State Department memo on Human Rights', *The New York Times*, 5 November 1981, Nexis UK, www.lexisnexis.com/uk/nexis, 3.
136 Nicolas Guilhot, *The Democracy Makers: Human Rights and International Order* (New York, Chichester: Columbia University Press, 2005), 180.
137 'Extracts from State Department memo on Human Rights', 1 (my italics).
138 Ibid. (my italics).
139 Ibid., 3.
140 'Extracts from State Department memo on Human Rights', 1.
141 Ibid., 3.
142 'Extracts from State Department memo on Human Rights', 2.
143 Ibid.
144 Ibid.
145 'Excerpts from Haig's address at OAS meeting', *New York Times*, 5 December 1981, Nexis UK, www.lexisnexis.com/uk/nexis, 1.
146 Ibid., 2.
147 Ibid., 2.
148 'Excerpts from Haig's address at OAS meeting', 2.
149 Ibid., 2.
150 Ibid., 2.

3 Democracy promotion and national security policy

On the night of 12 December 1981, several days after Haig's speech to the OAS recommending the creation of a Central American democracy institute, the Polish government declared martial law in order to reassert its control over Polish society and remove the threat to its power posed by Solidarity. Soon, communications between Poland and the outside world were severed and factories were placed under military discipline.[1] In addition, more than 6,000 Solidarity leaders and activists were arrested, including Lech Walesa,[2] and the union was suspended, seeming to bring the country's experiment with political pluralism to an abrupt end. This was the catalytic event that brought the idea of a global campaign of democracy promotion embracing action in the Soviet bloc and the Third World into the policymaking debate within the administration. The more strident calls for the support of dissident movements in Eastern Europe which resulted from the Polish government's actions triggered a process which resulted in the proposal of a government-sponsored strategy of democracy promotion to be implemented by US private groups.

This proposal, in turn, brought the strategic and organisational tensions involved in pursuing such a campaign to the forefront of the policy debate in the administration and resulted in horizontal conflicts between the hard-line Reaganite group of policymakers and the more pragmatic State Department. The primary tension was strategic, as the issue of democracy promotion was superimposed over the pre-existing policy differences between these two groups over policy towards the Soviet Union and pro-US authoritarian regimes. The Reaganites wanted to prosecute a geopolitically limited campaign aimed at using democracy promotion to weaken and undermine pro-Soviet governments and the government of the USSR internally as an element of a 'centred' Cold War strategy, while maintaining support for pro-US dictatorships. In contrast, the State Department favoured a wider strategy of using democracy promotion to enhance containment in the Third World by transitioning pro-US dictatorships to more stable democratic governments, while creating internal problems for the USSR in its zone through the support of dissident groups and movements. The operations that State advocated both in the Third World and the Soviet bloc were thus compatible with its existing focus on a 'de-centred' Cold War strategy of containing Soviet expansionism. Thus, tensions over how democracy

72 *Democracy promotion and national security policy*

promotion could be used as a vehicle to pursue US national security interests were incorporated into the existing strategic debate over how to fight the Cold War most effectively.

The projected implementation of programmes aimed at strengthening political groups overseas on a wide scale necessarily required the creation of a new state–private network to implement them. However, the injection of US non-state actors into the campaign complicated the strategic tension by adding an organisational one. While the use of such domestic private groups had operational advantages for the United States government, some degree of government control would clearly be needed to manage the gap between private interests, whether these were expressed as the promotion of democracy for ideological, rather than strategic, reasons, or the sectional interests of the groups concerned, and the more narrow and specific national security interests of the US. The choice of either a 'centred' strategy based on operations against the Soviet bloc only or a more 'de-centred' one based on the containment of Soviet power through the support of democratic movements globally, including the Soviet bloc, implied the exercise of different degrees of control over non-state actors by the government. Each contending faction within the administration attempted to institute a pattern of state–private relationships favourable to its own strategy. The distribution of power in the administration and the attitude of the President would exercise the most influence on the model of democracy promotion that emerged from this struggle.

Martial law in Poland and the shift towards democracy promotion

The declaration of martial law in Poland had a profound impact on the development of democracy promotion, as the crisis in Eastern Europe brought the disagreements over anti-Soviet strategy within the administration between those who were focussed on weakening and undermining communist control of the Soviet bloc internally and those who gave priority to strengthening the 'Free World' instead into the open and made it a matter of urgency to resolve them. The tough response of the Reaganite faction, and the divisions this caused within the administration, created the context in which a global campaign of democracy promotion was proposed to the President. It is necessary to examine this context to fully understand why an expansive campaign of democracy promotion was proposed at this point.

Economic and political warfare proposals

The immediate effect of the crisis was to strengthen the Reaganites in their calls for a political and economic assault on the Soviet bloc. This campaign could be prosecuted as a crusade for democracy, as in the Polish case US national security interests and pro-democratic rhetoric intersected and reinforced each other. Richard Allen, the former National Security Advisor, who had recently left the

Democracy promotion and national security policy 73

administration after a minor corruption scandal but continued to serve on the President's Foreign Intelligence Advisory Board, showed this link when he asked rhetorically: 'Are we not now presented with a beautiful opportunity to raise the cost suddenly and dramatically and seize the high ground?'[3] In addition to this ideological reinforcement, the Reaganite faction found they had more space in which to push for punitive actions against the USSR and Poland because while the US government as a whole had been focussed on the possibility of a Soviet invasion of Poland, there was no pre-existing consensus on what action to take in the event of a crackdown by the Polish government.[4]

The Reagan administration imposed a range of sanctions on Poland in the wake of martial law, suspending talks over a long-term grain agreement with the USSR and placing an embargo on the export of scientific and technical equipment to the Soviet Union.[5] Dobson argues that President Reagan's motivation in imposing these measures was limited to sending a clear message of disapproval to Moscow;[6] however, the Reaganite faction in the administration wanted to go further. This hard-line group, composed of William Casey, William Clark, the Deputy Secretary of State, and Caspar Weinberger, together with second-tier policymakers such as NSC staffers Richard Pipes and Norman Bailey, Weinberger advisor Richard Perle and Assistant Secretary of Commerce for Export Administration Lawrence Brady, wanted to institute more punitive measures, including declaring Poland in default on the debt it owed to Western banks.[7] The aims of such a policy were to wage economic warfare by reducing the Soviet's economic capacity to build up and maintain its military forces[8]. As noted in the previous chapter, this Reaganite desire for economic warfare preceded the Polish crisis, as Casey had argued that economic problems and political unrest made the Soviet bloc vulnerable in May 1981, long before the crisis had come to a head. However, the new political atmosphere that the crisis had created gave the hard-liners more political space in which to press for the adoption of a tough policy towards the Soviet bloc.

The Reaganites had found a tangible target for US economic warfare measures in the Urengoi gas pipeline, which was intended to transport Soviet natural gas to Western Europe and was being part-financed by a number of Western European countries. It was thought that embargoes on the equipment the Soviets needed to construct the pipeline would hurt them by depriving them of foreign currency earnings and damaging the Soviet economy.[9] This was a long-standing cause of disagreement within the administration, which had not been able to agree on the parameters for restricting the export of the technology the Soviets required to complete the pipeline: Haig had pressed for the adoption of the least restrictive guidelines possible in 1981 in order to gain Western European support for the policy, while NSA Richard Allen pushed for tougher measures.[10] The Polish crisis changed this dynamic and allowed the hard-liners to push for the harsher measures they favoured on the grounds that sustained economic warfare could cause the collapse of the USSR.[11] On 29 December, the Reagan administration suspended export licences for pipe-laying equipment to the Soviet Union. The Department of Commerce then decided, seemingly unilaterally, that any

74   *Democracy promotion and national security policy*

such sanctions, if applied, should be retroactive and applicable to US subsidiaries.[12] While these actions were insufficient to meet the maximal programme of the Reaganites, they were certainly a step in the right direction.

This decision opened up a potential fault line between the US and its allies, as it meant that companies in Western Europe manufacturing pipe-laying equipment under licence from US firms would also be subject to the ban or risk having secondary sanctions imposed on them, and that contracts already signed would have to be abrogated.[13] However, the largest fault line which opened up was in the administration itself. While Weinberger, Casey and other hard-liners wished to forge ahead with tough sanctions, up to and including a complete Western trade embargo on Poland and the USSR, Haig was initially cautious, fearing that too strong a response could trigger direct Soviet intervention in Poland.[14] He also feared that the imposition of such tough sanctions could damage the NATO alliance. Although, as Supreme Allied Commander in Europe, he had also opposed the pipeline when it was first begun, and for the same reasons as the Reaganites,[15] as Secretary of State he recognised that the Western Europeans had already invested a great deal in the pipeline project, both in terms of money and planning, and that they were unlikely to withdraw from it or buckle to US sanctions.[16] In Haig's view, maintaining a strong NATO alliance was more important than spending valuable allied goodwill to achieve a goal which might prove to be unattainable. The Secretary argued in his memoirs, written shortly after he left the administration in 1982, that 'In the Polish crisis we were not seeing the collapse of the Soviet empire. Moscow's difficulties with the Poles were a sign of trouble and decay, but the situation was not irreversible.'[17] US pressure on Western Europeans to abrogate economic relations which they stood to profit from greatly in the service of an uncompromising anti-Sovietism, which was not part of their ideological worldview would probably serve the interests of the USSR more than the USA in the long run by driving a wedge between the US and its allies.[18]

Haig was supported in this stance by State Department officials with responsibility for foreign economic policy such as Myer Rashish, the Undersecretary of State for Economic Affairs, and Robert D. Hormats, his successor, who argued that US attempts to impede the pipeline could result in a rupture of the Western alliance.[19] However, the State Department was not unified on this question, with the Bureau of Political–Military Affairs and the Policy Planning Staff taking a more hard-line position.[20] This brought the Reaganites and more pragmatic State Department officials into direct collision; one faction wanted to push for economic warfare in the belief that this could weaken the Soviets and possibly begin the process of destabilising the regime; the other saw little prospect of seriously harming the Soviets through sanctions and believed it was more important to preserve the Western alliance. At an NSC meeting on 26 February, Haig called for pipeline equipment to be exempted from any sanctions imposed, while Caspar Weinberger called for sanctions on the equipment to be applied retroactively and extraterritorially.[21] The Secretary of State managed to delay the imposition of tough sanctions by sending a State Department mission

Democracy promotion and national security policy 75

to Western Europe to persuade the Western European leaders to fall into line with the US approach,[22] but he was not hopeful.[23] The issue remained open as Reagan decided to wait for the results of the mission before making a final decision.

Although sanctions were a key area of disagreement, the conflict within the administration went beyond them to include the issue of political operations in the Soviet bloc itself, as the Reaganites also began to push for greater US support of Solidarity now that the worst possible consequences of such support becoming known to the Soviets had materialised anyway. At a meeting of key policymakers shortly after the declaration of martial law Richard Pipes, the NSC's hard-line anti-communist Director of Eastern European and Soviet Affairs, suggested that the US government should begin covertly funding Solidarity in order to make sure that the organisation survived to spread its example to the Baltic States and Russia itself. The idea was strongly supported by Weinberger, Casey, Clark and the President,[24] and in late February Casey discussed a programme for covert funding of Solidarity aimed at ensuring the union's survival as an effective underground organisation with Reagan.[25] Although proposals to channel US government aid to Solidarity were strongly opposed by Haig, who felt that the Soviets would not tolerate such actions,[26] the crackdown had invalidated his previous arguments against US support of Solidarity to a large degree.

The administration's new human rights doctrine: the positive track

This move to greater militancy in supporting anti-Soviet democratic groups behind the Iron Curtain was paralleled in the sphere of policy and ideology by a shift in the Reagan administration's Human Rights doctrine from the use of the concept as a rhetorical device to criticise foreign governments to a policy of intervening to support private democratic groups. The new doctrine was announced in the State Department's annual 'Country Reports on Human Rights and Practices' for 1981, submitted to Congress at the end of January 1982. Although such Country Reports were normally submitted to Congress at the end of the year in question, the 1981 Country Reports were submitted at the end of January 1982 rather than December 1981, clearly placing them after martial law had been declared in Poland. The reason for this late submission was the disorganisation in the State Department's Bureau of Humanitarian Affairs caused by the fact that the administration had been unable to get its own appointee, Elliott Abrams, confirmed until the end of October 1981.

The introduction to the Country Reports posited a new goal for US Human Rights policy, stating that the punishment of abuses

> must be accompanied by a second track of positive policy with a bolder long-term aim: to assist the gradual emergence of free political systems. It is in such systems that we can most realistically expect the observance of human rights across the board.[27]

76 *Democracy promotion and national security policy*

Whereas the administration's previous guidelines for the use of Human Rights in US foreign policy, laid down in November 1981, had focused on the rhetorical use of the concept to solidify the Western alliance system and delegitimise the USSR internationally, the doctrine unveiled in January 1982 called on the US to take positive steps to alter political systems abroad.

This ideological melding of Human Rights and democracy promotion subsumed the task of safeguarding Human Rights within the idea of promoting democracy abroad and transformed the campaign for Human Rights into a struggle over the shape of political systems in foreign countries. As a leading neoconservative analyst of Human Rights policies argued several years after this shift, 'The struggle for human rights, far from being, as Carter and his aides proclaimed, indifferent to political systems, is fundamentally a struggle about political systems.'[28] Thus the doctrine of Human Rights was transformed from the Carter administration's policy of advocating cautious reforms in existing dictatorships into an ideology legitimating US efforts to intervene in and shape the internal political structure of other countries that had been missing since the scandals and crises of the late 1960s and 1970s.

However, while this was a significant shift, impelled by the Polish crackdown, it was not the defining shift towards a policy of democracy promotion. Instead, it opened up further questions about whether such a policy should and could be pursued against all dictatorships, or whether it would be limited to enemy states. While the policy was couched rhetorically in universal terms, its practical strategic focus was the USSR and its allies. The Country Reports which discussed the new policy had been produced under the aegis of Elliott Abrams, the recently-confirmed head of the Bureau of Humanitarian Affairs, a strongly anti-Soviet neoconservative who believed that 'The greatest threat to Human Rights is the Soviet Union and its allies'.[29] The announcement devoted a great deal of criticism to the Soviet Union, arguing that

> ... it is a significant service to the cause of human rights to limit the influence the USSR (together with its clients and proxies) can exert. A consistent and serious policy for human rights in the world must counter the USSR politically and bring Soviet bloc human rights violations to the attention of the world over and over again.[30]

It also singled out Poland's actions for criticism, stating that, 'The recent suppression of the Solidarity labor movement in Poland constitutes a massive violation of the [Helsinki] Final Act.'[31] In contrast the document did not devote such harsh criticism to violations in friendly countries, beyond reiterating the position of the November 1981 memo that 'hard choices' between Human Rights and other US objectives were sometimes necessary in dealings with such regimes.[32] The impression is of a policy which remained more concerned with the Soviet bloc than dictatorships allied to the United States.

This impression is strengthened by Abrams' subsequent explanation of the policy in a speech to the Council on Foreign Relations several days after the

Democracy promotion and national security policy 77

Country Reports had been published. While Abrams spoke about the need to influence pro-US dictatorships in the direction of democracy, he argued that the interests of the US and Human Rights were served through maintaining strong relationships between the US government and friendly dictatorships. This was important to prevent communist takeovers which, he argued, would be more damaging to the cause of Human Rights than the current regimes.[33] The speech outlined no concrete strategy for promoting democracy in non-communist dictatorships, instead making an argument for the support of such regimes which was based on the short-term strategic interests of the United States. This was the Human Rights doctrine towards allied dictatorships advanced in the memo of 1981, not the new doctrine articulated in early 1982. Abrams' actions were consistent with his words; one of his first acts as head of the Bureau was to certify that the Human Rights situation in El Salvador had improved, thus allowing military aid to be disbursed in January 1982.[34]

The second key aspect of the doctrine was that it outlined a method for building democracy in dictatorships through connections with private groups abroad, referred to as 'Building Freedom'. This meant that the US would lend support to private 'pockets of freedom', which could then spread to the whole society. These 'pockets of freedom' included

> labor unions, churches, independent judicial systems, bar associations and universities. *Where we do not have leverage over the shape of an entire society, we can nourish the growth of freedom within such institutions.*[35]

Further support for the idea that the policy of promoting democracy and Human Rights was focussed on the Soviet bloc is the inclusion of 'labor unions and churches' as 'pockets of freedom' to be supported by the US, as these institutions constituted the leadership of the anti-communist movement in Poland. However, neither the Country Reports nor Abrams himself spelled out exactly how private groups overseas could be mobilised. While Abrams conceded the freedom of US private groups to protest against Human Rights abuses in allied states if they wished,[36] his speech contained no ideas on the role of domestic private groups in building democracy abroad.

The Polish crisis had impelled a shift towards a more confrontational posture towards the Soviet bloc embracing economic warfare and a renewed push to provide US covert support to Solidarity. This specific shift was reflected in the reformulation of Human Rights into a doctrine legitimating the support of private groups overseas to build democratic systems. However, it had not resulted in the delineation of a coherent strategy. Instead, this change opened up the strategic and organisational questions connected with any such effort to further discussion. While the impetus seemed to be behind a strategy of democracy promotion focussed on the USSR and its allies, the idea of 'Building Freedom' offered room for manoeuvre, as it only articulated the policy in general terms and contained no organisational blueprint for how the policy could be implemented. These omissions were used to argue for

78 *Democracy promotion and national security policy*

a much more expansive campaign of democracy promotion implemented by private groups.

A strategic and organisational framework for democracy promotion in the Soviet bloc and the Third World

Up until March 1982 it seemed that the initiative within the administration had passed to the Reaganite faction. However, the fact that this group had advanced no organisational solution to the problem of 'Building Freedom' through indigenous private forces provided space for others to push their own priorities. A solution to the organisational problem was offered by Alexander Haig in early March; however, rather than seeking merely to enable the Reaganite policy, Haig proposed his solution in the context of a campaign of democracy promotion which merged the support of friendly forces in the Soviet bloc and democratic movements in pro-US authoritarian states in the Third World, bringing these two contentious tracks of policy together. This widening of the targets, together with the diplomatic complications such an expansive campaign could give rise to, made the organisational structure which he had advocated in December 1981 – the Betancourt Institute – obsolete and made implementation by US private groups a necessity. Haig's ideas thus put organisational flesh on the bones of the idea of 'Building Freedom', while also tying it to his own geopolitical priorities, moderating the Reaganite proposals for the support of democratic groups behind the Iron Curtain while seeking to replace their calls for anti-Soviet economic warfare with a democracy promotion campaign.

Haig's proposal was made in a memo to the President on 8 March, several months after the Polish declaration of martial law and while the controversy over sanctions within the administration continued. It took as its starting-points the two geopolitical cases that had preoccupied the administration for the previous 12 months – Poland and El Salvador – and generalised the approach to be deployed in each into a more integrated strategy to be deployed within both friendly and enemy dictatorships. Haig's argument that 'In non-communist countries we need to help moderate democratic forces as the best long-term protection against communism'[37] was clearly an expanded version of the State Department's approach to the conflict in El Salvador which had been generalised to encompass a new US approach to Third World dictatorships. It also reversed the typical response of the national security bureaucracy to political change in allied states by arguing that, rather than opening the way to communism, greater political freedom would actually create more stable regimes, which were better able to withstand communist pressure. Such an approach would go beyond the Kirkpatrick Doctrine and begin to implement the Bureau of Human Rights' more positive policy in the Third World. However, Haig went beyond this focus on the Third World to propose democracy promotion in the Soviet bloc by arguing that '[w]e can help to keep the Soviets preoccupied with problems inside their existing empire (rather than expanding further) by giving practical assistance to democratic and nationalistic forces and thus going on our own political

Democracy promotion and national security policy 79

offensive',[38] with Poland cited as the concrete example. This expansion of democracy promotion to take in the Soviet bloc went further than the proposals of the 1970s, or Douglas' and Samuels' article of 1981.

This citing of the Soviet bloc as a possible target of political operations appears to indicate that Haig had abandoned his opposition to the tougher Reaganite policy. However, it is clear from a close reading of the memo that Haig's acceptance of anti-Soviet political operations was motivated by his desire to limit and manage their impact, rather than a genuine conversion to the Reaganite viewpoint that such operations could help to undermine Soviet control of Eastern Europe and the USSR. Haig's comment that democracy promotion programmes in the Soviet bloc would limit further Soviet expansion makes it clear that the support of democratic forces within the Soviet bloc was aimed at boosting containment by tying the Soviets up with domestic difficulties, not overthrowing or transforming Marxist governments. Haig accepted the proximate goal of the Reaganite strategy – instability in the Soviet bloc – as part of his own strategy but did not believe that the US was capable of significantly undermining or transforming bloc governments. Thus, the State Department's general strategy had not evolved from a policy of containing the USSR to one of undermining the internal control of communist governments within the bloc.

Given the disagreements between the US and its NATO allies which he feared over the issue of economic sanctions, Haig might have agreed to political operations to head off the more serious threat of the tough sanctions the Reaganites proposed, which he believed to be dangerous to the Western alliance. In fact, the Secretary of State argued that, 'The use of this political tool [of containment] is no less effective than military and *economic* leverage, and is much less costly and risky.'[39] Haig's proposal was made several days before the State Department's mission to Western Europe referred to above, which was aimed at developing a coherent Western position on economic sanctions towards Poland and the Soviet Union, was due to leave. At this point Reagan had not definitively ruled on the scope of such sanctions, meaning that there was still an opportunity to influence the outcome of this process.

Haig's proposal of a gradual approach was also aimed at limiting the dangers posed by a democracy campaign to short-term US interests. This gradual approach was to apply to the targets of the strategy as a whole, as '[o]bviously there are constraints as to what we can do towards both communist and non-communist countries in the immediate future'. However, specifically, a 'pragmatic and careful' approach would be best to avoid pushing the Soviets into dangerous counter-actions or 'alarming our European allies with visions of an all-out effort to destabilize Eastern Europe and the Soviet Union itself';[40] all consequences of a more aggressive policy towards the Soviet Union which Haig had predicted and feared. Thus, the long-term approach advocated by Haig would make political operations within the Soviet bloc more acceptable to himself and other State Department officials. He also argued for a gradual campaign in the Third World, stating that an immediate and all-out campaign might

80   *Democracy promotion and national security policy*

'destabili[ze] non-democratic friends'[41]. Such an approach might also make a campaign in the Third World easier to sell within the administration, as the Reaganite NSC was intensely worried that pushing pro-US dictatorships into liberalising measures precipitately could lead to rifts between them and the United States which radical forces could profit from, as these policymakers believed had occurred in Nicaragua in 1979.

This wider strategy required a new instrumentality to implement it, as the expansion of the remit of democracy promotion from Central America to Eastern Europe rendered the organisational form that Haig had championed to the OAS in December 1981 – a democracy training institute to be run as a multi-governmental organisation through the OAS – insufficient. Such a limited institute could not be used to carry out democracy promotion operations outside the Western Hemisphere. Instead of this multi-governmental approach, Haig turned to the solution which had been advocated by the non-state actors; a non-governmental democracy promotion organisation. A strategy of democracy promotion which was to be deployed simultaneously in the Third World and in Eastern Europe needed as much freedom of action as possible, both from bureaucratic constraints within the policymaking apparatus and from interference from other countries. This freedom of action, which would be used to achieve US national security interests and not those of a coalition such as the OAS, would clearly best be provided by an organisation located outside the Executive, and one that was solely American.

The requirement for a plausibly deniable and credible organisation to implement democracy promotion programmes on a global basis, then, pointed to the foundation of a new state–private network focussed on political action rather than ideological or cultural projection. The use of a private organisation could also resolve the organisational problems that the Reagan administration could experience in pursuing democracy promotion in both the Third World and the Soviet bloc. The fact that the actions of such a private instrumentality could not be blamed on the US government would defuse accusations of American interference from other countries.[42] Such a capability would be valuable for operations aimed at Poland or the Soviet Union, allowing the US to stave off charges of US political meddling from these countries, or at least make them less credible to the rest of the world, and providing a more plausibly deniable channel for the funding of groups behind the Iron Curtain such as Solidarity. In the Third World, outsourcing democracy promotion to a non-governmental body would allow the US government to preserve working relationships with friendly dictators until they fell or the time came to replace them. A non-governmental instrumentality would also be more credible and acceptable as an ally to the foreign private groups it sought to shape and influence than a government program, as Douglas and Samuels had previously argued.

A private instrumentality represented an organisational solution to the policy tensions inherent in State's new strategy of pursuing a long-term programme of democracy promotion in both enemy states and allied dictatorships. However, the fact that the new private organisation would require Congressional funding,

Democracy promotion and national security policy 81

as well as private money, to engage in a 'major, sustained and professional effort'[43] represented a potential threat to its credibility as a body separate from the US government. Haig did not consider this question in depth, merely asserting that '[t]he Europeans and the Soviets use such "private" institutions for political operations without serious problems.'[44]

The new state–private network that Haig was calling for was already in the process of formation. State Department personnel had already been in contact with the non-state democracy promoters, who noted that State's proposal 'reflects a line of thinking developed in the State Department with some input from the APF' as a result of 'several private meetings which included Doctor Michael Samuels, International Director of the Chamber of Commerce and Mr Mark Palmer, Deputy to the Under-Secretary for Political Affairs at the State Department'.[45] Many of the points made by Haig in his proposal were derived from arguments used by these democracy promoters previously. Haig's argument that 'the United States is organized to give economic and military assistance, but we have no institutions devoted to political training and funding'[46] was derived from the article co-authored article by Michael Samuels and William Douglas in 1981.[47] Haig also uses the analogy of Western European political assistance to the Portuguese Socialist party used in Samuels' proposal and refers to other European efforts, possibly the West German foundations whose example was championed by George Agree. He also proposed a non-governmental Institute for Democracy along the lines previously suggested by Samuels.[48]

This proposed recourse to a state–private institution to implement national security programmes re-opened the strategic and organisational questions, which had bedevilled the previous state–private network. The President's response to Haig's proposal clearly showed the strategic and organisational tensions which would have to be negotiated to make privately-implemented democracy promotion a reality. This response took several weeks to materialise and when it did, on 2 April, it was channelled through William Clark, the administration's new National Security Advisor and a long-standing collaborator of the President. While Reagan was interested in the concept he was unsure how such an expansive strategy of building democracy abroad could be implemented in conformity with the particular national security interests of the United States. Strategically, Reagan wanted to know how the operations of the institute could be squared with the US need to maintain good relations with friendly dictators; a prime concern for the Reaganites within the administration. This was linked to the organisational question, as the President also wanted to know how the actions of a private organisation could be tied to US national security priorities while remaining credible enough to be effective and who would make operational decisions.[49] The administration did not want to create a private democracy institute which might escape Executive control and pursue actions which were not in line with US national security interests as it conceived them. All of these questions had a bearing on whether a non-governmental institute for democracy could be used effectively to support US national security interests.

Designing an overt state–private network

Reagan's queries led to further meetings between State Department representatives and the democracy promoters in order to discuss how a credible and effective state–private organisation could be created to implement a campaign of democracy promotion. The key discussion occurred on 6 April when the APF directors met with Mark Palmer, the Deputy Undersecretary for Political Affairs, to discuss the question of organisational structure. Palmer was a key player in the convergence between non-state actors interested in democracy promotion and the US government, and had played a role in bringing the democracy promoters to the attention of the Department, meeting with Michael Samuels before Haig's proposal of 8 March. Born in 1941 in Ann Arbor, Michigan, as a student Palmer had been a civil rights activist for the Student Nonviolent Co-ordinating Committee and a Freedom Rider for the Congress of Racial Equality before spending time in the Soviet Union as an exchange student. He had joined the Foreign Service in 1964 as a career official and was posted to Moscow as a consular officer, before returning to Washington to continue work in the State Department.[50] Palmer went on to play key roles in the history of US democracy promotion; first, as an advocate for the project within the State Department, then by supporting Hungarian dissidents during his tenure as US ambassador to that country from 1986–1990. After leaving government service, Palmer served on the boards of private think thanks and organisations connected with the non-state democracy promotion community such as Freedom House and the Council for a Community of Democracies.

Palmer's time in the USSR had convinced him that change within the Soviet bloc was possible, and he arrived at the April 1982 meeting committed to an expansive campaign for democracy that included the USSR. However, he also believed that such action needed to proceed in tandem with negotiations, and that it should not be pushed so obviously or rapidly that it led to Soviet countermeasures which would destroy the groups the United States was trying to help.[51] For these reasons, and to decide how operations could be carried out under similar constraints in the Third World, discussion at the APF meeting turned on how an effective government-funded private democracy foundation could be created.

The problems to be solved were similar to those that had led to the creation of the initial state–private network organisations in the late 1940s; the US state needed private allies whose actions would be more flexible, plausibly deniable and credible than the actions of national security agencies. However, the problem was more complex in the 1980s, as the shift to an overt relationship between the government and private groups threatened to tar any new democracy foundation as merely an arm of the national security bureaucracy. George Agree stated this problem clearly in a memorandum he circulated to the APF directors prior to the meeting:

> An American institution for contact with democratic forces abroad along the lines of the State Department memo will need the utmost credibility to be effective. Attacks on its motivations and insinuations as to its control are inevitable.[52]

Democracy promotion and national security policy   83

Palmer's solution was to make 'the initiative … independent or outside the executive branch'.[53] The APF should form a key part of the new democracy promotion infrastructure, as it was already known to foreign party leaders and would be more easily accepted overseas and domestically than a totally new institution. In addition, it already had the tax-exempt status necessary to make the most of any government funding.[54]

However, government funding of the APF alone would be insufficient to wage a democracy campaign that was to include actions by other groups such as unions and business associations. What was needed was an effective umbrella structure that would be credible and would allow a number of different private groups to fold their sectional interests into a coherent strategy to promote democracy. Both the State Department and the APF agreed in principle with the State Department's idea that:

> While the American Political Foundation would be one beneficiary of funds from this new Institute … clearly the Institute needs to be a separate and much larger effort. But both parties should be on its board, along with other important elements like the AFL-CIO, a representative of the press, etc.[55]

Thus, the conception went beyond political action by the APF focussed on party-building abroad to embrace the umbrella foundation concept proposed by Douglas and Samuels in 1981. Palmer and Agree fixed on the example of the West German party foundations as a model of how US private groups could act together to promote democracy overseas in a credible way.[56] Agree had first lobbied for instrumentalities on the pattern of the West German foundations in 1977 and rearticulated his arguments in favour of them now. These foundations, although they were in fact and in the public perception, party-connected, were legally separate entities to the parties, operating independently of the parties, and able to receive private as well as government funding. Agree argued that the US institutions should be structured in exactly the same way, as this would facilitate their acceptance in countries in which the German foundations already operated; moreover, it would be difficult to attack the credibility of the US entities without also attacking that of the German foundations.[57]

The structure also needed to effectively unify private interests into a coherent and effective campaign to promote democracy. For the APF, the choice was between partisan government-funded party institutes along the lines of the West German instrumentalities, or one bipartisan foundation. It was this question that provoked disagreement. Agree and the Palmer argued that the US should create one bipartisan party foundation rather than following the West German model of a separate foundation for each party. Agree had argued for this when setting up the APF originally and Palmer's position on this was clear; the State Department supported the creation of a bipartisan institute on the model of the APF, arguing that a bipartisan structure would help to overcome factional differences between and within the parties, as the promotion of democracy could act as an ideological rallying point which all the participants agreed with.[58] The APF's Republican

84 *Democracy promotion and national security policy*

Chairman, William Brock, also supported the idea, believing a bipartisan institute would be more acceptable to Congress. It would also serve to maintain the focus of operations on democracy promotion rather than sectional group interests, as neither of the two parties would be able to conduct any democracy promotion operations the other was opposed to. While the position was generally accepted, Charles Manatt, the Democrat vice-chairman of the APF, questioned the viability of the idea of a bipartisan foundation and argued for separate party foundations.[59]

While these conflicts over the connection between democracy promotion and partisan interests would grow in importance in the future, however, they were muted at this stage. All agreed that the most pressing matter was to convince the Reagan administration to back the creation of a private democracy promotion organisation. To accomplish this, the State Department accepted the vehicle put forward by Michael Samuels in his proposal of 1980; a study that would help to build political consensus in favour of the plan. Palmer offered $200,000 from the Human Rights division of AID to finance this research.[60] The commission would employ area and political specialists to investigate existing international political activity by others, problems and opportunities for the US, and recommend pilot projects, a three-year plan of operations, a structure for the new institute and a financing plan.[61] Finally, Palmer urged haste, as the State Department wanted to include an announcement of the study in Reagan's forthcoming speech to the British Parliament in June.[62]

Democracy promotion and US Cold War priorities

Although the State Department and the APF had agreed on how private groups could be operationalised in the emerging campaign for democracy relatively easily, the Department's attempt to sell its design within the administration encountered resistance. The primary difficulty was strategic disagreements with Reaganites on the NSC, who feared that the Department and its private allies would press pro-US dictators hard enough to alienate them while failing to exert strong pressure on the Soviets. These strategic disagreements translated into competing organisational models for the democracy promotion effort, as the degree of the state control required was directly linked to how far an expansive democracy promotion campaign was seen to clash with particular US national security interests.

Some progress had been made towards convergence between the different factions. The State Department's acceptance of the Reaganites' proximate goal in the Soviet bloc – to support anti-communist political movements – opened the way to some accommodation over Soviet policy. By April 1982 the NSC had also come to accept, however reluctantly, the State Department's strategy of containment through democratisation in Central America, with a policy summary dated 6 April stating that

> We have an interest in creating and supporting democratic states in Central America capable of conducting their political and economic affairs free

from outside interference.... In the short run we must work to eliminate Cuban/Soviet influence in the region, and in the long run we must build politically stable governments able to withstand such influences.[63]

However, although the Reaganites had acknowledged the logic of State's position in the case of Central America because a strategy of '[b]uilding democratic political institutions capable of achieving domestic political support'[64] could ease the passage of the military aid the NSC sought for the pro-US Salvadoran junta through Congress, this grudging acceptance of the need to build democracy in an allied state in one region did not mean these Reaganites were willing to have this strategy generalised to other right-wing dictatorships in the Third World. The fact that the APF's organisational history, Douglas and Samuels' article and the Department's plans before martial law had been declared in Poland had focussed on democratising allied Third World dictatorships may have made Reaganites in the NSC suspicious that State's plans for political warfare against the Soviet bloc were a fig leaf covering an obsession with promoting democracy in pro-US dictatorships. This debate emerged in full force after the Department reported to the NSC on its response to Reagan's three concerns after its meeting with APF, on 13 April 1982.

State's reply tried to manage the Reaganites' concerns by restating the anti-communist rationale for the democratisation of Third World dictatorships, arguing

While we often need to support non-democratic friends in the near term, over the long term most dictatorships are unstable and we should lay the foundation for a stable democratic successor. If we do not, we are leaving the field open for the communists.[65]

The State Department also attempted to distance itself from the Carter administration's Human Rights campaign, which many in the administration blamed for 'losing' Iran and Nicaragua:

[t]he long-term institution-building nature of the institute's programs would be a far cry from the human rights policies of the previous administration, which were punitive in approach and demanded immediate results.[66]

The policy of promoting democracy in the Third World would be a long-term effort aimed at building the private institutional precursors of a democratic regime from the ground up rather than a top-down attempt to pressure unsavoury dictators to reform. NSC staffer Dennis Blair summed up the 'basic idea' of the project in this area as

to give the United States an additional instrument for dealing with authoritarian regimes.... We need a way to operate openly in support of moderates who are trying to build the structure of democracy – political parties, trade unions, media, etc.[67]

86   *Democracy promotion and national security policy*

While William Casey was a strong supporter of the idea, however, the NSC was split over it, with some staffers fearing that promoting democracy in allied regimes would damage the national security of the United States. NSC official Norman Bailey, a hard-liner who had championed tough sanctions on the USSR in the wake of Polish martial law, feared that such programmes would lead to diplomatic problems with friendly dictatorships, arguing that

> [State's memo] does not answer the question of how one trains labor leaders, journalists and others from friendly dictatorships without damaging our relationships with those dictatorships. In fact, a statement is made that 'we should lay a foundation for a stable democratic successor.' I know of no dictators who would take kindly to that particular suggestion.[68]

Bailey also objected that such a campaign would dilute the US government's focus from contending with the Soviet Union, complaining that '[State's memo] ignores the problem of building democracies in communist countries completely.'[69] The State Department had not been asked to expand on this topic in William Clark's memo of 2 April, so the criticism was unwarranted. However, the comment illustrates the centrality of narrow anti-Sovietism to the Reaganite worldview.

These strategic disagreements had a direct bearing on debates over what the relationship between the private groups and the state should be. Clearly some level of government control would be needed, as there was no guarantee that once the organisation had been established and the private groups had received government funding they would pursue the national interests of the United States rather than carrying out actions based on their own ideologies or interests. However, a level of government control that was too visible would erode the advantages of plausible deniability and credibility with democratic movements overseas that the democracy institute was expected to provide.

This problem recalled the tension between exercising the control of private groups receiving government funding necessary to ensure their actions conformed to national security objectives and providing them with the level of autonomy required for them to appear fully independent of the government that had been a constant and unresolved feature of the state's relationships with private groups before 1967. However, this tension was more difficult to resolve in the early 1980s because the state–private relationship could not be kept covert due to the lingering effects of the 1967 crisis. The challenge was then to create an institution that would receive government funding overtly but which 'could avoid being seen as an agency of the US government, while acting in a complementary way to government policies.'[70]

The lack of strategic consensus within the administration over the targets and end-goals of a democracy promotion campaign complicated this task, as different administration factions proposed organisational models with differing mixes of state control and private autonomy commensurate with their own strategies. The State Department's more geopolitically expansive strategy meant that the US government would have to exert less control over private partners, as the fact that the State Department and the APF agreed on the promotion of democracy in both enemy and allied states meant that the activities of private groups engaged in democracy promotion would not need to be limited to specific regions. In contrast, the NSC's focus on a more narrowly anti-Soviet strategy indicated that a greater level of control would be needed in order to restrain private actions in pro-US dictatorships. Significantly, no faction in the administration called for full private autonomy.

The State Department's solution to this autonomy/control dilemma was to begin building long strings of control into its relationship with the APF which would not be apparent to a casual observer but which would enable the 'light touch' direction needed to deploy private groups within the Department's more expansive strategic framework. Such control could be exercised through government leverage over the internal political dynamics of the organisation. To this end, the Department recommended that the new democracy foundation's voting procedures be structured so that a two-thirds majority of board members would be required to approve operations, with each party being given 40 per cent of the votes, to ensure the party of the administration could ensure consistency with government policy.[71] State's 13 April report reassured other government officials that

> The Foundation is viewed as independent, as are similar but government-funded foundations of the German political parties. However, it cannot as a practical matter stray far from government policy.[72]

This mode of control was similar to the 'ringed autonomy', which Stonor Saunders argues the CIA had used to restrict the activities of its private partners within defined limits in the 1950s and 60s; private groups would be given latitude over day-to-day operations, but rogue actions could be effectively vetoed due to the government's influence over the foundation.

Some Reaganite staffers felt that this mode of control would be either unworkable or too damaging to the US' existing relationships with pro-US dictatorships, however. According to Bailey, the State Department's suggestions for controlling the democracy foundation would only serve to destroy its credibility:

> [The State Department memorandum's] suggestions as to maintaining the myth of independence from the government are ludicrous.[73]

Two other NSC officials, William Stearman and Carnes Lord, argued that 'the body will be "tainted" as an arm of the US government', thus destroying its credibility, 'yet the government will not have complete control',[74] increasing the possibility of rogue actions. These criticisms implied that the project was unrealisable because the autonomy/control problem was unresolvable.

The NSC's solution, rather than abandoning the project, was to sacrifice a measure of credibility to the need for control and to devise an organisational

88 *Democracy promotion and national security policy*

solution for corralling a private democracy promotion foundation into its own anti-Soviet strategy in May. The power of the Council, together with its ability to impose its Reaganite views on the other foreign policymaking agencies in the Executive, had been greatly increased by the departure of Richard Allen as NSA in November 1981.[75] Unlike Allen, who had reported to the President through White House aide Edwin Meese his replacement, William Clark, reported to Reagan directly. Clark's relationship with the President and his access to Reagan made the NSC a far more important player in the administration.[76]

In May, Clark tied the strategy of promoting democracy, and so the proposed institute, to a concerted ideological offensive against Soviet communism then being planned in the National Security Council.[77] This planned campaign for the projection of democratic ideology represented an expansion of Project Truth beyond Western Europe to incorporate anti-Soviet propaganda action on a global scale. Clark merged this propaganda initiative with the proposed democracy foundation by embedding his call for 'political training, organization and financial support for pro-Western forces' with 'international campaigns on issues like Afghanistan and Poland', 'covert political action programs' and 'USICA communications efforts',[78] elements of the NSC's campaign. This action diluted State's project by connecting it explicitly with a strategy focussed exclusively on direct anti-Sovietism, rather than the creation of democratic regimes as firewalls to Soviet expansion. It also diluted the emphasis on building democratic systems abroad by merging it with programmes, which aimed to deploy democratic ideology as a counterforce to communism in a way which was more reminiscent of the pre-1967 state–private network's approach of projecting democracy ideologically than the new proposals which Douglas, Agree and Samuels had made. In contrast to this focus on direct anti-Sovietism, Clark made little mention of the idea of strengthening democratic groups in allied authoritarian states to enable them to create more stable regimes, aside from an isolated reference to 'strengthen[ing] democracy in both communist and non-communist countries.'[79] Thus, as of May 1982 the projected Institute for Democracy was contained within a larger programme that emphasised political and propaganda confrontation with the Soviet Union and communist ideology, rather than a campaign aiming at political transformation in both friendly and unfriendly dictatorships.

The anti-Soviet vision: rollback and liberalisation

Clark's situating of the projected state–private democracy promotion network within the context of a propaganda and political campaign against the Soviet Union was consistent with the wider framework for Soviet policy, which was taking shape within the administration. This framework was moving beyond the concept of containment to posit more radical goals, such as a rollback of Soviet power outside the borders of the USSR and attempts to reduce the dominance of the Soviet communist party within the Soviet Union itself. The link between democracy promotion and this tougher anti-Soviet strategy was made clear in NSDD-32 and then announced publicly by Reagan in a major speech in Britain.

Democracy promotion and national security policy 89

NSDD-32: rollback and reform in the Soviet Empire

NSDD-32 was the Reagan administration's first attempt at generating a coherent national security strategy, after over a year in office. The process of drafting it had begun in February 1982, when Reagan signed off on an NSSD which tasked Clark's NSC to develop an overarching framework for national security policy.[80] While the preparatory study upon which it was based had been carried out by an interagency group consisting of the NSC, the State Department, the CIA, the Joint Chiefs of Staff and the Department of Defence,[81] the final document reflected the views of the Reaganite faction.[82]

The objectives for US national security policy outlined in NSDD-32 clearly went beyond the State Department's focus on containment to include a more aggressive anti-Soviet campaign that posited different objectives towards different elements of the Soviet Empire. The policy contained in the NSDD envisioned a campaign of rollback directed against Soviet-allied states in the Third World, with the document calling upon the US to 'contain and reverse the expansion of Soviet control and military presence throughout the world'.[83] Within the Soviet bloc in Eastern Europe, the administration would conduct political action to 'encourage long-term liberalizing and nationalist tendencies'[84] – a formulation which echoed Haig's language in his 8 March proposal. The campaign also included efforts to weaken the USSR domestically 'by forcing the USSR to bear the brunt of its economic shortcomings',[85] as hard-liners had called for in the wake of the Polish declaration of martial law. Although the bulk of the document consisted of discussion of US military posture, rather than further discussion of a clear strategy for achieving these objectives, NSDD-32 clearly indicated that a tough policy of seeking to roll back Soviet advances and to affect the balance of political forces within Eastern Europe and the USSR itself through political intervention within these states was gaining ascendancy within the administration. While the document did not set out a clear strategy for US political operations directed against and within the Soviet bloc, it did posit objectives that such operations could be used to attain.

A rare speech given by Clark at Georgetown University on 21 May 1982 to explain the new strategy clarified the ideological basis of the policy by couching it in the context of a struggle for democracy in the Soviet bloc. Clark stated that '... collectivism and the subordination of the individual to the state' constituted a 'bizarre and evil episode of history.... We have something better to offer – namely freedom.'[86] He was also forthright about the administration's goal of using US national security policy to encourage reform in the USSR by 'convince[ing] the leadership of the Soviet Union ... to seek the legitimacy that only comes from the consent of the governed ...'.[87] White House aides, speaking to journalists after the speech, further characterised the policy towards the Soviet bloc as an 'active ... campaign aimed at reform in the Soviet Union and dissolution or at least shrinkage of the Soviet empire'[88] It was clear that political action and propaganda programmes oriented towards the spread of democracy would play a role, alongside other forms of intervention, in the administration's anti-Soviet strategy.

90   *Democracy promotion and national security policy*

Despite this democratic rhetoric and the similarity to Haig's language in the description of the political operations to be conducted, however, the document did not call for an expansive strategy of democracy promotion, as the objective of pressuring regimes to reform or altering regime types was not set with regard to non-communist dictatorships in the Third World. There was some recognition of the roots of Third World instability and the Soviet exploitation of it:

> Unstable governments, weak political institutions, inefficient economies, and the persistence of traditional conflicts create opportunities for Soviet expansion in many parts of the developing world.[89]

However, the document detailed no strategy to solve this problem through political methods. Instead, the paper remarked blandly that supporting greater trade and investment in the Third World which could lead to greater development and 'the growth of humane social and political orders' would be sufficient.[90] Nowhere were the political problems of Third World regimes analysed or a solution proposed, beyond this piece of economic determinism. Thus, democracy promotion in the Third World was not an integrated part of this Reaganite grand strategy; in contrast, democracy promotion activities directed against the Soviet bloc were clearly linked to attempts to reduce Soviet power or alter the regime through propaganda and the support of anti-Soviet political movements. This integration of democracy promotion into the administration's pre-existing plans for a campaign to deploy democratic propaganda against the Soviet Union and its allies and then the codification of this strategy in the administration's new national security framework represented a defeat for the State Department's strategy of containment and thus the NSDD did not have a great deal of support from higher-level Department officials, especially Haig.[91] However, the Secretary of State's power within the administration was declining, and there was little he could do to block it at this stage.[92]

Reagan's Westminster address

The Department also failed to exercise a controlling influence over the content of the President's address to the British Parliament, scheduled for June, which was drafted during May. The first draft of the speech, written by Reagan speechwriter Aram Bakshian, had contained the idea of supporting foreign civil society groups, the 'infrastructure of democracy'[93] but had been criticised by hard-liners such as Richard Pipes for being too soft on the Soviet Union.[94] A further draft was then produced by another speech-writer, Anthony Dolan, which was much stronger in its criticism of the USSR.[95] This draft incorporated material from a memo on Soviet policy written by Richard Pipes almost a year earlier, which argued that the USSR was in the throes of a revolutionary crisis.[96] This perception of Soviet weakness was of key importance to the hard-liners, as it formed the basis of their belief that the Soviet Union could be undermined or transformed due to its vulnerability.

Democracy promotion and national security policy 91

Reagan's address at Westminster, given on 8 June 1982, is seen as a foundational moment in the history of US democracy promotion, and rightly so. In it, the President set support for democratic parties and civil society groups overseas as a goal of US policy, explaining to his British audience that

> The objective I propose is quite simple to state: to foster the infrastructure of democracy, the system of a free press, unions, political parties, universities, which allows a people to choose their own way to develop their own culture, to reconcile their own differences through peaceful means.[97]

However, the wider context in which these remarks were delivered indicates that the President had in mind the vision set forth by Clark and in NSDD-32 – a combined campaign of propaganda and political action to be directed by the US government and focussed on the Soviet Union – rather than the conception of a privately-implemented campaign to support the growth of democratic organisations in both the Soviet bloc and the Third World proposed by the APF, its private allies, and the State Department.

The speech was first and foremost an anti-Soviet address that portrayed the Cold War not as a geopolitical conflict, but as an ideological conflict that pitted freedom and democracy against communist totalitarianism. In a sense, it was the opening shot in the anti-Soviet propaganda campaign envisaged by the NSC. The President was vocal in his support for Solidarity and his criticism of the Soviet domination of Eastern Europe, and his argument that the advance of freedom would leave Marxist-Leninist ideology on the 'ash-heap of history'[98] left no doubt that the primary target of the burgeoning crusade for democracy would be the Soviet bloc and communism. Reagan was careful to describe his call for a democratic campaign against the Soviet Union as a 'plan and hope for the long term'[99] rather than an effort that would bring immediate results, partly in order to reassure his audience, but there could be little doubt that the final goal was to transform the Soviet regime. In effect, Reagan was calling for a campaign to produce a Western victory in the Cold War by ideologically defeating Marxism-Leninism and altering the totalitarian Soviet regime. In contrast, the President made little mention of concrete US assistance for democratic reform in the Third World. It is true that the President discussed recent democratic change in India and Nigeria, and the February 1982 elections in El Salvador.[100] However, these examples were included to argue that history was moving in the direction of democracy rather than communism, not to argue for active US support for democracy promotion outside the Soviet bloc, which clearly received a lower priority. Thus, the speech largely focussed on the democratisation, or at least the liberalisation, of the Soviet Empire, rather than the wider campaign proposed by the non-state democracy promoters and supported by the State Department. There were also organisational differences between the ideas championed by the democracy promoters and the President, as Reagan's announcement of a crusade for democracy by both the US government and the private sector indicated that the private groups involved were to function alongside governmental

92 *Democracy promotion and national security policy*

organisations within a campaign shaped by government objectives, rather than as fully autonomous actors.[101] The campaign presented by Reagan, then, was at odds with the original vision of democracy promotion in strategic and organisational terms.

Nevertheless, Reagan did announce the study that the APF and the State Department had lobbied for in the speech:

> The chairmen and other leaders of the national Republican and Democratic Party organizations are initiating a study with the bipartisan American [P]olitical [F]oundation to determine how the United States can best contribute as a nation to the global campaign for democracy.[102]

This announcement came in the wake of a letter sent to Reagan by the APF leadership several days before the speech which further explained the goals of the projected study into democracy promotion methods as the examination of 'how to handle the tension between maintaining friendly relations with current governments while sowing the seeds of democratic successors' and 'how to encourage domestic pluralistic forces in totalitarian countries'.[103] Reagan also referred to other planned initiatives, such as a meeting of parliamentarians organised by the Council of Europe to take place in Strasbourg which could discuss methods of promoting democracy, and a conference on free elections to occur in Washington later in the year.[104] However, as was pointed out by commentators at the time and more recently in an in-depth analysis of the speech, these proposals for studies and further meetings did not represent the announcement of a clear strategy for the promotion of democracy.[105] The key weakness of the speech was that it posited an overarching objective but explained no tangible way in which it could be achieved, leaving the crucial question of what form a campaign for democracy would take unanswered.

Conclusion

The entry of the concept of privately-implemented democracy promotion into the policy debate within the Reagan administration had brought the strategic and organisational tensions inherent in the effort to the surface and divided policymakers over how a campaign aimed at building democratic structures overseas through the support of private groups could be integrated into the national security strategy of the United States. Behind these divisions lay two competing policy visions; the 'de-centred' strategy of tough containment espoused by the State Department and the more 'centred' strategy of rolling back Soviet influence and pressuring the USSR to reform championed by many Reaganite policymakers in the NSC. Both groups wished to limit the campaign proposed by the private sector; the Reaganites by focussing on the Soviet bloc rather than noncommunist dictatorships, the State Department by seeing democracy promotion operations in the USSR as an additional tool of containment rather than a serious attempt, no matter how long term, to liberalise the system.

Attempts to limit the campaign, either in terms of geopolitical focus or final objectives, translated into attempts to exercise control over private sector democracy programmes to bring them into conformity with US goals; however, the different objectives of groups of policymakers called for differing modes of control. The State Department's more expansive campaign called for light methods of control, while the Reaganites' more narrow vision of a campaign focussed on communist regimes required a stronger dose of government supervision. The merging of the original private conception with the administration's anti-Soviet strategy, as laid out in NSDD-32 and Clark's plan for a range of political action and propaganda programs, together with Reagan's focus on the narrowly anti-Soviet dimension of democracy promotion in his speech, indicated that as of June 1982 the more geopolitically limited conception was ascendant in the administration. This placed the idea of strengthening democratic groups in pro-US dictatorships to act as successors to the sitting regimes, which had emerged before the widening of the campaign to include the Soviet bloc, in danger of being de-emphasised. However, the President's announcement of government funding for the APF's study, coupled with the fuzziness over how the idea for the campaign would be translated into practical actions, meant that there was still a possibility that a more expansive strategy could be pursued.

Notes

1 Timothy Garton Ash, *The Polish Revolution: Solidarity* (London: Penguin Books, 1999), 273–275.
2 Gregory Domber, 'Supporting the Revolution: America, Democracy and the End of the Cold War in Poland, 1981–1989' (PhD thesis, George Washington University, 2008), accessed 29 August 2014, http://transatlantic.sais-jhu.edu/ACES/ACES_Working_Papers/Gregory_Domber_Supporting_the_Revolution.pdf, 209–216, 335–350, 410–411, 123.
3 Quoted in Jerry W. Sanders, *Peddlers of Crisis: The Committee on the Present Danger and the Politics of Containment* (Boston, MA: South End Press, 1983), 322.
4 Alexander Haig, *Caveat: Realism, Reagan and Foreign Policy* (New York: Macmillan Publishing Company, 1984), 247.
5 Alan P. Dobson, 'The Reagan Administration, Economic Warfare, and Starting to Close Down the Cold War', *Diplomatic History* 29, no. 3 (2005): 552, accessed 3 August 2012. doi: 10.1111/j.1467–7709.2005.00502.x.
6 Ibid.
7 Ibid., 534 and 537.
8 Raymond L. Garthoff, *The Great Transition: American-Soviet relations and the End of the Cold War* (Washington DC: The Brookings Institute, 1994), 549.
9 Peter Schweizer, *Victory: The Reagan Administration's Secret Strategy that Hastened the Collapse of the Soviet Union* (New York: The Atlantic Monthly Press, 1994), 105–106.
10 NSC, 'Minutes of National Security Meeting on East-West Trade Controls', 16 October 1981, DDRS, accessed 7 July 2013.
11 Dobson, 537.
12 Haig, *Caveat*, 254.
13 Dobson, 544.
14 Haig, 251.

94 *Democracy promotion and national security policy*

15 Ibid., 252.
16 Ibid., 252–253.
17 Ibid., 250.
18 Ibid., 255
19 Philip J. Funigiello, *American-Soviet Trade in the Cold War* (Chapel Hill: University of North Carolina Press, 1988), 264, note 6, and Bernard Gwertzman, 'Debate on Curbs against Moscow to go to Reagan', *New York Times,* 20 February 1982, http://web.lexis-nexis.com/executive.
20 Funigiello, Ibid.
21 Domber, 410–411, 148–149.
22 Dobson, 544
23 William P. Clark, 'Memorandum for the President: Terms of Reference for High-Level Mission to Europe on Soviet Sanctions', undated, DDRS, accessed 7 July 2013.
24 Schweizer, *Victory*, 69.
25 Ibid., 75.
26 Ibid., 69.
27 State Department Bureau of Human Rights and Humanitarian Affairs, 'Country Reports on Human Rights Practices', 1982, *Readings in Security Assistance: A selected bibliography of articles of current interest*, accessed 16 March 2011 www. disam.dsca.mil/Pubs/Indexes/Vol%204–4/Abrams.pdf, 97.
28 Joshua Muravchik, *The Uncertain Crusade: Jimmy Carter and the Dilemmas of Human Rights Policy* (Washington DC: American Enterprise Institute for Public Policy, 1986), 59.
29 Quoted from 'Abrams, State's Human Rights Chief, Tries to Tailor a Policy to Suit Reagan', *The National Journal*, 1 May 1982, http://web.lexis-nexis.com/executive, 6.
30 State Department Bureau of Human Rights and Humanitarian Affairs, 'Country Reports on Human Rights Practices', 97.
31 Ibid., 91.
32 Ibid., 97.
33 Elliott Abrams, 'United States Human Rights Policy', *Readings in Security Assistance: A selected bibliography of articles of current interest*, 10 February 1982, accessed 16 March 2011, www.disam.dsca.mil/Pubs/Indexes/Vol%204–4/Abrams. pdf, 86–89.
34 'Abrams, State's Human Rights Chief', 5.
35 'Country Reports on Human Rights Practices', 98. My italics.
36 Abrams, 'United States Human Rights Policy', 87.
37 Alexander Haig, memo to the President, 8 March 1982, DDRS, accessed 11 December 2006, 2.
38 Ibid., 2.
39 Haig to the President, 2. My italics.
40 Ibid.
41 Ibid., 2.
42 Haig to the President, 3.
43 Ibid., 3
44 Ibid.
45 APF, 'Minutes of 1982 Annual Meeting Board of Directors of American Political Foundation', 6 April 1982, Folder 3: APF Minutes, Box 1, George E. Agree Papers, LOC, 1.
46 Ibid., 1.
47 Michael A. Samuels and William A. Douglas, 'Promoting Democracy', *The Washington Quarterly* 4, no. 3 (1981): 53, accessed 30 May 2012, http://dx.doi.org/10. 1080/01636608109451791.

Democracy promotion and national security policy 95

48 Ibid.
49 Memo, William Clark to Alexander Haig, 2 April 1982, Folder 11 (5), Box OA 90304, Robert Kimmitt Files, Ronald Reagan Presidential Library, Simi Valley, California, hereafter RL.
50 Robie M. H. 'Mark' Palmer, interviewed by Charles Stuart Kennedy for *The Foreign Affairs Oral History Collection of the Association for Diplomatic Studies and Training*, 30 October 1997, accessed 31 July 2013, www.adst.org/OH%20TOCs/Palmer,%20Mark.toc.pdf, 27–39; 93.
51 For these views see Ibid., 99 and 134.
52 Memo, George Agree to APF Board of Directors, 5 April 1982, Folder 3: APF Minutes, Box 1, George E. Agree Papers, LOC, 1.
53 APF, Minutes of 1982 Annual Meeting, 6 April 1982, 2.
54 Ibid., 3.
55 State Department, 'American Support for Democratic Forces', attached to Minutes of May 1982 Meeting of Board of Directors of American Political Foundation, Folder 3: APF Minutes, Box 1, George E. Agree Papers, LOC, 4.
56 APF, Minutes of 1982 Annual Meeting, 6 April 1982, 1.
57 Agree to APF Board of Directors.
58 APF, Minutes, 6 April 1982, 2.
59 Ibid.
60 Ibid., 3.
61 Agree to APF Board of Directors, 5 April 1982.
62 APF, Minutes, 6 April 1982, 1.
63 Quoted from 'National Security Council document on policy in Central America and Cuba', *New York Times*, 7 April 1982, LexisNexis, http://web.lexis-nexis.com/executive, 1.
64 Ibid., 2.
65 Memo, L. Paul Bremer to William Clark, 13 April 1982, Folder 11 (5), Box OA 90304, Robert Kimmitt Files, RL, 2.
66 Ibid., 3.
67 Memo, Dennis Blair to William Clark, 19 April 1982, Folder 11 (5), Box OA 90304, Robert Kimmitt Files, RL.
68 Memo, Norman A. Bailey to Dennis Blair, 14 April 1982, Folder 11 (5), Box OA 90304, Robert Kimmitt Files, RL.
69 Ibid.
70 Memo, Bremer to Clark, 2.
71 Ibid.
72 Ibid.
73 Memo, Bailey to Blair.
74 Memo, Blair to Clark.
75 Lou Cannon, *President Reagan: The Role of a Lifetime* (New York: Simon and Schuster, 1991), 193.
76 Paul Lettow, *Ronald Reagan's Quest to Abolish Nuclear Weapons* (New York: Random House, 2005), 62–63.
77 Thomas Carothers, *In the Name of Democracy: US policy towards Latin America in the Reagan Years* (Berkeley and Los Angeles, California: University of California Press, 1991), 201.
78 Memo, William Clark to the President, 12 May 1982, Folder 11 (5), Box OA 90304, Robert Kimmitt Files, RL.
79 Ibid.
80 Paul Lettow, *Ronald Reagan's Quest*, 63.
81 Ibid., 64.
82 Ibid., 68.
83 White House, NSDD-32: Basic National Security Strategy, Federation of American

96 *Democracy promotion and national security policy*

Scientists, hereafter FAS, 20 May 1982, accessed 5 May 2007, www.fas.org/irp/offdocs/nsdd/nsdd-32.pdf, 1.
84 NSDD-32: Basic National Security Strategy, 2.
85 Ibid.
86 Quoted from Lettow, *Ronald Reagan's Quest*, 69.
87 Ibid., 70.
88 Quoted from Helen Thomas, 'Reagan Approves Tough Strategy with Soviets,' United Press International, 21 May 1982, Nexis UK, http://web.lexis-nexis.com/executive.
89 NSDD-32: Basic National Security Strategy, 2.
90 Ibid., 1.
91 Lettow, *Ronald Reagan's Quest*, 68.
92 Ibid.
93 Robert C. Rowland and John M. Jones, *Reagan at Westminster: Foreshadowing the End of the Cold War* (Texas A & M University Press: United States of America, 2010), 43, 48.
94 Richard Pipes, *Vixi: Memoirs of a Non-Belonger* (New Haven and London: Yale University Press, 2003), 196–197, 199.
95 Rowland and Jones, 44.
96 Pipes, 196–197, 199.
97 Ronald Reagan 'Address to the British Parliament,' 8 June 1982. *Miller Center*, accessed 17 May 2008, http://millercenter.org/scripps/archive/speeches/detail/3408.
98 Ibid.
99 Ibid.
100 Reagan, 'Address to the British Parliament.'
101 Ibid.
102 Reagan, 'Address.'
103 Letter, William Brock, Charles T. Manatt and Richard Richards to Ronald Reagan, 4 June 1982, Folder 1: APF Correspondence, Box 1, George E. Agree Papers, LOC, 2.
104 Ibid.
105 Rowland and Jones, *Reagan at Westminster*, 71, 93–97.

4 Building a consensus for democracy promotion

Reagan's speech to Parliament of 8 June announcing a US effort to support democracy by both the US government and private organisations brought the issue of US democracy promotion out of the meetings of the APF and the administration and made it a public matter, while at the same time opening questions about what form the campaign would take and what its objectives would be. This provided the non-state democracy promoters with greater opportunities to agitate for their own concepts, while also bringing a wider foreign policy elite outside the administration consisting of the press, former government officials and Congress into the debate.

This more public process quickly exposed divergences between the administration and forces outside it over whether the goal of promoting democracy would be translated into a narrow campaign aimed at hostile states and political groups, where there was a clear ideological and strategic correspondence between support for local democrats and US national security interests, or whether US interests would be substantially redefined to embrace the promotion of democracy in dictatorships friendly to the US; or, indeed, redefined still more widely, to include the promotion of democracy on a global scale. These groups also had different blueprints for the type of organisational structure most appropriate for conducting an overt campaign of democracy promotion.

To advance the project, it was necessary to engineer consensus between the national security bureaucracy, non-state democracy promoters and Congress over both the strategic role of democracy in US foreign policy and the organisational relationship between non-state groups and the government. Although debates on both strategy and organisation proceeded concurrently, the key factor was the role of democracy promotion in US strategy, as the agreement reached on this factor would determine the organisational framework. Strong convergence between the administration and non-state democracy promoters meant that the latter could be trusted with more autonomy; conversely, serious divergences on strategy between these two groups would lead the administration to attempt to keep tighter control of the process. Organisationally, the need for a measure of control had to be balanced against the need to create an effective organisational framework for the campaign, which would be credible with foreign democrats. The administration, non-state groups and Congress would need to converge

98 *Building a consensus for democracy promotion*

over these strategic and organisational issues to make democracy promotion a reality. All of the groups involved in this process accepted that promoting democracy was a legitimate function of US foreign policy; however, the administration's failure to engineer this necessary consensus placed the project in jeopardy.

Differing visions of democracy promotion

Reagan's speech triggered a public debate on how the US could best promote democracy, as well as efforts by the administration to refine its vision of a campaign waged in the American interest behind closed doors, which highlighted key differences in how the groups involved conceptualised democracy promotion. Outside the administration, those members of the democracy promotion coalition who supported a wider ideological vision aimed at stimulating the growth of democracy on a global basis and figures in Congress who supported an even-handed campaign against both dictatorships of the Left and Right found common strategic and organisational ground. In contrast, the administration remained focussed on a campaign to combat Soviet communism, which was to be coordinated by the US government.

The wider foreign policy establishment's vision of democracy promotion

The wider foreign policy establishment weighed in immediately before and after the speech in favour of a more expansive democracy promotion campaign carried out under private auspices. Even before the delivery of the speech, the *New York Times* editorialised in favour of 'a quango to promote democracy in developing countries and, where possible, in communist countries'.[1] Far from seeing the project as solely an anti-Soviet campaign, the *Times* believed that democracy promotion should be aimed at dictatorships of both the right and left.[2] Several weeks after the speech David Newsom, a former Carter administration official who had served as Undersecretary of State for Political Affairs, argued that the Reagan administration's insistence on targeting Eastern Europe and the USSR would only increase Soviet paranoia with little chance of success. He was also sceptical over the administration's willingness to support democrats in allied dictatorships such as Argentina, Chile, Pakistan and the Philippines but argued that a refusal to do so would destroy the credibility of the campaign.[3]

The founders of democracy promotion also entered the debate. However, rather than becoming embroiled in a strategic discussion over whether the campaign should be implemented in a narrow fashion against the Soviet empire or in a more expansive fashion to also take in friendly dictatorships, they articulated a more global ideological vision. In an interview given in early July, George Agree stated that, 'We would be building democratic structures, not becoming involved in electing specific individuals.'[4] According to Agree, democracy promotion activities would consist of support to civil society groups such as the training of local democrats to run voter registration campaigns, efforts to boost union organising and conferences on democracy.[5] This vision side-lined the question of whether democracy promotion should be used to pursue tangible strategic goals such as containing Soviet power in the Third World through support of democratic forces in pro-US Third World dictatorships or more direct confrontation of the Soviet Empire through political operations. Instead, Agree's formulation subsumed these issues within a pro-democratic campaign which would secure the US over the long-term by building a world order in conformity with its internal system. Such a campaign was in line with the more expansive instincts of the wider foreign policy elite, but not limited by them.

The democracy promoters and the wider foreign policy establishment also agreed that the best implementing mechanism for the campaign would be a non-governmental structure similar to the West German party foundations. Taking the democracy campaign out of the hands of government would make the effort more credible to foreign democrats and also institutionalise a wider approach, not the narrow anti-Sovietism of the NSC. The APF provided the organisational model for a privately-implemented effort by promoting the advantages of the West German party foundations, which were now explained to a wider audience in a newspaper article written by William Brock at the end of July. According to Brock, while West Germany had many private labour and cultural organisations engaged in development work abroad, 'only its party-related foundations have the motivation and expertise to help critically important institution-building in the political area that other foundations shy away from.'[6]

Although Brock mentioned the fact that the West German foundations had aided democratic parties against the Portuguese communists in the 1970s, his discussion of the utility of the foundations was couched primarily in terms of building democracy, not merely opposing communism.[7] This approach was compatible with Congressional Democrats' suspicions of the strong, ideological anti-Sovietism which characterised sections of the Reagan administration. An aide to Senator Edward Kennedy stated the Democrats' position succinctly:

> Our concern is that it not become an exercise in Reaganitis.... We want to see the sophisticated European model adopted and not a return to the 1950s hardline (sic) anti-Communist politics.[8]

Newsom also believed that the best implementing mechanism for a campaign for democracy would be US civil society groups, commenting that

> It is when we move out from the campuses and the think tanks within this country to the rhetoric and guided programs of a government-financed effort abroad that we increase the risks and lose credibility.[9]

There was clearly substantial support in Congress and among elite opinion leaders for a democracy campaign which would function on an expansive rather than a narrow basis. This in turn fitted in with the more idealistic conceptions of democracy promoters such as Agree, who aimed at a global campaign of

100 *Building a consensus for democracy promotion*

democracy untied to either containment or a tougher policy of confronting the Soviet Empire. Furthermore, in terms of organisation some groups and figures outside the Executive saw private and governmental programmes as competing models for the implementation of the project, rather than complementary ones.

The administration's vision of democracy promotion

Within the government, on the other hand, democracy promotion was conceived of as an umbrella concept for a campaign of public diplomacy and political action aimed at combatting the growth of communism in the Third World and Western Europe, and US financing of opposition forces in the Soviet Empire. National Security Advisor William Clark, reporting on a meeting between the new Secretary of State, George Shultz, who had recently replaced Haig after a sharp disagreement on sanctions policy towards the Soviet bloc, Casey, Wick and Robert McFarlane, the Deputy National Security Advisor, on implementing the President's speech, described the objectives as 'strengthen[ing] the forces of democracy throughout the world and ... more effectively engag[ing] in the competition of ideas and values with the Soviets and their allies.'[10] The grounding of the campaign in national security priorities rather than the imperative of developing democratic structures on a global basis is clear from the fact that, rather than focussing exclusively on nations which did not have existing democratic systems, one of objectives of the new democracy policy was to counter Soviet propaganda aimed at undermining the US' democratic allies.[11] This aspect of the policy represented an integration of the objectives of the Project Truth campaign in Western Europe into the democracy promotion campaign. This effort to guard against increasing Soviet influence in states which were already democratic was clearly linked to safeguarding US national security interests rather than the conception of creating democratic systems overseas in countries which were not yet democratic on a global basis.

The administration was also at odds with the emerging public consensus in its conception of the role of non-state groups in the emerging campaign. It wanted the co-operation of private groups in its effort in order to make its projected anti-Soviet campaign more credible with foreign democrats. Clark, reporting on the meeting between high level officials after the speech, reported, 'Some of the public funds ... would be allocated to private US organizations which could conduct certain programs overseas more easily than the USG.'[12] However, in the administration's conception these private groups were expected to work alongside government instrumentalities as part of the administration's campaign rather than being in control of an autonomous global effort. Clark's memo makes this clear, stating, 'We ... have to create some new programs ... to provide support and training to democratic forces. The private sector must be energized to join us in this effort.'[13] The implementing structure for the campaign for democracy would be a Special Planning Group composed of representatives of government agencies such as the State Department and the USIA, not a board of private citizens directing a US version of the German Party foundations. The campaign

Building a consensus for democracy promotion 101

was seen as a reconfigured, overt state–private network programme with a command centre located in the administration, not within a private institution.

State and non-state convergences and divergences

In order to implement a campaign prosecuted jointly by the state and private groups, it was necessary to bridge the gap between the differing conceptions of democracy promotion held by each group. The task of engineering convergence was made more complicated by the fact that the democracy promotion coalition itself was not a unitary actor, but contained groups and actors whose conception of the democracy campaign ranged from a focus on clear strategic and tactical objectives to a framework anchored more by universalistic idealism. The necessary convergence was easiest to achieve when the government and private groups were able to focus on specific and limited programmes and most difficult to create when the actors involved focussed on their differing frameworks for democracy promotion.

State–private agreement proved easiest to engineer in the case of the AFL-CIO, which had officially joined the APF's democracy promotion coalition in the wake of the President's speech. The AFL-CIO was eager to join the new political action effort in order to regain the level of funding and operational flexibility it had enjoyed as a member of the CIA-guided state–private network before 1967. Although the union had received US government funding through AID after the collapse of the network, legal restrictions had limited it to funding projects which were ostensibly non-political.[14] AFL-CIO officials had tried to solve this problem in the 1970s by proposing the creation of a non-governmental foundation on the pattern of the West German Party foundations.[15] Participation in the democracy project was a way for the union to gain the funding it required to pursue its more political objectives.

However, an agreement over targeting with state officials was necessary because although the union was strongly anti-communist it was also engaged in a project that was not necessarily connected to US national security objectives: the building of a global network of 'free trade unions' patterned after the AFL-CIO itself and under its influence. American labour had its own priorities and interests, and disagreements between the union and the national security bureaucracy stretched back to previous programmes carried out in co-operation with the CIA. These disagreements continued into the 1980s; a State Department briefing paper on AALC, the AFL-CIO's training foundation for African trade unionists, noted that

> AALC, because of its strong fraternal outlook on union-to-union linkages with African unions, has on occasion appeared to view advice from State, AID, and/or Labor Department as making unwarranted intrusions into African labor union matters.[16]

Such tensions might re-emerge within the democracy project. However, when the union began to submit requests for funding for political operations to be

102 *Building a consensus for democracy promotion*

included within the ambit of the administration's democracy campaign in August 1982, it and the national security bureaucracy were able to reach a limited consensus over specific operations in Western Europe, the Soviet bloc and the Third World without having to give ground on their wider strategic objectives.

This convergence was strongest over the AFL-CIO's proposed programmes for Western Europe, where the union and the US government had worked together in the beginning of the Cold War on programmes to support pro-US unions and undermine communist political and cultural influence. There was also minimal disagreement between the State Department and the NSC over US objectives. The AFL-CIO requested funds for the backing of pro-US and anti-communist unions and parties such as the centre-right French trade union Force Ouvière in its campaign against the communist-led CGT and the Inter-University Union (UNI), a small youth group composed of French faculty and students which contested university elections with communist groups and distributed propaganda in favour of Solidarity and the mujahideen.[17] Funding these groups also served the interests of the AFL-CIO, which had begun funding Force Ouvrière in the late 1940s, first with its own money and then with assistance provided by the CIA.[18] The operations would also clearly serve the larger US purpose of strengthening Western European allegiance to NATO, a key objective of the administration since the inception of Project Truth in August 1981.

Convergence over the Soviet bloc was also comparatively simple because the AFL-CIO and the administration held the same near-term goal of supporting dissident organisations. Both had already been working towards these goals, although separately. The AFL-CIO had been involved in providing low-level private support for Solidarity in Poland since 1980, and requested funds from the administration to be channelled to the Solidarity Co-ordinating Committee in Brussels,[19] formed by Solidarity exiles in the West after the declaration of martial law in Poland at the request of leaders still within Poland to lobby for Western assistance for the embattled union.[20] Reaganites within the administration had been seeking such an arrangement since 1981, while the State Department had agreed to a degree of democracy promotion in the Soviet bloc in Haig's March 1982 memo to Reagan.

Convergence over operations to be carried out in the Third World was the most difficult aspect of the process, because the history of state–private co-operation here differed to that in Western Europe and the Soviet bloc. Whereas in these regions US interests clearly dictated the support of democratic forces, the US had had no political grand design for its intervention in Third World political systems and had supported democrats or dictators as short-term US interests dictated. Thus, while the AFL-CIO had been implementing political operations in the Third World since the 1950s, as had the US government state apparatus, the approach taken was a more disjointed one in which overseas groups were supported purely on the basis of anti-communism, not necessarily due to their democratic credentials. Policy towards the Third World was also more subject to intra-administration disagreement due to the uncertainty over whether such operations should merely continue the previous focus on combatting communism or be widened to include the support of democratic successor groups in pro-US authoritarian states.

Explicitly anti-communist programmes put forward by the AFL-CIO seem to have provoked little debate within the administration. One example of this is the union's plan to channel funds to pro-Western forces in Nigerian trade unions to help them combat the communist leadership of the National Labor Centre. The union argued that this pro-Western group had 'the potential to turn the tables and take control of the NLC, or barring that to at least establish a counter-force in the country' but that it required assistance to accomplish this.[21] The State Department supported this assessment, claiming that although the NLC's leadership was in the hands of communists, '[t[his could be turned around with money. One half the affiliates of the current National Center are friendly moderates who could build their support and dominate the National Center.'[22] The picture was similar in Latin America, where the AFL-CIO requested funds to support The Seaman and Waterfront Workers Union of Grenada, headed by Eric Pierre, '[which] is the only organized opposition to the Marxist government of Maurice Bishop.'[23] The State Department agreed that the union, 'the only hopeful opposition to Bishop'[24], should be supported. There was also agreement on the need to support pro-US unions such as the CTP in Peru against its communist and leftist competitors and the CUS against the Sandinistas in Nicaragua.[25] These operations would have appealed to the NSC's strong anti-communism as well.

While the state and the AFL-CIO were able to converge over union programmes directed at Third World communists, programmes aimed at dictatorships allied to the US had the potential to be much more divisive. In contrast to operations against enemy states such as Grenada, NSC support of AFL-CIO programmes in countries such as Chile and South Africa could not be taken for granted due to the organisation's fears that mounting democracy promotion operations in friendly dictatorships could damage diplomatic relations with them and weaken the US' position in the Cold War, or even weaken the regimes internally and provide opportunities for domestic communist movements to grow in power. In South Africa, the AFL-CIO requested money to support newly-formed black trade unions, arguing that these organisations would probably have 'an immense impact on the economic, social and eventually political structure of the country.'[26] The union also requested funds to support a Chilean union, the UDT, described as 'only democratic and anti-communist workers organization in opposition to the Pinochet government'[27] The State Department supported the funding requests for these operations for reasons of national security. Support for democratic unions in South Africa would prevent an alliance between leftist political organisations and labor groups to oppose apartheid. The Department did not believe that the apartheid system was stable and that '[d]uring [the] eventual blow-up, we want to have labor stay in our camp.'[28] Regarding the proposal for Chile, the Department commented that 'We need to do the same thing we did in Venezuela in the '50's.'[29] Expanding on this, the Department noted that ORIT, a Latin American labour confederation funded by the AFL-CIO in the 1950s had

104   *Building a consensus for democracy promotion*

employed large numbers of organizers, particularly democratic elements forced into exile by the Perez Jimenez dictatorship in Venezuela. These individuals were instrumental in setting Venezuela on a pro-Western course when the Perez Jimenez dictatorship fell and democracy was re-established.[30]

Thus, the State Department was clearly in favour of AFL-CIO programmes aimed at supporting groups in pro-US authoritarian states. While administration hard-liners based in the NSC and other agencies had often been unconvinced that such programmes were in line with US national security objectives, a basis for agreement existed due to the fact that these programmes were aimed at preparing democratic groups to compete for power with Soviet-funded groups after the collapse of pro-US dictatorships, not at funding them to destabilise the sitting regime. The opportunity for convergence between the union and all sections of the national security apparatus clearly existed if a list of operations could be agreed upon and definite limits to these set.

This accommodation over specific cases linked to the administration's three key theatres for democracy promotion – Western Europe, the Soviet bloc and the Third World – was a useful starting-point for the development of consensus between the state and non-state actors. However, it did not amount to the generation of the strategic and organisational framework, which the campaign for democracy required to avoid the prosecution of operations on a piecemeal basis. Efforts to create a more systematic approach and durable structure fostered the emergence of tensions between the tough anti-Soviet approach of hard-liners within and outside the administration and the more even-handed or ideologically pro-democratic positions articulated by other elements of the non-state democracy promotion coalition and their bureaucratic allies.

This tension was demonstrated in political manoeuvring over the direction of the APF's study on democracy promotion, which was then in the process of being organised. Unlike the AFL-CIO, the parties had put forward no clear programme proposals besides the vague statement in the APF's letter to Reagan of 4 June that they would focus on building democratic movements in totalitarian states and preparing democratic successors in other regimes. They also lacked an extensive track record of foreign operations that officials could scrutinise for clues to their future behaviour. This lack of specificity caused concerns among Reaganites that the APF would be 'soft on communism' rather than pursuing actions in line with their own hard-line anti-Sovietism. This led to attempts to establish informal control over the organisation's projected study of democracy promotion to co-opt the APF into the strategic priorities of the Reaganites.

To this end, former Reagan administration NSA and current Republican National Committee foreign policy advisor Richard Allen attempted to keep William Brock, Chairman of the APF, from playing a leadership role in the study announced in Reagan's June speech. Brock was viewed by the Reaganites as being 'an ideological soft spot in the Republican Party'[31] and had also backed Haig against them over the question of more extensive sanctions on the USSR in

Building a consensus for democracy promotion   105

response to the Polish declaration of martial law in the early months of 1982.[32] In addition, he was linked to the State Department's more even-handed approach to dictatorships of both the left and right. An anonymous member of the APF study group commented that, 'Dick Allen doesn't want Bill Brock and the State Department playing a role in this thing.'[33] Allen was nominated as a member of the study board by Richard Richards, Chair of the RNC,[34] apparently with White House backing,[35] but did not succeed in excluding Brock from involvement. This episode illustrates the fears of hard-line anti-communists over the direction of non-state democracy promotion operations.

Even more threatening than this lack of specificity from organisers such as Brock, however, were the views of intellectuals who had helped to shape democracy promotion such as William Douglas and George Agree. These figures had a tendency to outline grand, ideologically-driven frameworks for democracy promotion which took an extremely expansive and long-term view of the relationship between democracy and US national security, rooted in the ideas both had put forward in the 1970s, when democracy promotion had existed as a grand concept divorced from day-to-day US national security concerns. The effect of this was to highlight the disjuncture between the state and non-state democracy promoters even further.

An example of this is the framework for democracy promotion which William Douglas set out in an article published in September 1982, which was clearly determined first and foremost by the need to promote democracy on a global basis as a form of government rather than US security needs. While Douglas began by arguing that democracy promotion could help to stabilise pro-US dictatorships, as he had done previously, he then went beyond this by arguing that a US democracy promotion organisation should also concentrate on areas or countries where democracy was in decay or where sectors of the population felt inadequately represented by existing democratic structures. Douglas argued that such a lack of representation was a long-term danger because it could lead to groups or classes abandoning electoral politics in favour of armed struggle, creating instability and, if they won, a dictatorial state. This could be averted by studying the political system of such a country for gaps of representation and then building political parties to fill them.[36] Douglas gave the example of Honduras, where there was no leftist party to represent the poor majority and argued that the construction of such a party with finance and political technology imported from the United States would help to stabilise the Honduran political system and avert another insurgency in Central America.[37]

This analysis was extremely far-sighted, but Douglas' recommended action in Honduras went far beyond the concept of a propaganda and political action campaign aimed at combatting Soviet influence, which was taking shape in the administration. It also went beyond the focus of the State Department on containment in US dictatorships threatened by insurgencies, as Honduras was already a democracy dominated by a pro-US elite and posed no foreseeable threat to US national security in the short or medium term. Douglas' ideological perspective, which was divorced in some respects from immediate national

106 *Building a consensus for democracy promotion*

security concerns, showed that the NSC's fears that an autonomous private effort to promote democracy would waste government funds on ideological projects instead of guarding US national security were not groundless.

This problem was not limited to Douglas, as clear differences over the nature and goals of the democracy project between George Agree and the US government surfaced in two parallel interviews, one with Agree and one with an unnamed state official, published in the US press in September 1982. In contradiction to Agree's earlier emphasis on building democratic structures rather than supporting individual candidates, the official stated that 'Some elements [of the democracy campaign] involve sophisticated campaign tactics' and mentioned CIA support of the Christian Democratic Party in the Italian elections of 1948 as a precedent for the democracy project.[38] This operation had been aimed at electing pro-US forces to safeguard US national security interests and block the Italian communists from taking power, rather than building democracy.[39] While the official went beyond a purely anti-Soviet framework in conceding that the democracy crusade could function in authoritarian states allied to the US,[40] it was clear that to the administration the campaign was aimed at resolving near-term US security issues. This differed clearly from the concept of democracy promotion as a long-term project to transform political structures on a global scale, although Agree conceded that 'We can't be doing things that would be seriously harassing to our own government's foreign policy, or it would jeopardise its own success.'[41] This strategic and ideological disagreement inevitably led to differences over how the project was to be organised and implemented. According to Agree the campaign would be implemented through groups outside the government and foundations rather than the state.[42] However, the official restated the administration consensus that it would be managed by an inter-agency group based in the White House rather than privately-controlled.[43] The fact that the interviews with Agree and the official quoted in the newspaper story had been separate indicated a lack of coordination between the state and non-state democracy promoters in addition to the conceptual differences between them.

Managing the conceptual gaps that existed between the administration and private groups had proven problematic by autumn 1982. Consensus was possible in cases where the NSC, State Department and private groups could focus on specific tactics and programmes to be run in specific countries to achieve clear national security aims. However, when this was not possible due to a lack of specific programme proposals by the non-state democracy promoters or a focus on grand ideological frameworks, the rift between the government and non-state forces widened. These disagreements over strategy were, in turn, linked to different organisational conceptions; whereas the administration, and particularly the Reaganites, believed that a campaign focussed on US security needs would be best implemented under government supervision, private groups favoured an autonomous implementing structure for their wider campaign. What was lacking above all was a clear strategic framework which incorporated the private groups into administration priorities.

Creating a strategic framework for democracy promotion

The administration moved to create this strategic framework in the second half of 1982. This required not only agreement between the state and private forces but also between contending factions within the administration over these aims. The administration held two consensus-building events in October and November 1982 to resolve these problems; a closed anti-Soviet strategy conference at the end of October and a public Conference on Free Elections in early November. Although both of these gatherings reached provisional agreements on how democracy promotion would be implemented tactically and what role US civil society groups might play in such efforts, the larger problem of reaching a consensus over grand strategic issues such as the final objectives of a campaign for democracy directed at the USSR or the targeting of democracy promotion in the Third World were not resolved.

The role of democracy promotion in anti-Soviet strategy

The anti-Soviet conference, the Conference on the Democratization of Communist Countries, was held in the State Department and focussed on generating tactics and programmes which the government and private groups could co-operate on to promote democracy in the Soviet Empire. In addition to government officials it included representatives of interested private and quasi-private groups. This private and quasi-private contingent included organisations that had functioned as part of the covert state–private network in the 1950s and 1960s before becoming quasi-autonomous overt organisations in the 1970s, such as Radio Free Europe and Radio Liberty. John Richardson, a former director of RFE and the President of Freedom House[44] and future Chairman of the National Endowment for Democracy also attended, along with prominent US academics and Sovietologists.[45] This private contingent also included the AFL-CIO[46] but not representatives of the APF, highlighting the fact that the democracy promotion coalition was a diverse group in which some members had closer ties to a more narrowly anti-Soviet vision than others.

The Conference was focussed on 'develop[ing] suggestions for more effective US Government and private sector program – to implement the broad initiatives set forth in the President's address to the British Parliament' with regard to the USSR, Eastern Europe and Third World communist countries.[47] The participants recommended that a two-pronged campaign of propaganda and political operations be launched against the Soviet Empire, using both governmental and private agencies.[48] The suggested strategy made a clear distinction between the Soviet Union itself and vulnerable satellite states and Soviet clients such as the Eastern European countries and Nicaragua. The propaganda element would be a long-term campaign focussed on developing consciousness of the benefits of the democracy in populations under communist rule without provoking a violent response.[49] This element was to be accomplished through governmental and quasi-governmental propaganda organisations such as the VOA and RFE,[50] as

108   *Building a consensus for democracy promotion*

increasing US broadcasting was seen as a key way to play on Soviet vulnerabilities because '[c]entrifugal forces abound within [the Soviet] empire, and our broadcasting, the largest component of our agenda, is the key weapon in encouraging these forces.'[51] The campaign would deploy further traditional methods of exerting psychological and cultural influence such as exchanges; the setting up of an institute as a home base for the most recent wave of Soviet émigrés; and the distribution of literature through both official and non-official channels, as 'most considered books and journals to be basic weapons in the competition of ideas.'[52] Many of these ideas harked back to propaganda components of the US 'Liberation' campaign to weaken Soviet rule over Eastern Europe during the late 1940s and 1950s; for example, a university for anti-communist refugees had originally been set up by the Free Europe Committee during the 1950s.[53]

The strategy towards clients and satellites such as Nicaragua and Poland, however, was more focussed on providing support to political groups within the target states, and so incorporated the deployment of US private groups into the campaign more extensively. The new Secretary of State, George Shultz, when speaking at the conference, clearly supported US aid for Solidarity, stating that he saw the rise of the organisation as beginning a new era of democratic reform and revolution,[54] and promised that the US 'will not ignore the individuals and groups in communist countries who seek peaceful change.'[55] The conference attendees also believed that in states where Marxist governments had not yet completely consolidated themselves, such as Nicaragua, 'the US (especially private groups) should be providing far more support to those elements still fighting for democracy.'[56] In general 'the participants advocated a substantially expanded role for non-governmental organizations; these can often be more effective than government.'[57] Private involvement was clearly required, as the actions against Poland and Nicaragua were far more political than those aimed at the USSR and so required greater plausible deniability to avoid harsh Soviet counter-actions. Thus, action by non-state forces was incorporated into the campaign against the Soviet Empire on a tactical basis.

The conference was able to produce a rough consensus over tactics and individual programmes, which incorporated action by private groups by leaving the final strategic objectives of the policy undefined. However, when the US government attempted to define a more cogent policy internally, the struggle over end-goals continued. The State Department's cautious approach to the idea of promoting democracy in the communist world was evident in administration discussions over NSDD-75, the administration's statement of anti-Soviet strategy, which had been drafted largely by the Reaganite NSC Director of Eastern European and Soviet Affairs, Richard Pipes.[58] Pipes, who was working for the NSC while on leave from his position as a Professor of History at Harvard, was a confirmed hard-liner. He had previously conducted consultancy work for the US government in 1976 as the Chairman of Team B, a group of analysts from outside the intelligence community who had been brought in to review the CIA's intelligence data and conclusions on the USSR by the Ford Administration. The Team's conclusions on the threat posed by the USSR were far bleaker than those

Building a consensus for democracy promotion   109

of the CIA's analysts.[59] He had also written extensively on the threat posed by the Soviet Union for the Committee on the Present Danger. The maximum period of leave that Pipes could take from his teaching position at Harvard was two years, and this period was nearly over, meaning that he would soon have to leave his government position. The NSDD on US Soviet strategy was to be his legacy to the administration. However, the process of creating the document proved to be contentious.

Disagreement centred over the goals for US policy outlined in NSSD 11–82, the policy study that NSDD-75 was based on. This study envisaged a confrontational posture towards the USSR that included ideological warfare and support for political movements within the Soviet Empire. In terms of Soviet client states the study echoed the objective of 'contain[ing] and revers[ing] Soviet expansion' by 'encourag[ing] long-term liberalizing and nationalist tendencies within the Soviet Union and allied countries' contained in NSDD-32.[60] According to the study, the US should 'not accept the idea that Communist rule is irreversible' in Soviet client states in the Third World and follow a policy of rollback by supporting 'democratic movements.... To ... bring about political change' in Third World allies.[61] There was a clear role for democracy promotion instrumentalities in this policy, as

> Long-term political cadre and organization building programs, long a strongly emphasized instrument of Soviet policy, must become a regular, and more developed, part of U.S. policy.[62]

However, the policy outlined towards the Soviet Union itself was more far-reaching than previous objectives. The drafting of the new NSDD on Soviet policy proceeded on the assumption, which Pipes had drawn up, that 'Soviet international behaviour is a response not only to external threats but also to the internal imperatives of the Soviet political, economic, social and ideological system.'[63] This implied that US national security could be enhanced by an effort to change the Soviet Union's internal system, and the study set the ambitious goal of 'promoting change within the USSR itself' through support for 'internal forces'.[64] This objective was to be accomplished through putting pressure on the USSR through economic sanctions[65] and a US ideological and political offensive, as 'US policy towards the Soviet Union must have an ideological thrust which clearly demonstrates the superiority of US and Western values' such as 'political democracy'[66]. This policy went beyond the previous US consensus conception of Cold War strategy, a fact that the study acknowledged:

> By identifying the promotion of evolutionary change within the Soviet Union itself as an objective of U.S. policy, the United States takes the long-term strategic offensive. This approach therefore contrasts with the essentially reactive and defensive strategy of containment ...[67]

This proposal combined the 'rollback' of Soviet control of territory outside the USSR itself with efforts to promote internal reform within the Soviet Union that

110   *Building a consensus for democracy promotion*

would reduce the power of the CPSU over Soviet society. To accomplish this, the US would have to strengthen its political action capability, including 'The President's London initiative to support democratic forces'[68] and to consider how political action could be used to influence Soviet policy.[69] It was clear that both governmental and private programmes aimed at the projection of democratic ideology and support for democratic movements would play a part in such a project.

The novelty of this new strategy of 'encouraging antitotalitarian [*sic*] changes' within the USSR itself was stressed by Clark in his presentation of the policy to Reagan and the National Security Council.[70] This goal went beyond the State Department's original concept that support for democratic forces in the Soviet bloc could assist the containment of Soviet power by focussing Soviet attention on domestic stability rather than expansion.[71] The study did qualify the goal of fostering change in the USSR by casting it as a long-term project which would interact with internal Soviet factors rather than a goal which the US could achieve alone and over a short span,[72] and also specified that the pursuit of negotiations with the USSR to achieve agreements on areas of mutual interest should be a track of US policy.[73] However, the Department still attempted to limit the goal of encouraging change within the Soviet system. Mark Palmer, the State Department's strongest supporter of democracy promotion, objected to the more extreme provisions for economic pressure[74] and the Department as a whole demanded changes to water down the goal of democratic transformation of the Soviet Union[75] in the document. This goal was summed up in the second objective listed for the administration's Soviet policy in the policy document that resulted from the study, NSDD-75:

> To promote, within the narrow limits available to us, the process of change in the Soviet Union towards a more pluralistic political and economic system in which the power of the privileged ruling elite is gradually reduced. The US recognizes that Soviet aggressiveness has deep roots in the internal system ...[76]

Pipes' original draft had been more radical and had not included the phrase 'within the narrow limits available to us', which had been inserted at the insistence of the State Department after a hard-fought battle between the two agencies.[77] CIA officials even feared that State would resist the implementation of the policy completely.[78] Pipes regarded State's editing of his document as 'timorous',[79] while NSC hard-liner Norman Bailey complained that the policies contained in NSDD-75 were 'bitterly opposed by other high-level administration figures and by whole bureaucracies in the Departments of State and Commerce.'[80]

While both the State Department and the NSC favoured mounting a political/ideological campaign for democracy against the Soviet bloc which would incorporate action by US private forces, they were divided over how this campaign was connected to US grand strategy towards the Soviet Union, how far to prosecute it and what its end-goals should be. The result was a compromise document that was not as hard-hitting as Pipes had hoped. However, a role for

Building a consensus for democracy promotion 111

democracy promotion towards the Soviet Union remained an element of the policy, and the rough consensus over operations enabled this element to move forward within the existing broad framework, even though problems of consensus over grand strategy remained.

The role of democracy promotion in US policy towards the Third World

A framework for democracy promotion operations in the Third World was also difficult to negotiate due to Reaganite fears that attempts to spread democracy in pro-US dictatorships would lead to their collapse and replacement by communist regimes. To build consensus on political operations in the Third World, the administration held a Conference on Free Elections at the beginning of November, several days after the Conference on the Democratization of Communist Countries. In contrast to the anti-communist event of October, which was held behind closed doors, this event was public and was attended by representatives from 34 countries,[81] many of which had recently democratised or re-democratised.[82]

As in discussions on the Soviet Empire, a clear role for private groups in the emerging campaign was envisaged, as the conference took as its starting point an idea that had been generated by the non-state democracy promoters in the 1970s and early 80s, and agreed that a process of democratisation of Third World dictatorships could begin by forging links between exiles, parties, labour groups, foundations and their US counterparts. US private groups would take the lead in these initiatives, as they would have the necessary credibility to liaise directly with foreign democrats.[83] However, this decision did not resolve the issue of whether the targets should be pro-US dictatorships threatened with communist revolution, Third World communist states such as Nicaragua and Grenada, or all non-democratic Third World states.

This fuzziness was shown in the remarks addressed to the conference by the President and Secretary of State George Shultz. The opening address given by Reagan stressed a non-partisan democratic idealism and avoided the sweeping denunciations of the USSR contained in the President's London speech in favour of putting forward a more inclusive and acceptable vision.[84] This approach was also followed by Shultz, who chose to stress the democracy campaign's positive aspects, stating that 'We are not here to challenge other countries but to offer our expertise'.[85] The Secretary of State made no reference at all to the USSR, communism or Marxism-Leninism during his speech. Elliott Abrams, the administration's Assistant Secretary for Humanitarian Affairs and Human Rights, took a more focussed approach, arguing that 'democracies tend to have the best human rights practices, communist regimes and military dictatorships tend to have the worst.'[86] However, Abrams did not stress the need for US authoritarian allies to reform and thus did not engage with the continuing strategic debate.

Jeane Kirkpatrick, on the other hand, took a clear position that couched the promotion of democracy as an anti-communist project and inveighed strongly against communism and Leninism, stating that:

112 *Building a consensus for democracy promotion*

> The idea that the will of the people can be better expressed through a revolutionary elite than through free elections is, of course, a fundamental tenet of Leninism. It is incompatible with democratic elections and democratic government ...[87]

Kirkpatrick devoted much of the second half of her speech to criticism of the Marxist FMLN guerrillas in El Salvador for opposing the March 1982 elections and of the Sandinistas for failing to hold elections in Nicaragua.[88] The speech was focussed very much on existing US security concerns in Central America and on the US' leftist enemies, not its rightist friends. In Kirkpatrick's formulation the enemies of democracy and the enemies of the US were one and the same. The outcome of the conference was general agreement on a gradualist policy of building up foreign civil society organisations such as unions and parties; however, as the targets of this initiative were not specified, each administration faction could read into it an affirmation of its own agenda.

By December 1982, the administration had moved into a rough internal convergence on a strategic framework and the role of private groups within this design. Rather than an independent effort which subsumed anti-communist operations in the Soviet bloc and efforts to build democratic movements in Third World dictatorships under the banner of promoting democracy, it envisaged a larger Project Truth which would go beyond Western Europe to launch a political and ideological assault on Soviet communism, coupled with political action and broadcasting initiatives aimed at the USSR itself. Although this agreement was sufficient to allow the programme to move forward, there were still areas of tension over the strategic objectives of the campaign which had not been fully resolved, such as whether actions against the Soviet bloc were to be aimed at the containment of Soviet power through stirring up internal dissent or promoting gradual change in the bloc countries' societies and the Soviet Union. In the Third World, the option of prosecuting a wider campaign that aimed at fostering the emergence of democratic systems in all Third World countries, including pro-US authoritarian governments, had not been adequately examined. While some officials spoke of a more even-handed campaign, others remained fixed on attempts to undermine Third World Marxist states opposed to the US, such as Nicaragua. The administration had failed to come to a clear internal agreement in both cases. However, despite this strategic fuzziness, there was enough general agreement within the administration that programmes should be mounted in them to allow the project to move forward. What the administration also required was a credible and effective organisational structure to carry it out.

Bureaucratic consensus and the organisational structure for democracy promotion

Concurrently with the debates over strategy discussed above, the administration turned its attention to creating an organisational structure to implement its

Building a consensus for democracy promotion   113

democracy campaign. Its clear preference was for a governmental structure to coordinate government and private programmes in the interests of US national security and allow the national security bureaucracy to manage any strategic tensions between it and these groups which arose, much as CIA funding and coordination of state–private network organisations had done before 1967. The outcome of the 1967 crisis indicated that in operational terms an overt structure would be more acceptable domestically than a covert one. It would also be more durable, as it could not be destroyed by public exposure. However, the decision to pursue such a structure to coordinate and fund the democracy campaign opened up a number of problems which the CIA had not had to face when co-opting private groups. First, the decision to locate the coordinating centre within the government made the process hostage to problems such as bureaucratic man-oeuvring or non-co-operation that had previously been mitigated by giving responsibility for such operations to a covert agency. Second, an overt pro-gramme would need to be acceptable to Congress in order to be voted the appro-priations it needed to function. The CIA's covert programme had not faced such a requirement.

There were also issues of credibility and plausible deniability involved in dis-bursing US government money overtly to US private groups, who would then channel these funds to private groups overseas, which could have an impact on the organisational structure for democracy promotion. Before 1967 private groups had been able to secure co-operation from their counterparts overseas more easily than government agencies because their receipt of government funds had been covert, enabling them to preserve their credibility as independent actors. In contrast, the shift to overt funding could make foreign private groups less willing to accept funding which they knew had ultimately originated in the US government. Overt funding of private groups overseas could also affect rela-tionships with foreign governments, who would object to US political interven-tion. This tension was further complicated by the fact that several of the programmes under consideration went beyond the pre-1967 state–private net-work's aim of projecting democratic ideology to focus on the more controversial objectives of training foreign opposition movements and providing groups and individuals overseas with the support and skills needed to alter foreign political structures.

The administration's need to anticipate Congressional reaction to its propos-als had an immediate effect on its choice of implementing structures for the cam-paign. The CIA's involvement was seen to be unacceptable to Congress due to the lingering effects of the 1967 crisis and the Agency was ruled out as an imple-menting structure for the campaign by Lawrence Eagleburger, State Department Undersecretary for Political Affairs, and Robert C. McFarlane, the Deputy National Security Advisor, at the end of August 1982, with the rationale that 'if we have the C.I.A. in this we can call it off right off the bat'.[89]

The obvious solution was to pass responsibility for supervision to another component of the bureaucracy; however, the difficulty with removing the CIA from the equation was that no other bureaucratic agency possessed the full legal

114 *Building a consensus for democracy promotion*

authority or the desire to implement the programme as a whole. One possible option might have been to fund and coordinate the programmes through AID, the Agency for International Development, which had channelled funding to the AFL-CIO's foreign operations after and to an extent a few years before the 1967 collapse of the state–private network. However, AID was not a sufficiently flexible channel for disbursing funds to private groups operating globally, as US groups accepting AID funding would only be able to operate in countries that had agreed to host AID programmes. This meant that, for example, the channel could not be used by the AFL-CIO in either Nigeria or South Africa, which the union saw as the key African countries for its strategy, as neither hosted AID programmes at that time.[90] In addition, AID's mandate to provide funds for developing countries meant that the organisation could not be used to channel funds to any European programmes, whether in the West or the East. Thus, funding the Solidarity Co-ordinating Committee would have been ruled illegal under AID's mandate. This would also apply to any other private groups attempting to fund operations outside the Third World with AID money, such as the APF.

These problems appeared before any operations had been specified, in relation to the APF's democracy study, which was to be funded from AID's Human Rights budget. In August George Agree had sent an outline and proposed budget for the study,[91] however, no contract was signed until the beginning of December 1982 due to conflicts with AID's geographical mandate and mission. The APF proposed funding for a study into methods for promoting democracy in 'other countries', however, AID proposed to fund an examination of methods for promoting democracy in 'developing countries' or 'non-developed countries',[92] in conformity with its mandate. This distinction was crucial, as the APF's study was not focussed only on the Third World,[93] and would include the Soviet bloc as well. Thus, the basic problem was that the AID funding channel was not flexible enough to implement either the expansive campaign favoured by the democracy promoters and the State Department or the more narrowly anti-communist strategy favoured by the Reaganites.

A further problem was that no national security agency had an operating mandate that allowed it to fund programmes aimed at the political transformation of other countries. AID's mandate authorised it to conduct programmes related to social and economic development, not political engineering, which meant that such political programmes would not be legally fundable by AID. In addition, many State Department officials believed that their organisation did not have sufficient legal authorisation to house or pass funding to political programmes.[94] This applied especially to those elements of the campaign which went beyond promoting the idea of democracy to encompass the support and training of political forces, such as the proposed Institute for Democracy in Central America, a key part of the government's strategy. In early November Walter Raymond, the NSC's Director of International Communications and a member of the Working Group charged with coordinating the emerging campaign, argued that

Building a consensus for democracy promotion 115

Part of this [implementation and funding] will be based on ensuring that the items selected are consistent with the authorization that comes with the money that will be available.... We may have difficulty creating democracy institutes in Central America ... if there is no existing authorization to which this can be tied.[95]

Added to this problem of legal authorisation was bureaucratic resistance by national security agencies to taking on more responsibility outside their key functions. A further concern for AID, as with the AFL-CIO programmes mentioned above, was that funding political programmes would take it too far outside its core mission. Raymond commented that 'Part of AID's concern is that a grant to the American Political Foundation would be somewhat "out of character" for AID.'[96] AID's obstructionism and attempts to limit the scope of the study and control the disbursement of funding continued into December, when Raymond successfully pressured the State Department to push AID to fund the study.[97] Most agencies also feared that taking on some responsibility for democracy promotion would force them to fund the programmes out of their own budgets, at least initially. The State Department was reluctant to extend its mission to democracy promotion, due to concerns 'about the impact on its budget if there is heavy pressure for resources.'[98] The NSC acknowledged that all other bureaucratic agencies were likely to make the same argument.[99] However, even if a solution to these bureaucratic problems had been found, such a solution would not have resolved the credibility problem which stemmed from funding such initiatives overtly through the government.

One possibility for resolving problems of bureaucratic management and credibility, especially for more political programmes which involved training leadership groups overseas, was private funding, which had been mentioned by William Clark in the meeting after Reagan's speech.[100] This idea was fleshed out into a 'Fund for Democracy' to be created through donations from prominent industrialists and foundations by Gerald Helman of the State Department, a member of the Working Group organising the democracy project, towards the end of November. Helman argued that government funds should go largely to government-sponsored and controlled projects, but that a private 'Fund for Democracy' could be used to fund non-governmental groups. The Fund should be created through a fund-raising campaign headed by the President, with letters distributed to potential donors. Once a core group had been formed, there would be a conference at the White House.[101]

This option was supported by USIA, which believed that it provided a way to work around the problem of bureaucratic mandates and solve the credibility issue for programmes which it was problematic to find an official home for in the US government. The agency argued that the Fund should be used for programmes which would be 'legally ambiguous' if executed by the government. In addition, the arrangement would serve to minimise the connection of more controversial programmes to the US government; something to be avoided 'for obvious credibility reasons.'[102] A lack of direct funding links to the government

116 *Building a consensus for democracy promotion*

would enhance the credibility of several of the more controversial programmes listed for financing under the private fund, including the Free Market Institutes which would later become the NED's Centre for International Private Enterprise and the ever-problematic Institute for Democracy in Central America,[103] eventually incarnated as the NED's School for Democracy in Venezuela.[104] In the end the initiative seems to have been insufficient. This put the ball back into the administration's court: some method of funding the programmes by the government would have to be found if the choice was between accepting reduced credibility for these programmes and failing to implement them.

By the end of 1982 the administration had run out of time to adequately resolve the problems of bureaucratic mandates, bureaucratic resistance, and credibility issues which the interagency process had thrown up and decided to include the appropriation for democracy promotion programmes in its 1984 budget, to be submitted to Congress in early 1983, in an attempt to have it approved in an off-election year. The campaign was to be presented as a bipartisan initiative, as this strategy had more chance of succeeding before campaigning for the 1984 Congressional elections began in earnest. It thus decided to forward the programmes it had already decided to implement, including more political efforts which were legally ambiguous, on to Congress for an appropriation vote, placed in one package: Project Democracy. This decision tied the project to the administration's relations with Congress and had an impact on the management structure chosen for the campaign, as the choice of agency to manage the Congressional appropriation would determine the strategy the administration chose to present the initiative to Congress.[105]

The command and control structure for Project Democracy

The agency chosen to manage Project Democracy was USIA, which would act as a 'lead agency' coordinating the entire effort. USIA would receive the Congressional appropriation, which it would then allocate to the projects that fell into its area of responsibility, while channelling funding to AID or the State Department to be spent on the components of the project located in those agencies. USIA was chosen as the implementing agency to solve the problems of legal mandates encountered with other bureaucratic agencies, as it could be argued that the bulk of Project Democracy fell under USIA's existing mandate.[106] Although the Information Agency did not have a mandate to conduct political activities, it did have one to conduct public diplomacy, which the administration defined extremely widely as being 'comprised of those actions of the US government designed to generate support for our national security objectives'.[107] This definition was vague and elastic enough to incorporate activities from propaganda programmes to training of political figures abroad. A further reason for placing the programme under USIA supervision was USIA Director Charles Wick's close relationship with the President.[108]

USIA, in turn, would be supervised by a Special Planning Group under the chairmanship of the National Security Advisor, which would coordinate all US public diplomacy and political action measures. The SPG would have four sub-committees reporting to it: the Public Affairs Committee, which would coordinate activities carried out to support INF missile deployments in Western Europe and against the nuclear freeze movement in the US;[109] the International Broadcasting Committee, which would manage international radio broadcasting, an important component of the administration's anti-Soviet campaign;[110] and the International Information Committee, which formalised the Project Truth Working Group.[111] The committee designated to manage Project Democracy was the International Political Committee, chaired by the State Department, with USIA as vice-chair.[112] The IPC was to be responsible for 'planning, co-ordinating and implementing international political activities' and countering 'totalitarian ideologies and aggressive political action moves undertaken by the Soviet Union or Soviet surrogates'.[113] The committee was also authorised to coordinate 'aid, training and organisational support for foreign governments and private groups to encourage the growth of democratic political institutions and practices'[114] through 'close relationship[s] with those sectors of the American society – labor, business, universities, philanthropy, political parties, the press – that are or could be more engaged in parallel efforts overseas.'[115] This placed both governmental and private programmes under the supervision of the International Political Committee and ultimately the Special Planning Group.

This command structure, which linked Project Democracy to efforts to persuade Western Europeans to accept INF deployments and the administration's broadcasting assault on the USSR, was clearly designed to implement an anti-Soviet agenda shaped by immediate national security crises rather than one tied to either an expansive strategy of democracy promotion connected to national security or a global campaign to build democracy. It also placed the democracy campaign under government supervision. It remained to be seen whether this arrangement would be acceptable to Congress.

Congress blocks Project Democracy

When placed before Congress by the Reagan administration in February 1983, Project Democracy was described as an effort to promote democracy through 'leadership training, education, building of democratic institutions, informational programmes and bolstering ties between American individuals and organizations and their foreign counterparts'[116] in Africa, Asia and Latin America, and to promote an ' "evolution … toward democracy" in the Soviet Union and Eastern Europe'.[117] It also incorporated action by private groups, who were to receive government funding. However, while Project Democracy represented the significant strengthening of US political action capability sought by NSDD-75, it did not constitute a coherent strategy for promoting the growth of democratic parties and political structures overseas. Instead, its programmes were a compendium of propaganda and exchange programmes, connected haphazardly with more political initiatives aimed at winning a 'battle of ideas' with Soviet communism, rather than building democratic systems overseas on a global basis. Project

118   Building a consensus for democracy promotion

Democracy encountered immediate problems in Congress during hearings held by the House Foreign Affairs Subcommittee on International Organisations and Senate Foreign Relations Committee due to the lack of strategic and organisational consensus between the administration and the legislature.

The core strategic disagreement between the administration and Congressional Democrats was over whether the campaign should be focussed on combatting Soviet ideological and political influence, mainly through the type of initiatives which had been conducted earlier in the Cold War through USIA and the CIA, or whether it should focus on promoting changes in political structures in enemy and allied dictatorships through new forms of political intervention. The fact that the administration's vision of democracy promotion was largely based on a desire to use democratic ideology to achieve near-term US national security goals and to combat communism, coupled with its failure to clearly demarcate its objectives with regard to Third World dictatorships friendly to the US, ensured a clash with Congressmen who favoured a wider campaign aimed at a long-term effort to foster democracy in all dictatorial states.

The basis of Project Democracy in US national security interests and anti-Sovietism was most apparent from the fact that programmes were to be conducted in Western Europe, a region which was already democratic, to support US military goals. Such programmes made sense only as a vehicle for US foreign policy in general, not for the promotion of democracy. For example, the 'Full Cycle' programme, in which European students were invited to the US on exchange visits and then encouraged to form committees to recommend participants for the next cycle of exchanges, and a proposal for teacher-training workshops and secondary school materials to create more support for NATO in the UK,[118] were aimed at increasing support in Western European civil society for US military deployments, and tied in to the administration's wider goal of shaping a 'successor generation' to maintain solid alliance links with Western European countries.[119] This was a goal only tenuously connected to democracy promotion, if at all. Democratic Party Senator Christopher Dodd summed up the incongruity of launching programmes to promote democracy in Western Europe by commenting that 'If [the Western Europeans] don't believe in democracy, we're in real trouble'.[120]

Congressmen on the House Foreign Affairs Subcommittee on International Organisations were also concerned about the larger issue of 'how US national interests and the even-handed spreading of democratic ideology might be reconciled in the conduct of the project'.[121] These concerns were raised by the fact that the activities focussed on the Third World were largely aimed at contesting communist ideology, rather than a more expansive effort to promote democracy. An example of this was the Central American Media Program, which consisted of a newspaper and radio facilities targeted at rural populations, i.e. those social sectors most likely to support the insurgents the US was arming the region's militaries to combat.[122] This activity was clearly aimed at indoctrinating Central American peasants against communism, not empowering them as democratic citizens. The exchanges proposed in the programme were also directed at

Building a consensus for democracy promotion   119

Marxist ideology and seemed to equate democracy with the United States. The rationale advanced for African–US scholar exchanges was to use democracy as a counter-ideology to Marxism, rather than to create democratic structures:

> … African faculties and significant segments of the student population tend to view the world through Marxist lenses and have little understanding or sympathy for democratic values and processes.[123]

In contrast to this focus on anti-communism, Project Democracy presented no clear plan to foster transitions to democracy in pro-US right-wing dictatorships and had few concrete programmes aimed at building democratic successor movements capable of taking power in these states. One of the few concessions to the danger of right-wing authoritarianism in the clutch of propaganda initiatives was a programme of seminars on democracy for military leaders, based on the idea that '[d]emocratization often depends on building positive attitudes towards democracy in present and future military leaders.'[124] Project Democracy would also contribute $1.7 million to the dictatorial government of Samuel Doe in Liberia to fund an election to return to civilian rule[125] and would fund the problematic Institute for Democracy in Central America, together with democracy institutes for other regions.[126] However, the Liberian programme was an isolated case, not an example of a grand strategy at work, and while the proposed Institute for Democracy in Central America seemed likely to become a reality, the Institutes for Democracy mentioned for other areas of the world were discussed only as future possibilities, not concrete realities.[127] These programmes were ad hoc responses to current problems and were not tied to a wider or more strategic approach.

The fact that the administration had put forward a number of anti-communist proposals but few initiatives focussed on building democracy in right-wing dictatorships was a serious stumbling block to the acceptance of the plan by Democrats on the House and Senate Committees. During George Shultz's testimony in support of the initiative, he was questioned by Democrat Congressman Stephen Solarz on whether the US would limit democracy promotion to unfriendly governments or whether it would promote democracy in allied dictatorships such as the Philippines, Chile, Taiwan and South Korea during his Congressional testimony in support of the programme,[128] with Solarz arguing that a policy of selective democracy promotion would destroy the credibility of the whole effort.[129] Shultz attempted to sidestep the issue, which was controversial within the administration as well as in the legislature, by stating that the aim of the campaign was not to support dissidents but to support the idea of democracy in general.[130] However, his answer was unsatisfactory to some, and the project began to be tagged as 'Project Right-wing Democracy'[131] by Senator Paul Tsongas and as a 'conservative ideological crusade' by Congressional Democrats.[132]

In contrast, criticisms made by Republican senators were more focussed on the ideological colouration of the US private organisations which were to receive funding, and Conservative Republican senators complained that the right-wing

120 *Building a consensus for democracy promotion*

private organisations they favoured were not slated to receive funding.[133] These objections were a direct consequence of the administration's decision to create an overt network, as under the pre-1967 model of covert funding provided by the CIA the national security bureaucracy had not had to make a case to Congress for the targeting of its programmes or the groups that would receive support.

The strategic objections put forward by Congressional Democrats translated into reservations over the organisational framework for the democracy campaign, as legislators feared that if the administration were responsible for its day-to-day management and coordination, it would focus on the anti-Soviet aspect of the campaign to the exclusion of its possible wider dimensions. This was possible due to the fact that, while the programme included participation by private organisations that would receive US government funding, rather than distributing block grants to private groups who would then work autonomously, the administration had created a government command centre for the programme and proposed to release funding for specific projects in fixed amounts. This mode of control was similar to that employed by the CIA to manage its private partners before 1967, and would have corralled private groups into the administration's priorities.

A further key problem was that the programme was to be managed by a close collaborator of the President and a man famed for his anti-communist pronouncements: Charles Wick. Wick could be expected to focus on anti-communism to the detriment of a more universal approach and was unpopular with many legislators due to their perception of his conservative bias. Walter Raymond frankly admitted this problem in a memo to William Clark on Congressional strategy:

> There is deep suspicion over the direction of USIA. Part of this stems from the Director and his approach to propaganda ... in terms of the 'democracy project' [Congress] do[es] not see either the Director or his staff as being sufficiently politically nuanced to manage this intricate program.[134]

Congressmen believed that Wick, with his black and white view of a world divided into communist enemies and US friends, would prosecute the project in a strident and propagandistic manner. This stemmed from Congressional discomfort with previous USIA propaganda operations such as Project Truth and the agency's 'multi-media blitz "Let Poland Be Poland"'.[135] Wick's description of the project as aimed at waging 'a war of ideas with the Soviet Union' clearly did not dispel this impression.[136] This problem extended beyond Wick, however, as legislators were also unhappy about the coordinating role of the Special Planning Group committees and the degree of government control of the project this implied. Both Republican and Democrat Senators feared that government involvement could damage the credibility of the enterprise and of US information and exchange programmes in general.

The management of the democracy promotion campaign by the national security bureaucracy also heightened concern that the programme represented a

Building a consensus for democracy promotion   121

resurrection of the previous state–private network, rather than a new approach completely divorced from covert operations. Wick was questioned closely in the Senate on whether the CIA was involved in Project Democracy and, if so, to what extent.[137] He was also interrogated over a Project Democracy programme which involved channelling $50,000 to the Inter-American Press Association through an intermediary organisation to bypass the association's prohibition on accepting funding from foreign governments. As far as one member of the Senate Foreign Relations Committee was concerned, 'This would appear to be a rather indelicate attempt to launder $50,000,' meaning that funds were to be transferred illegally and covertly.[138] This action was reminiscent of the manner in which the CIA had transferred funds to US civil society groups without the knowledge of many of the members of such groups before 1967 and fuelled suspicions that the administration was attempting to pursue illegal covert actions through the Project Democracy framework. This was unacceptable to Congress. It was also short-sighted, as carrying out covert operations under the Project Democracy banner would inevitably lead to a gap between the democratic message of the Project and its operating principles similar to the ideological gap which had delegitimised the state–private network in 1967, repeating the cycle of operation, destruction and attempted resurrection.

Rather than a serious effort to build democracy in other countries, legislators began to see Project Democracy as simply a multimillion dollar propaganda campaign that was 'sure to give us trouble' or to argue that other countries would merely consider it 'mischief making', with these criticisms emerging from both parties.[139] Several Congressmen argued that it would be better to administer the democracy campaign through a 'semi-autonomous non-governmental organization' rather than the national security bureaucracy,[140] with Robert Kastenmeier opining that '[Project Democracy] may have legitimate functions if it were in private, non-governmental agencies'.[141] At the end of the Senate hearing on Project Democracy, Wick had to decline the offer of a shredder for his organisational charts from its Republican Chairman, Charles Percy.[142]

Conclusion

From this point onward Project Democracy seemed unlikely to be approved by Congress. The opposition to the programme in the legislature was partly due to its poor organisational framework. The unwieldy structure of a lead agency distributing funding to other participating agencies under the supervision of two committees at different levels led to Congressional feeling that such an organisational framework simply could not work. The government funding and coordination of the project also risked destroying the credibility of the project as a serious attempt to promote democracy, rather than a propaganda effort directed at achieving US interests. There was no guarantee that private groups or political movements overseas would be willing to accept government funding dispensed by an initiative managed and coordinated by the US national security bureaucracy. These organisational problems were partly a result of the legal and

122 *Building a consensus for democracy promotion*

bureaucratic constraints faced by the administration in its attempts to resurrect a state–private network previously run covertly through the CIA and to implement it overtly through governmental structures and agencies that had not been designed to manage such a programme.

However, the overarching reason for the failure of Project Democracy was the clash between two visions of democracy promotion held by different sections of the foreign policy elite. The campaign presented by the Reagan administration mobilised an abstract concept of democracy promotion to combat the spread of Soviet communism ideologically and to legitimate propaganda and political initiatives that sometimes had little connection to creating democratic systems in dictatorial countries. It was the narrow nature of this campaign, focussed on the support of the Reagan administration's national security objectives, which required a command centre within the government to supervise the actions of the private groups mobilised by it to conform to these priorities. However, this command centre was proving detrimental to Project Democracy's credibility with Congress. In contrast, many Congressional Democrats favoured an expansive campaign aimed at supporting democracy in dictatorial regimes friendly to the United States as well as enemy dictatorships, and believed that such a campaign would be best implemented by removing day-to-day control from the Reagan administration, whose strident anti-Sovietism they were suspicious of, and vesting it in private groups. The problems experienced by Project Democracy opened a space for the non-state democracy promoters to put forward their own implementing structure – the National Endowment for Democracy – which was tied to a wider campaign of democracy promotion likely to be much more acceptable to Congress.

Notes

1 'A Quango for Democracy?' *New York Times*, 6 June 1982, Folder: Press, Box 1, George E. Agree Papers, LOC.
2 See Ibid.
3 David Newsom, 'Reagan's crusade for democracy', *The Christian Science Monitor*, 2 July 1982, Folder: Press, 1979–1984, Box 1, George E. Agree Papers, LOC.
4 Susan Trausch, 'Private group would aid young democracies', *Boston Globe*, 13 July 1982, Folder: Press, 1979–1984, Box 1, George E. Agree Papers, LOC.
5 Ibid.
6 William E. Brock III, 'Reagan's campaign for democracy – and the German example,' *The Christian Science Monitor*, 27 July 1982, Nexis UK, www.lexisnexis.com/uk/nexis.
7 Ibid.
8 Quoted from Trausch, 'Private US group would aid young democracies'.
9 Ibid.
10 Memo, William Clark to the President, undated, 1982, DDRS, accessed 11 December 2006, 2.
11 Anonymous, document beginning 'The Democracy Initiative, a government-wide, inter-agency program', November 1982, Box OA91162, Folder: 11/82, Box OA91162, Walter Raymond Files, RL.
12 William Clark, memo to the President 1–2.

13 Ibid., 1.
14 Michael A. Samuels and William A. Douglas, 'Promoting Democracy', *The Washington Quarterly* 4, no. 3 (1981): 55.
15 Dale Good, interviewed by Thomas D. Bowie for *The Foreign Affairs Oral History Project: Labor Series, Association for Diplomatic Studies and Training*, 1 June 1996, accessed 13 July 2013, www.adst.org/OH%20TOCs/Good,%20Dale.toc.pdf, 5–6.
16 State Department, 'The African American Labor Center and Its Activities in Africa', undated, Folder 11/82, Box OA91162, Walter Raymond Files, RL.
17 Anonymous, Document beginning 'In response to request ...', August 1982, Folder 11/82, Box OA91162, Walter Raymond Files, RL, 1.
18 Trevor Barnes, 'The Secret Cold War: The C.I.A. and American Foreign Policy in Europe, 1946–1956: Part I', *The Historical Journal* 24, no. 2 (1981): 404, 413, accessed 29 October 2005, www.jstor.org/stable/2638793.
19 Anonymous, Document beginning 'In response to request ...', 3–4.
20 Idesbald Goddeeris, 'Lobbying Allies? The NSZZ Co-ordinating Office Abroad, 1982–1989', *Journal of Cold War Studies* 13, no. 3 (2011): 87–88, accessed 26 October 2014, doi: 10.1162/JCWS_a_00143.
21 Anonymous, Document beginning 'In response to request ...', Attachment II, 2.
22 State Department, 'African American Labor Center,' undated, DDRS, accessed Oct. 14, 2009.
23 Anonymous, Document beginning 'In response to request ...', Attachment I, 1.
24 State Department, 'AFL-CIO Labor Institutes: American Institute for Free Labor Development,' undated, Folder 12/82, Box OA91162, Walter Raymond Files, RL, for details.
25 Anonymous, document beginning 'In response to request ...', Attachment I, 1–2.
26 Ibid., 2.
27 Ibid.
28 State Department, 'AFL-CIO Labor Institutes, Attachment: African American Labor Center (AALC)', undated, Folder 12/82, Box OA91162, Walter Raymond Files, RL.
29 State Department 'American Institute for Free Labor Development'.
30 Anonymous, 'Labor Programs: Overview: (4) Assistance to International Labor Bodies', undated, Folder 11/82, Box OA91162, Walter Raymond Files, RL.
31 'Democracy in Action', *New York Times*, 17 August 1982, Folder: Press, Box 1, George E. Agree Papers, LOC.
32 Alan P. Dobson, 'The Reagan Administration, Economic Warfare, and Starting to Close Down the Cold War', *Diplomatic History* 29, no. 3 (2005): 544, accessed 3 August 2012, doi: 10.1111/j.1467–7709.2005.00502.x
33 Ibid.
34 APF, Minutes of 1982 Third Meeting Board of Directors of American Political Foundation', 19 August 1982 Folder 3: APF Minutes, Box 1, George E. Agree Papers, LOC.
35 'Democracy in Action'.
36 William A. Douglas, 'Helping Democracy Abroad: A US Program', *Freedom at Issue*, September–October 1982, Folder: Press, Box 1, George E. Agree Papers, LOC, 17.
37 Ibid., 18–19.
38 Memo, NSC to Scott Thompson, United States Information Agency & Richard Stilwell, Department of Defense, 22 September 1982, Folder 09/82–10/82, Box OA91162, Walter Raymond Files, RL, 3.
39 Kaeten Mistry, 'The Case for Political Warfare: Strategy, Organisation and US Involvement in the 1948 Italian Election', *Cold War History* 6 no. 3 (2006): 314, accessed 30 September 2014, DOI: 10.1080/14682740600795451; Scott Lucas, *Freedom's War: The US Crusade against the Soviet Union 1945–56* (Manchester:

124 *Building a consensus for democracy promotion*

Manchester University Press, 1999), 43–47; and Christopher Andrew, *For the President's Eyes Only: Secret Intelligence and the American Presidency from Washington to Bush* (London: Harper Collins Publishers, 1996), 171–172.

40 NSC, memo to Scott Thompson, 4.

41 Ibid.

42 Ibid., 3.

43 Ibid.

44 Richard M. Weintraub 'Shultz Kicks off a 'Crusade for Freedom', *The Washington Post*, 19 October 1982, LexisNexis, http://web.lexis-nexis.com/executive.

45 Cable, George P. Schultz to all diplomatic posts, Folder 09/82–10/82, Box OA91162, Walter Raymond Files, RL.

46 Weintraub, 'Shultz Kicks off a "Crusade for Freedom"'.

47 Cable, George P. Schultz, 1.

48 Ibid.

49 Ibid. 1.

50 Ibid.

51 Anonymous, 'Introduction to Program Book: Political Action', Folder 09/82–10/82, Box OA91162, Walter Raymond Files, RL, 4.

52 Ibid.

53 Giles Scott-Smith, 'The Free Europe University in Strasbourg: U.S. State–Private Networks and Academic "Rollback"', *Journal of Cold War Studies* 16 no. 2 (2014): 77–107, accessed 22 June 2014, doi:10.1162/JCWS_a_00452.

54 Facts on File, 'Shultz sees Democratic Revolution', Facts on File, 22 October 1982, LexisNexis, http://web.lexis-nexis.com/executive.

55 Weintraub, 'Shultz Kicks off a "Crusade for Freedom"'.

56 Ibid., 2.

57 Cable, George P. Schultz, 1.

58 Richard Pipes, *Vixi: Memoirs of a Non-Belonger* (New Haven and London: Yale University Press, 2003), 188.

59 Murray Friedman, *The Neoconservative Revolution: Jewish Intellectuals and the Shaping of Public Policy* (New York: Cambridge University Press, 2005), 143–144.

60 White House, 'NSDD-32: Basic National Security Strategy', FAS, 20 May 1982, accessed 5 May 2007, www.fas.org/irp/offdocs/nsdd/nsdd-32.pdf, 1–2.

61 White House, 'Response to NSSD 11–82: US Relations with the USSR', 6 December 1982, *Central Intelligence Agency Freedom of Information Act Electronic Reading Room Historical Collection on Ronald Reagan, Intelligence and the End of the Cold War*, hereafter CIA FOIA Reagan, accessed 26 September 2014, www.foia.cia.gov/sites/default/files/document_conversions/17/19821206.pdf, 36.

62 Ibid.

63 White House, 'NSSD 11–82: US Relations with the USSR', 21 August 1982, CIA FOIA Reagan, accessed 26 September 2014, www.foia.cia.gov/sites/default/files/document_conversions/17/19820821.pdf.

64 NSC, 'Response to NSSD 11–82', 23.

65 Ibid., 26.

66 Ibid., 30.

67 Quoted from Ibid., 23.

68 White House, 'Response to NSSD 11–82', 31.

69 Ibid., 32.

70 Paul Lettow, *Ronald Reagan's Quest to Abolish Nuclear Weapons* (New York: Random House, 2005), 79.

71 Memo, Alexander Haig to the President, 8 March 1982, DDRS, accessed 11 December 2006, 2.

72 White House, 'US Relations with the USSR,' 21.

73 White House, 'Response to NSSD 11–82,' 23.

Building a consensus for democracy promotion   125

74 Pipes, *Vixi*, 201.
75 NIO USSR-EE, 'Memorandum for Director of Central Intelligence: NSC meeting on US policy toward the Soviet Union', CIA FOIA Reagan, accessed 26 September 2014, www.foia.cia.gov/sites/default/files/document_conversions/17/19821214.pdf. See also Ambassador Thomas W. Simons Jr., interviewed by Charles Stuart Kennedy for *The Foreign Affairs Oral History Collection of the Association for Diplomatic Studies and Training*, 22 July 2004, accessed 13 September 2014, http://adst.org/wp-content/uploads/2012/09/Simons-Thomas-W1.pdf, 115.
76 White House, 'NSDD-75: US Relations with the Soviet Union', 17 January 1983, FAS, accessed 20 April 2012, www.fas.org/irp/offdocs/nsdd/nsdd-075.htm, 1.
77 Pipes, *Vixi* 201; Lettow, *Ronald Reagan's Quest*, 78–79.
78 NIO USSR-EE, memo to Director of Central Intelligence.
79 Pipes, 201.
80 Norman A. Bailey, 'The Strategic Plan That Won the Cold War: National Security Decision Directive 75', 1998, *Hispanic American Center for Economic Research* accessed 6 August 2012, www.hacer.org/pdf/Bailey001.pdf, 10.
81 'President Campaigns for Free Elections', *Washington Post*, 5 November 1982, http://web.lexis-nexis.com/executive.
82 David D. Newsom, 'Can democracy be promoted around the world?' *The Christian Science Monitor*, 24 November 1982, LexisNexis, http://web.lexis-nexis.com/executive, 1.
83 Ibid.
84 Ronald Reagan, 'Conference on Free Elections', *Public Papers of the Presidents*, 4 November 1982, Nexis UK, www.lexisnexis.com/uk/nexis.
85 State Department, 'Current Policy No. 433: Promoting Free Elections', November 1982, State Department Current Policy Records: Statements: Records 1981–1989 Box 3, RL.
86 Ibid., 5.
87 Ibid., 4.
88 Ibid., 3–4.
89 Jeff Gerth, 'Problems in Promoting Democracy', *New York Times*, 4 February 1983, Nexis UK, www.lexisnexis.com/uk/nexis, 2.
90 Anonymous, Document beginning 'In response to request ...', Attachment II, 2.
91 George E. Agree, 'Support for Democracy Outline Feasibility Study', attached to letter, George Agree to Peter McPherson, 27 August 1982, Box 1, Folder 1: APF Correspondence, George E. Agree Papers, LOC.
92 Compare letter, L.E. Stanfield to George Agree, 'Grant No. OTR-0098-G-SS-3029–00', 1 December 1982, with same document, 'APF PROPOSED REVISIONS', both attached to APF, Minutes of 1982 Fourth Meeting Board of Directors American Political Foundation, 16 December 1982, Folder 3: APF Minutes, Box 1, George E. Agree Papers, LOC.
93 APF, Minutes of the Fourth Meeting Board, 3.
94 Memo, Walter Raymond to Robert McFarlane, 3 December 1982, Project Democracy Folder 4, Box OA90304, Robert Kimmitt Files, RL, 2.
95 Memo, Walter Raymond and Peter Sommers to Robert McFarlane, 3 November 1982, DDRS, accessed 11 December 2006.
96 Memo on Project Democracy, Walter Raymond, 24 Nov 1982, DDRS, accessed 11 December 2006.
97 Memo, Walter Raymond to William Clark, 9 December 1982, DDRS, accessed 11 December 2006.
98 Memo, Walter Raymond to Robert McFarlane, 3 December 1982, 2. See Morton H. Halperin, *Bureaucratic Politics and Foreign Policy* (Washington DC: The Brookings Institute, 1974), 56–58 for a discussion of how budgetary considerations play into organisational decisions on whether to take on new functions.

126   *Building a consensus for democracy promotion*

99   Memo, Raymond to McFarlane, 3 December 1982, 2.
100   Memo, Clark to the President, undated, 1982, 1–2.
101   Gerald Helman, 'Paper on private sector funding', 22 November 1982, Folder 12/82, Box OA91162, Walter Raymond Files, RL.
102   Memo, Robert Kiernan to W. Scott Thompson, 28 December 1982, Folder 12/82, Box OA91162, Walter Raymond Files, RL, 1.
103   Ibid., 2.
104   William I. Robinson, *Promoting Polyarchy: Globalization, US Intervention and Hegemony* (Cambridge: Cambridge University Press, 1996), 180.
105   Walter Raymond, memo to Robert McFarlane, 8 December 1982, DDRS, accessed 11 December 2006.
106   Walter Raymond, memo to Robert McFarlane, 3 December 1982.
107   White House, 'NSDD 77: Management of Public Diplomacy Relative to National Security', 14 January 1983, FAS, accessed 17 May 2011, www.fas.org/irp/offdocs/nsdd/nsdd-077.htm, 1.
108   Thomas Carothers, *In the Name of Democracy: US Policy towards Latin America in the Reagan Years* (Berkeley & Los Angeles: University of California Press, 1991), 201.
109   Ibid., 2.
110   Ibid., 3.
111   'NSDD 77', 2.
112   Ibid.
113   Ibid., 2.
114   Ibid., 2.
115   'NSDD 77', 2.
116   R. Gregory Nokes, 'Shultz Unveils "Plan to Promote Global Democracy"', The Associated Press, 23 February 1983, Nexis UK, www.lexisnexis.com/uk/nexis, 1.
117   R. Gregory Nokes, 'untitled', The Associated Press, 23 February 1983, Nexis UK, www.lexisnexis.com/uk/nexis, 1.
118   Steve Steiner, 'Democracy and Public Diplomacy: An Inter-Agency Program', attached to memo, Steve Steiner to Robert D. Blackwill, undated, Folder: Democracy Initiative (2), Box 91753, Steve Steiner Files, RL, 38, 39 and 5.
119   Laurien Alexandre, *The Voice of America: From Détente to the Reagan Doctrine* (Norwood; New Jersey: Ablex Publishing Corporation, 1988), 103–104.
120   Patricia Koza, 'untitled', United Press International, 3 March 1983, Nexis UK, www.lexisnexis.com/uk/nexis.
121   USIA, 'Testimony of Secretary of State George Shultz before the House Foreign Affairs Subcommittee on International organizations on February 23, 1983', Project Democracy: Folder 2, Box 90301, Robert Kimmitt Files, RL, 1.
122   Anonymous, 'Project Democracy', undated, Folder 6: Reports and Proposals, Box 1, George E. Agree Papers, LOC, 31.
123   Ibid., 25.
124   Anonymous, 'Project Democracy', 8.
125   Ibid., 17.
126   Ibid., 15.
127   Ibid., 9.
128   R. Gregory Nokes, 'Shultz Unveils "Plan to Promote Global Democracy"', 1; Bernard Gwertzmann, 'Skeptics pelt Shultz with Queries on Reagan's "Project Democracy"', *New York Times*, 24 February 1983, Nexis UK, www.lexisnexis.com/uk/nexis, 2.
129   R. Gregory Nokes, 'untitled', 2.
130   Don Oberdorfer, 'Lawmakers Voice Skepticism on US "Project Democracy"', *Washington Post*, 24 February 1983, Nexis UK, www.lexisnexis.com/uk/nexis, 2.
131   Mary McGrory, 'Promoting the "Infrastructure of Democracy," With Charts', *Washington Post*, 3 March 1983, Nexis UK, www.lexisnexis.com/uk/nexis, 1.

Building a consensus for democracy promotion   127

132 'Untitled', The Associated Press, 16 March 1983, Nexis UK, www.lexisnexis.com/uk/nexis

133 Jeff Gerth, 'Problems in Promoting Democracy', *New York Times*, 4 February 1983, Nexis UK, www.lexisnexis.com/uk/nexis, 1; and Cord Meyer, 'USIA's effort to promote democracy', *Washington Times*, 4 March 1983, Folder: Press, 1979–1984, Box 1, George E. Agree Papers, LOC.

134 Memo, Raymond to Clark, DDRS, accessed 11 December 2006, 1.

135 Ibid.

136 Patrick E. Tyler, 'USIA Chief Questioned On "Project Democracy"' *Washington Post*, 3 March 1983, Nexis UK, www.lexisnexis.com/uk/nexis, 1.

137 McGrory, 2.

138 Tyler, 2.

139 R. Gregory Nokes, 'untitled', 1.

140 USIA, 'Testimony of Secretary of State George Shultz', 2.

141 E. Michael Myers, 'untitled', United Press International, 23 February 1983, Nexis UK, www.lexisnexis.com/uk/nexis, 2.

142 McGrory, 'Promoting the Infrastructure of democracy', 3.

5 The foundation of the National Endowment for Democracy

The lack of consensus over Project Democracy threw the emerging campaign for democracy into disarray. Congress' objections to an overt government-supervised programme aimed largely at combatting Soviet communism spurred a re-thinking of the effort, which created an opportunity for the non-state forces associated with democracy promotion to fill the bureaucratic and strategic gap left by the failure of the administration's effort by presenting their own vision to Congress.

In order to succeed, these non-state democracy promoters needed to solve the immediate problems which had proven so damaging to Project Democracy by presenting a strategic framework for US political operations overseas capable of generating consensus and an organisational blueprint which would be both credible and effective. For these actors, the stakes went beyond the Reagan administration's immediate goal of launching an anti-Soviet propaganda campaign in support of its foreign policy, as the goal of creating a non-state US democracy promotion organisation extended back to the ideas first put forward by William Douglas in the early 1970s, and then modified and elaborated by George Agree and Michael Samuels. The more long-range goal was to create an overt state–private network and harness this to the new objective of building democratic systems overseas through support for foreign political parties and groups. In order to accomplish this, it was necessary to devise a set of concepts – ideological, strategic and organisational – which would allow for a re-convergence of the state and private actors on an overt basis and resolve the problems of bureaucratic inconsistency and blockages which had been a consistent feature of US attempts to pursue political reform in other societies.

The requirements that the new democracy promotion institute be overt, government-funded and credible meant that the democracy promoters had to consider three keys audiences. The first two were internal to the United States: Congress, which favoured an expansive campaign of democracy promotion, and the Reagan administration, which was more concerned with narrower US security goals. Broad approval from both of these actors would be necessary to create a new democracy institute, unlike the pre-1967 period, when funding could be dispensed to US private groups covertly through the state–private network. The third key audience was foreign democratic groups and leaders. In

The foundation of the National Endowment for Democracy   129

order to secure their co-operation with future democracy promotion programmes, non-state democracy promoters needed to design an organisation which was not too closely linked to the US government, so that these foreign democrats could co-operate with it without sacrificing their credibility as authentic nationalists within their own societies. Finally, it was necessary to maintain a balance of power between the various private groups connected to the study in order to preserve the internal consensus of the growing non-state democracy promotion community.

The democracy promoters were successful where the national security bur-eaucracy had failed; they produced an organisation capable of carrying out overt political operations abroad that would be acceptable to the administration and Congress. This was achieved largely by de-emphasising strategic questions and instead focussing on building consensus around an ideological commitment to the promotion of democracy and the organisational structure recommended by the group. The fact that the ideological concept of global democracy promotion de-emphasised debates centred on whether to pursue a narrow anti-Soviet strategy or a broader one also focussed on friendly dictatorships meant that all groups could see the programme as acceptable in terms of their own priorities, while the non-state nature of the initiative served to defuse the bureaucratic problems which had complicated the plan to fund overt programmes through Project Democracy. However, the failure to resolve the strategic question, together with the fact that the design approved by Congress contained important organisational weaknesses, increased the danger that democracy promotion would prove to be a fragmented enterprise driven by a mix of democratic ideo-logy, sectional interests and partisan perceptions of US interests.

Designing the National Endowment for Democracy: strategy, effectiveness and partisan interests

The study on US democracy promotion tactics and methods that had been announced by Reagan in his London speech produced a blueprint for a non-governmental implementing structure for US democracy promotion to be placed before Congress – the National Endowment for Democracy. This study, referred to as the Democracy Program, was tasked by AID with researching current gov-ernmental and private initiatives to support democracy in the US and the West as a whole, identifying democratic groups to be supported overseas, recommending programmes and tactics for supporting such groups, and examining new mecha-nisms for promoting democracy.[1] It also represented an opportunity for the democracy promoters to solidify the concepts put forward by Douglas and Samuels in their 1981 article by deciding the extent to which new democracy promotion programmes should support democratic groups in US-allied dictator-ships and hostile states, and what the balance would be between aiming programmes at short-term targets of opportunity and fostering long-term polit-ical development. However, the study did not generate a strategic framework based on either the needs of democratic forces overseas or US interests; more-over, the organisational design it produced for the Endowment was shaped by

130　*The foundation of the National Endowment for Democracy*

the preconceptions of the non-state democracy promoters and the partisan interests of the groups participating in it, rather than on a clear, evidence-based assessment of the effectiveness of competing structural models in promoting democracy overseas.

The Democracy Program: a focus on organisational issues

The Democracy Program study was funded by the administration through the AID Human Rights budget, as promised to the APF by Mark Palmer in April 1982. Although it proceeded concurrently with the Reagan administration's planning for Project Democracy, the Democracy Program was largely a self-contained effort overseen by an Executive Board consisting of non-state democracy promoters such as William Brock, Charles Manatt, Michael Samuels, former officials of the Reagan administration, such as Richard Allen and of the Carter administration, such as Anthony Lake, and legislators such as Dante Fascell and Christopher Dodd.[2] The study was directed by Professor Allen Weinstein of the Centre for Strategic and International Studies, a respected historian. Weinstein was also Executive editor of the *Washington Quarterly*, which had published William Douglas' and Michael Samuels' article, 'Promoting Democracy', and a stalwart anti-communist and neoconservative.

Weinstein presided over what was, as of January 1983, a four-power coalition. The non-state democracy promotion community had broadened beyond the two parties in the wake of Reagan's speech, when the Republicans and Democrats had been joined in their project by the AFL-CIO. These three were then joined by representatives of the US Chamber of Commerce in January 1983, after Michael Samuels had sold the idea of a role for US business in democracy promotion to the Reagan administration's Project Democracy Working Group.[3] Thus, the key private actors that Douglas and Samuels had called on to participate in a semi-private democracy promotion organisation in their 1981 article worked together on the study, which had been originally conceived of as a vehicle for generating initial democracy promotion programme proposals and building consensus in the Executive and Congress to support the creation of a democracy promotion foundation by Michael Samuels in 1979.[4]

However, the study did not consider the strategic and tactical dimensions of democracy promotion in any great depth, focussing instead on the generation of an organisational model for private democracy promotion by US groups. It spent little time considering how democratic successor groups could be built up in authoritarian regimes, although, according to the programme's leaders, it did consider how such movements could be helped in totalitarian states. This information was omitted from the interim report which the study presented to Congress in April 1983 to make its case for government funding for the National Endowment for Democracy,[5] presumably so as not to re-open the strategic question with legislators and thus jeopardise the organisation's funding.

Debate over strategic and tactical matters was further minimised by the time constraints that the study operated under. Like the Reagan administration, the

The foundation of the National Endowment for Democracy 131

study leaders believed that the chances of securing bipartisan support in Congress for legislation for a new democracy promotion organisation would be damaged if their programme were not presented before the legislature entered the forthcoming mid-term election cycle. The legislative timetable for the programme was discussed in the first Executive Board meeting on 16 December 1982, and in March 1983 Weinstein warned the study staff that 'we are racing the Congressional clock in completing our work.'[6]

These time constraints meant that important research which could have informed decisions on democracy promotion and the design of the Endowment was not completed before the group's recommendations were presented to Congress. For example, the group had done no more than cursory research on the US government agencies and programmes already functioning in its areas of interest – a condition of its AID funding[7] – to consider whether the new endowment might duplicate these programmes. In addition, none of the regional reports on prospects for democracy promotion in Africa, East Asia, South Asia, Latin America and the Middle East had been finished, and the study group also lacked a clear conception of the roles the four core groups – the two parties, labour, and business – would play tactically in the promotion of democracy.[8] When the model for the NED was drawn up as a non-governmental umbrella organisation which would disburse funding to four separate democracy foundations to be run by business, the AFL-CIO, the Democrats and the Republicans, reports on the roles of business and labour in democracy promotion were uncompleted, and reports on the role of the Democratic and Republican parties in democracy promotion had not even been begun.[9]

The organisational model for the NED was recommended with no clear strategy underpinning it, no cognisance of how it would fit organisationally with governmental efforts, no clear understanding of what programmes it would follow to promote democracy on a regional basis, and no clear conception of the role the four core groups would play in promoting democracy. Instead, the blueprint for the organisation was based largely on the plan produced in 1981, rather than new research carried out by the study group, which tended to see the study as a vehicle for realising this preconceived vision.

The influence of partisan interests on the Democracy Program

The tendency of the study participants to see it as a vehicle for the creation of a political action capability for each of the four core groups was reinforced by its domination by staffers linked to these groups. Aside from Weinstein, the only full-time staffers on the study were four Assistant Directors, each of whom had been chosen by and owed allegiance to one of the four core groups. These four Assistant Directors were: Republican Keith B. Schuette, a former aide to Alexander Haig; Democrat politician John P. Loiello; John D. Sullivan of the US Chamber of Commerce; and AFL-CIO designee Eugenia Kemble, assistant to Albert Shanker of the American Federation of Teachers, which had funded and supported Solidarity's Information Office in New York before and after martial

132 *The foundation of the National Endowment for Democracy*

law in Poland.[10] These staffers 'were nominated by, and intended to represent the interests of, these four groups'[11] and later stated that the study:

> was *not* a feasibility study in the academic sense but instead was a study to work out a mechanism by which labor, business, and the two political parties could conduct programmes abroad promoting democratic institutions and processes.[12]

The dominance of the four core groups within the study created a tension between the need to maintain the coalition by satisfying the partisan interests of these groups and the design of an effective and credible organisation, which erupted in disagreements over whether two party foundations should be created, or whether the Republicans and Democrats should work together in one bipartisan foundation.[13]

This disagreement had first emerged in a low-key fashion at the APF's board meeting of April 1982, when George Agree and Mark Palmer had argued that the interests of both democracy promotion and US security pointed to the creation of a bipartisan political party foundation which would be able to overcome partisan differences between the parties by focussing on the common goal of promoting democracy, whereas Charles Manatt, the APF's Democrat vice-chairman, had argued in favour of partisan foundations. The initial agreement over a bipartisan party foundation began to change in February 1983, as the prospect of creating organisations that would receive government funding grew more apparent. Agree became concerned about the direction the study was heading in and raised a series of questions about what type of structure would be most appropriate for conducting party-related activities through the NED with William Brock and Charles Manatt, now Chairman and co-Chairman of the Democracy Program.

Although Agree proposed three possible organisational options – partisan institutes, one bipartisan institute or some combination of these two options[14] – it is clear that he favoured one bipartisan institute. He had been a supporter of a bipartisan institute since the foundation of the APF, which was itself a bipartisan organisation, and he offered a series of arguments for the creation of a bipartisan NED party institute connected to the operational effectiveness and credibility of the NED. A bipartisan structure would minimise factionalism within the parties by joining both together in a common goal – promoting democracy. It would also enable a long-range, consistent policy to be pursued through alternations of party control of the Executive and Congress. In addition to this, it would enhance the operational effectiveness and credibility of the institute for democracy, as the party of the administration could not be seen as its agent and would not, in fact, be able to undertake rogue actions dictated by its party colleagues in the Executive. At the same time, the pursuit of party-related activities through a bipartisan institute meant that there was less chance of the parties drifting into embarrassing ideological alliances overseas, or of their actions being used as campaign issues.[15] This was of key importance during the early 1980s, when Republicans and

Democrats often sharply disagreed over policy towards Central America. Thus, a bipartisan institute would serve the wider cause of democracy promotion and hopefully be more credible, both inside the US and with democratic movements overseas. Finally, Agree warned that partisan party foundations might prove unacceptable to Congress and so damage the chances of creating the NED.[16]

In February, Agree merely recommended that competing structural models for the new organisation be placed before the Executive Board of the study, which would then be able to make an informed choice.[17] Although his ideas had the support of important Board members such as Lane Kirkland, President of the AFL-CIO, and William Brock,[18] they provoked a rift between Agree and Charles Manatt. Agree's perception of the problem was that the Democrat party leaders were concerned that under his scheme their own party foundation would be unable to act alone to pursue its partisan interests. His understanding of this issue is clear from the compromise solution he suggested; the creation of international departments for the two parties through which they could pursue these interests, leaving the democracy institute untainted by partisan operations.[19]

Despite the APF President's efforts, competing structural models were never put before the Executive Board of the Study or the APF Board in order to enable board members to make an informed choice, as he had asked.[20] Neither were the arguments for bipartisan versus partisan party foundations ever put to Congress, as the question was omitted from the interim report which explained the structure of the NED to legislators. Instead, Agree charged, the decision to create partisan Democratic and Republican Party institutes was made behind closed doors 'through unofficial dealings among a few leaders'.[21] Several months later, Agree was removed as President of the APF by a small group of directors, which included Manatt.[22] The wider project of promoting democracy was being diluted by more partisan considerations, even if, as Agree had warned, this placed the approval of the organisation by Congress in jeopardy.

The drive for a measure of operational independence on the part of the four core groups also led to the creation of a weak supervisory framework for their activities. The legislative framework for the National Endowment for Democracy itself, the body tasked with disbursing funding to the core groups, contained few structural constraints on the operations of these groups. According to a Congressional staff analysis, the legislation which created the NED prohibited no activities to its constituent groups, gave the Endowment no control over the money which would be disbursed to the four cores, and provided no safeguards against misuse of its funds by them.[23] The four groups were not accountable to the NED, or to Congress, and did not have to either obtain advance approval for their activities or report them after the fact; unlike the West German party foundations which the NED's Republican and Democratic Party institutes claimed to have modelled themselves on.[24] In addition, although there was a requirement for the NED itself to be audited, there was no such requirement for the four groups.[25] The analysis pronounced 'the Endowment is a toothless tiger', 'merely a pass-through with no control whatsoever over the use of funds by the party institutes, or the business and labour institutes for that matter.'[26] Clearly,

134 *The foundation of the National Endowment for Democracy*

real power lay with the four core groups, who would gain funding through the Endowment.

The Democracy Program study had originally been instituted to investigate how US civil society groups in general could contribute to the promotion of democracy alongside government, and to generate concepts for initial programmes. However, the core groups' focus on creating an instrumentality which would offer them a degree of operational independence under the umbrella of democracy promotion was pursued even when it impeded the creation of an effective organisation, or the prospect that the study group's blueprint would be acceptable to Congress. This resulted in decisions which had the potential to impact democracy promotion in a practical way, as the weakness of the supervisory powers granted to the National Endowment for Democracy increased the likelihood that rogue actions unrelated to the promotion of democracy would be undertaken by one or more core groups. Instead of unifying their interests and subsuming them within the wider project of democracy promotion, the core groups had merely allied to pursue these sectional interests through the NED framework. In addition, in the rush to create the organisation the core groups failed to consider Agree's warning that partisan party foundations might be unacceptable to Congress.

Consensus between the democracy promoters and the administration

The Reagan administration, particularly its Reaganite faction, had previously shown reservations about allowing democracy promotion operations to be carried out by private groups without government supervision, due to fear that these groups would carry out actions which did not contribute to US national security. However, when the study group submitted its findings to Congress, it was able to include a letter from William Clark, dated 14 March 1983, which stated that the effort to create the NED was strongly approved by Reagan.[27] In addition, when the NED legislation later came under fire in Congress dissenting legislators received phone calls from Reagan administration officials urging them to change their minds.[28] The administration's strong support for the Endowment was largely a pragmatic response shaped by several factors.

Due to the difficulties which Project Democracy faced on the Hill, the administration needed another option for the pursuit of political programmes overseas and may have seen the National Endowment for Democracy as a more Congress-friendly channel for political operations. The democracy promoters explicitly offered just such a channel for the implementation of elements of Project Democracy. The interim report presented to Congress on democracy promotion as part of the effort to create the NED in April 1983 makes this plain by arguing that:

> Several of the bipartisan programmes previously recommended in the Reagan Administration's 'Project Democracy' initiative, for example, could be ... co-ordinated through the Endowment.[29]

The foundation of the National Endowment for Democracy   135

This offer provided the administration with an avenue through which some of its own programmes could be implemented. Indeed, given the level of Congressional opposition to Project Democracy, this was probably the only realistic way in which some of its objectives could be pursued.

Beyond this general picture, the Reagan administration and several of the core groups shared similar ideological preoccupations and specific objectives. The strongest immediate convergence was between the administration and the AFL-CIO, facilitated by the strong ideological anti-communism which both shared. Many of the proposed activities for the Free Trade Union Institute, the AFL-CIO-controlled democracy promotion foundation which would receive government funding through the Endowment, were described in the study group's report to Congress in anti-communist terms; for example, the case for the expansion of labor exchanges was made by stating that 'The size and scope of the Soviet bloc operation in this field should offer a clear incentive.'[30] FTUI planned to go on the offensive against the WFTU,[31] a global trade union federation dominated by unions controlled by Soviet bloc governments and, most importantly, to support the organisation of free trade unions in communist countries[32] because 'the Solidarity experience may foreshadow possible future events elsewhere in the communist world'.[33] Support for Solidarity and for the growth of non-communist trade unions elsewhere in the Soviet bloc, if possible, was a key objective for those elements of the Reagan administration focussed on liberalising communist countries.

More globally, the administration had a clear idea of the priorities the AFL-CIO would likely follow if provided with funding from the detailed proposals for operations to be carried out in the Soviet bloc, Western Europe and the Third World submitted by the union for inclusion in Project Democracy. When supporting the proposal of the NED to Congress the administration displayed a clear bias towards the FTUI. When the NED legislation was introduced to Congress it already contained budget amounts earmarked for the use of the four foundations and, at the Reagan administration's insistence, FTUI was given the lion's share of the money[34] – $13.8 million, as compared to $5 million each for the Republican and Democratic party foundations and $2.5 million for the Center for International Private Enterprise.[35]

The party institutes could also help to achieve the administration's foreign policy goals, as they could assist in the promotion of democracy in Central America. The whole administration supported reform in pro-US Central American regimes such as El Salvador, whether to strengthen containment by creating more legitimate governments or to remove Congress' objections to increased US military aid for the region. This particular strategic rationale for democracy promotion represented an enduring convergence between the government and the non-state democracy promoters: it had been cited in Alexander Haig's first proposal for a private democracy promotion instrumentality in March 1982, in Thomas O. Enders' speech on Central American policy of July 1981 and in Douglas' and Samuels' article of several months before.

The administration and the democracy promoters were co-operating in the planning of a programme to reinforce this objective as the structure of the

136 *The foundation of the National Endowment for Democracy*

Endowment was being generated and presented to Congress. This initiative, 'Inter-American Leadership Development', had been developed by State Department officials in the Bureau of Inter-American Affairs from a programme proposed by ARA in March 1983.[36] It consisted of 'seminars and training for politicians and staffs of democratic political parties and other democratic organizations in the respective regions'[37] on democratic party organisation, fund raising, fiscal management, and campaign planning, organisation and execution,[38] all of which would clearly strengthen the organisations whose representatives attended them, giving them an advantage in the struggle to take power in their home countries. The project seems to have shifted from governmental to private sponsorship between March and May 1983; whereas at the end of March it was discussed at an International Political Committee meeting as a governmental/State Department initiative,[39] on 21 May the project was being formally discussed in Caracas by a state–private delegation consisting of State Department officials, Allen Weinstein and Congressmen Barnes and Lagomarsino, who were enthusiastic supporters of the NED in the House vote later on that year.[40] The Central American programme indicated that there was a basis for co-operation between the administration and the NED.

The fact this programme had been generated in the State Department, not by the study board, however, indicates the final factor enabling administration support of the Endowment: the lack of new specific programme proposals from the study board. More than convergence over one programme or core foundation, this lack of specifics worked to the advantage of the non-state democracy promoters, who were able to offer wide statements about continuing Project Democracy, promoting democracy and opposing communism but few specifics on strategy or programmes which the administration could disagree with. The fact that the study group had ignored the strategic question and its failure to produce proposals for specific programmes in specific countries minimised flashpoints for disagreement between it and the Reagan administration. While uncertainty about what the private components of the nascent democracy promotion network would do had contributed to administration reservations about the project previously, the atmosphere created by Congressional reluctance to support Project Democracy over-rode these concerns and transformed the private groups' strategic fuzziness into a strength.

Selling the National Endowment for Democracy to Congress

After reaching agreement among themselves and with the administration, the non-state democracy promoters had to engineer consensus with Congress over their concept to receive funding; an action that private groups receiving covert government funding before 1967 had never had to undertake. This was the point at which Project Democracy had failed, due to its links to the state, which had made Democrats wary that it would be implemented in line with the Reagan administration's strategic preoccupations rather than broader American interests. Such links could also damage the project's credibility and effectiveness by making it appear to be the

The foundation of the National Endowment for Democracy 137

puppet of the national security bureaucracy to foreign populations. In order to foster Congressional approval for their design, the democracy promoters portrayed their blueprint as the natural fulfilment of the US' historic mission to promote democracy overseas, while stressing the operational advantages of a non-governmental organisation to the cause of promoting democracy through overt action.

The interim report: a vehicle to generate consensus

The vehicle used to persuade Congress to agree to government funding of the NED was an interim report of the Democracy Program study group, 'The Commitment to Democracy', which was presented to legislators on 18 April after being hurriedly drafted the preceding weekend by the Democracy Program staff. The document was created at the insistence of Dante Fascell,[41] a long-time supporter of private political action abroad. Fascell had been involved in the unsuccessful attempt to create a US Institute for Human Rights under the Carter administration in the late 1970s and was the Chairman of the Helsinki Commission, concerned with monitoring Soviet Human Rights practices. He was well-positioned to assist in the creation of the Endowment, as both a member of the Executive Board overseeing the Democracy Program study and the Chairman of the House Foreign Relations Subcommittee on International Organisations,[42] a committee whose support could have an impact on Congress' attitude towards the NED. The democracy promoters managed to guide their proposal through the minefield that had swallowed Project Democracy by using this report to foster a consensus over their own vision of democracy promotion.

The interim report was able to generate a consensus in favour of the creation of the Endowment, first, through an appeal to the US sense of democratic mission shared by Congress. This ideological framework had served as the basis for the consensus necessary both among US elites and between elites and the population for new strategic commitments and/or new policies to be pursued during the pre-Vietnam period of the Cold War. To re-forge such a consensus, the interim report opened with a collection of five quotes on the subject of democracy and the promotion of democracy overseas by the US, beginning with Abraham Lincoln, progressing to President Truman, 1940s Republican Senate leader Arthur Vandenburg, then moving on to a quote from Reagan's 8 June speech expressing his support for the study and Democratic Speaker of the House Thomas O'Neill, who also expressed his support for the Democracy Program study.[43] These quotes portrayed a continuum of US thought on democracy stretching from the Gettysburg address to the foreign policy problems of the 1980s, while the choice of quotes from both Republicans and Democrats conveyed an impression of bipartisanship. The introduction to the report also deployed this ideological tactic, linking the democracy promotion organisation proposed by the study group to the course of American history:

Throughout our national experience, Americans have rarely asked whether they should assist democracies elsewhere in the world, only how such support

138 *The foundation of the National Endowment for Democracy*

> could be provided most effectively.... From the early years of the American nation to its recent decades of global involvement, the United States has honoured a commitment to supporting the democratic ideal and those who uphold it, first in Europe, and more recently throughout the world.[44]

Of course, promoting democracy was a broad and undefined goal, which did not necessarily demand the particular organisational structure of four core institutes sheltering under a government-funded umbrella foundation the report went on to recommend. However, the report's ideological language linked the specific organisational structure put forward in it, which had been forged through prior negotiations between the four core groups, to a historic sense of mission with broad appeal throughout the US elite and US society.

Democratic idealism also performed an important function in providing an alternative rallying point to agreement over a list of specific programmes, and one that could be readily and rapidly deployed in the absence of hard data on specific actions the new democracy promotion foundation would conduct. Questions surrounding the targeting of Project Democracy programmes had been responsible for a great deal of Congress' unhappiness with the idea, due to the suspicions of Democrats that the structure was primarily aimed at Soviet communism, not at all dictatorial regimes. It had also led to Congressmen engaging in criticism of the whole project based on the fact that they disagreed with particular programmes to be run under it, such as the democracy promotion programmes to be run in Western Europe. The Democracy Program report avoided this problem almost completely by including no specifics on the strategy or programmes the NED would pursue. As noted previously, the only substantive strategic issue that the study group had discussed was how to foster democratic forces in totalitarian states, meaning the USSR and its clients and allies. However, discussion of these issues was omitted from the report presented to Congress, as it was felt to be 'inadvisable'.[45] Without a programme list, there was little scope for strategic objections to be raised.

The proposal of a number of democratic tasks for the NED rather than a strategic framework or specific programmes further de-emphasised strategic or tactical disagreements. These tasks were 'to encourage free and democratic institutions throughout the world through private sector initiatives', 'to facilitate exchanges', 'to promote United States nongovernmental participation ... in democratic training programmes', 'to strengthen democratic electoral processes abroad' and 'to encourage the establishment and growth of democratic development in a manner consistent with the broad concerns of United States national interests'.[46] These broad missions gave few specifics as to where the Endowment would focus its efforts, what type of regimes it would target and what programmes it would run to promote democracy. The missions largely represented broad goals rather than ways of achieving them, giving a hazy picture of what the Endowment would actually do in practice.

Similarly, the organisation of the report into sections dealing with the structure of the Endowment itself and that of each of its four core foundations, rather

The foundation of the National Endowment for Democracy 139

than other possible organising frameworks such as a discussion of the prospects for democracy promotion by region, served to focus Congressional attention on organisational structures rather than strategy or programmes. The NED's vagueness on this score meant that Congressmen and Senators could read their own strategic preferences into the organisation's list of missions and rhetoric. This vagueness helped to generate consensus over the basic organisational concept of a private umbrella foundation. Thus, the study group's strategic fuzziness actually facilitated the adoption of the NED by Congress; the exact opposite of the effect the Reagan administration's presentation of more specific programme data had had on Congress' attitude towards Project Democracy.

The advantages of a democracy promotion NGO

Congressional reservations about the implementation of democracy promotion were further defused by the emphasis placed throughout the report on the status of the NED as a non-governmental organisation, which served a number of functions. First, the de-linking of the campaign for democracy promotion from the Reagan administration organisationally served to calm Congressional fears that it would be a vehicle for the pursuit of the administration's partisan objectives. The report argued that the organisational structure of the NED would guard against such an outcome, as:

> The independent nature of the Endowment will insure that the programmes it funds promote the long-term, bipartisan interests of the United States rather than short-term partisan ends.[47]

The key point was that the command and control centre for the reconfigured democracy campaign would be located outside the state, in the National Endowment for Democracy, rather than in the Reagan administration's International Political Committee. This organisational de-linking of democracy promotion from the Reagan administration was necessary to ensure that Congress would not block the proposal for fear that it would be used to pursue the administration's narrow policy goals.

De-linking the National Endowment for Democracy from the state, in broader terms, also helped to overcome fears that democracy promotion would be used as a cover for covert operations unconnected to the promotion of democracy. This was important, as some Congressmen had already articulated fears that Project Democracy could and would be used as a cover for such covert operations. Furthermore, the method by which democracy promotion was to be funded in the structure the report was proposing – government money disbursed to a private umbrella foundation, which would then distribute the money to private groups – seemed remarkably similar to previous state funding of private groups through foundations manipulated by the CIA. For example, the CIA had funded a number of private groups and individuals in the state–private network through a dummy foundation concocted by the Agency,

140   *The foundation of the National Endowment for Democracy*

the Farfield Foundation.[48] The study group would need to avoid suggesting such parallels if it were to succeed.

The interim report was careful to not imply such comparisons by discussing previous covert funding of US private groups at length, preferring to locate the NED in a context of previous private efforts to promote democracy abroad from which the CIA was omitted.[49] Although the report also contained a short history of the AFL-CIO's foreign operations, the question of CIA funding was not raised.[50] This careful approach was necessary to avoid reigniting the controversy created by the exposure of the CIA's links to US citizen groups in 1967, in which Congress had taken a strong stand against what it perceived to be the infiltration and manipulation of US democratic groups by secretive government organisations to serve Cold War objectives, an activity thought to be subversive of the US' domestic democratic system. The drawing of such a parallel between the previous state–private network and the National Endowment for Democracy could have destroyed the new organisation's credibility with Congress as a non-state actor devoted to democracy promotion.

In addition to producing domestic credibility with Congress, the report also argued that the non-governmental organisational model that it put forward would be a superior vehicle for the prosecution of overt democracy promotion programmes overseas due to its greater credibility with foreign democrats than the governmental Project Democracy structure. The report made this point effectively by stressing the autonomy of the NED from the national security bureaucracy:

> 'If aid came from a foundation with genuine autonomy, supervised by a board of respected American and foreign figures,' the New York Times editorialized shortly after the President's London speech, it could be as uncontroversial as that already provided by private foundations.... Change 'foundation' to 'Endowment', provide for an American board but one which would work in 'cooperation with foreign figures' on jointly agreed upon programmes, and the description matches the proposal before us.[51]

Clearly a non-governmental instrumentality would be more credible than government agencies and would be more likely to gain the co-operation of foreign democrats within nationalistic Third World societies, where the open dispensing of funds by the NED 'might be perceived as a more recognizable, and hence more acceptable, source of funding than, for example, a political foundation functioning as a State Department, USIA, or AID grantee.'[52] Such an arrangement would serve to defuse accusations of neo-colonial behaviour that could accompany efforts by a US government agency to promote US values or support political groups in the Third World. It would also safeguard the credibility of foreign groups receiving funding in their own societies, as providing such funding through an NGO would make it more difficult for their opponents to paint them as puppets of the US government. This was an important operational consideration, if NED actions were to help democratic groups overseas rather than hinder them.

The foundation of the National Endowment for Democracy   141

In order to build and preserve this credibility the National Endowment for Democracy and its core institutes were established by the democracy promoters themselves rather than being created by act of Congress, as had been originally planned, with legislation only being required to provide funding for the NED.[53] Both the National Republican Institute (NRI) and the National Democratic Institute (NDI) were set up in April 1983,[54] while the Centre for International Private Enterprise (CIPE) was set up in June.[55] The AFL-CIO's Free Trade Union Institute (FTUI) pre-existed the NED, having been set up during World War Two to channel funding to European trade unionists, first from the AFL-CIO and then from the CIA in the early years of the Cold War.[56] The FTUI was resurrected in 1978 but had become largely dormant due to lack of funding.[57] Thus, the NED and all four of its constituent foundations had been set up before its Congressional funding was finally legislated at the end of 1983. The creation of the Endowment through private action rather than state legislation enhanced its credibility as an independent civil society organisation, not a component of the state apparatus.

Finally, the report argued that the status of the NED as a non-governmental foundation would also solve the bureaucratic problems and blockages that could arise during an effort to overtly fund democratic groups abroad through the state apparatus, such as the lack of legal authorisation for national security agencies to implement such programmes. These problems had already been clearly demonstrated by the bureaucratic considerations the administration had had to grapple with merely to design Project Democracy. The operational problem was that 'direct *government* grantees would probably be precluded by State, USIA or AID enabling legislation from engaging in many of the political exchange, training and democratic institution-building programmes called for by the charter of the National Endowment for Democracy ...'[58] The study group solved this problem by simply recommending that all funds appropriated for the Endowment and disbursed by it to other US groups be exempt from any legislative restrictions on the State Department, USIA or AID which would impair the ability of the Endowment or its four core groups to achieve their objectives.[59] The hiving off of such programmes to a non-governmental instrumentality solved the bureaucratic problems which had bedevilled attempts to institute new overt state–private network relationships which had occurred in the aftermath of the 1967 scandal, during the attempt to create an Institute for Human Rights under the Carter administration, and during the Reagan administration's more recent attempts to design an effective operating framework for Project Democracy.

Unsolved problems

The report seemed to put forward a plausible case for Congressional approval of the NED; however, it did gloss over two serious weaknesses inherent in the new structure. First, as noted by Conry, the Endowment's credibility overseas as an NGO pursuing a broader mission than the achievement of current US policy

142   *The foundation of the National Endowment for Democracy*

goals was built on the argument that government money that first passed openly through the NED and then either directly to foreign groups or indirectly, to one of the Endowment's four core groups and then to a foreign group, would cease to be government money on this journey.[60] One of the key functions of the National Endowment for Democracy itself was to serve as a 'pass-through', which put another structure between the government and the groups which received funding. However, the fact that NED's funding still ultimately originated from the US government left it vulnerable to attacks on its credibility.

The second weakness related to the NED's domestic credibility with Congress. The problem was that the report did not set out a clear case for the creation of two partisan party institutes, preferring to omit debate over whether one bipartisan or two party foundations would be more credible and effective at promoting democracy overseas. The report attempted to head off this question, which had created division within the democracy promotion community, by stating that:

> This proposal for creating two political foundations under the National Endowment for Democracy umbrella, therefore, rejects the question – 'Why have a Democratic and a Republican foundation?' – in favour of another query: 'Why were they not created long ago, considering their utility in our own political system?'[61]

The recommendation to create two partisan party foundations could have seemed out of place in a report that consistently appealed to bipartisanship in order to create a Congressional consensus in favour of the Endowment. This was clearly the intent of the report's title and sub-heading 'The Commitment to Democracy: A Bipartisan Approach'. The final section of the report is titled 'Why Now? Toward a New Bipartisanship'.[62]

The report made its case for Congressional support for democracy promotion by asking the legislature to support an organisation rather than a list of programmes; one which would be independent of the government and so able to pursue the goal of promoting democracy overtly in a way which was credible, effective and bipartisan. However, the study group did not fully resolve the credibility problem posed by government funding of the Endowment, and did not adequately consider the problems that the NED's fragmented organisational structure might raise. Its approach to convincing Congress to fund the programme largely turned on presenting the organisational structure it had agreed upon as the natural fulfilment of the historic US aspiration to promote democracy overseas so as to de-emphasise more detailed objections.

The Congressional debate over the National Endowment for Democracy

The funding legislation for the National Endowment for Democracy was forwarded to Congress in mid-1983 as part of a larger bill which also contained

The foundation of the National Endowment for Democracy 143

appropriations for US overseas broadcasting, to provide more funding to the Asia Foundation, an ex-CIA proprietary which dispensed grants to private groups in its region of concern, and to pay the general running expenses of the foreign service.[63] The section of the legislation concerned with the NED proposed a lump sum to be delivered to the Endowment. Funding was already allocated to the four core institutes in the bill: as noted above, $13.8 million was earmarked for the FTUI, the AFL-CIO's democracy institute; $5 million each for the National Republican Institute (NRI) and the National Democratic Institute (NDI), the party foundations; and $2.5 million for the Center for International Private Enterprise (CIPE), the US Chamber of Commerce's democracy institute.[64] The approach deployed by the democracy promoters was largely successful in shaping the Congressional debates over whether to approve funding for the National Endowment for Democracy. However, the organisational structure of the Endowment provoked Congressional debate that altered the balance of power within the democracy promotion coalition when the NED became active.

The strategic fuzziness that characterised the Interim Report was an asset in convincing Congressmen to support the idea of an NGO to promote democracy. While Congressional supporters of the NED such as Dante Fascell and Congressmen Barnes and Lagomarsino referred to the Endowment as a modification of Project Democracy, the majority of Congressmen possessed almost no information on the concrete programmes it would run. According to various Congressmen involved in the debate on the National Endowment for Democracy in the House of Representative in June 1983, the targets of the NED were, variously, 'authoritarian governments', 'totalitarianism', 'Marxism' and 'international communism', and various examples of the utility of private groups in promoting democracy were advanced in regard to El Salvador and Poland.[65] Without programme data legislators could not be sure of this and were merely making assumptions.

This vagueness served a positive function, as without detailed information regarding what the NED would do, there was little for strategic critics to challenge. Concrete issues such as the strategic framework and the programmes the organisation would implement were subsumed under the concept of democracy promotion. Clement Zablocki, the Chairman of the House Foreign Affairs Committee, argued that if Congressmen supported an amendment to the bill tabled by a critic of the Endowment, 'they will be supporting totalitarian, undemocratic, nondemocratic countries.'[66] This vague terminology, which could have included the USSR and Chile, framed the debate as a simple question of whether Congressmen were in favour of or opposed to the promotion of democracy. Thus, democratic ideology minimised discussions over strategy and provided a focal point for the generation of consensus in support of the Endowment.

Although the abstract ideological concept of democracy promotion was successful in securing Congressional consensus on the basic idea of a foundation to spread democracy, it failed to silence debate over the NED's organisational structure. A small number of Congressmen such as Jack Kemp, a conservative

144 *The foundation of the National Endowment for Democracy*

Republican, had little faith in the NED's ability to promote democracy in the interests of the US and argued that:

> USIA is the natural existing organisation, fully staffed and qualified, to manage Project Democracy ... the committee bill would remove Project Democracy form [*sic*] USIA control. ... I do not think that the creation of an autonomous bureaucracy serves the purposes of the project.[67]

However, this was a minority objection. For other critics, the NED's key weak point was its funding by the US government, which called its independence and credibility into question. It was this issue of government funding for US democratic civil society groups, and the state control and direction of these groups that such funding could imply, which had made the continuation of covertly-funded state–private network operations unacceptable in 1967.

Similar objections were now made by Republican Congressman Hank Brown, who argued that while he supported private attempts to promote democracy overseas with private money, 'there is a real problem on making [democratic civil society groups] dependent upon ... and ... answerable to the Government'.[68] In Brown's judgement the government funding of private groups, especially the political parties, posed 'a real danger to the whole concept of democracy itself'.[69] As well as the threat to democratic institutions, there was also the danger that government funding would 'destroy [the groups'] effectiveness'[70] at promoting democracy overseas. This point was enlarged upon by another opponent of the Endowment, who argued that such government-funded institutes linked to the parties, AFL-CIO and Chamber of Commerce 'will be viewed ... as an extension ... of the Federal Government.'[71] Despite the study group's attempt to create a new overt approach to overseas political operations that was more credible than previous covert approaches, the issue of government funding remained the weak point of its design and could not be disposed of unless the democracy promoters were willing to rely completely on private donations; an approach which they had seen as unworkable since the 1970s. These objections to the NED's general organisational principle were supplemented with more specific criticisms of the political parties, which were seen as lacking in foreign policy expertise and liable to take partisan positions in overseas elections.[72] The structure chosen by the study group over George Agree's objections meant that this was theoretically possible, whereas choosing to found a bipartisan party institute would have avoided this difficulty.

These criticisms led Brown to propose amendments that would excise the funding for the Endowment from the legislative package the Reagan administration had forwarded to Congress for approval. His first amendment called for all provision for the NED to be removed from the bill. This amendment was defeated due to legislators' acceptance of the goal of promoting democracy overseas.[73] However, support for the Endowment's removal had been broadly bipartisan, and it was defeated by only 21 votes.[74] Brown then introduced two further amendments; one which would remove the earmarking of funds for the new

The foundation of the National Endowment for Democracy   145

Republican and Democratic Party institutes, and one which would remove earmarking for the business and labour foundations. The amendment to terminate the earmarking for CIPE and FTUI failed due to the prestige the AFL-CIO enjoyed on the Hill for effective conduct of foreign political operations: one Congressman argued that 'In the international arena, organized labor has been an effective ally of everything that we are trying to do to protect the security of this country and our allies.'[75] However, the amendment to eliminate the earmarking for the party institutes, NDI and NRI, was passed rapidly.[76] Brown's amendment to de-fund the parties was supported by liberals, moderates and conservatives, rather than being supported by one political current only.[77] Although this funding was subsequently restored by the Senate, it was deleted again by the House just before the legislation funding the NED was signed into law.[78] While this change did not mean that the party foundations would be prohibited from receiving any of NED's funding, it did mean that they would have to compete for it on the same basis as other US private groups outside the NED coalition by forwarding individual project proposals to the Endowment's Board for evaluation, rather than having a lump sum which they could use to plan and fund their operations.

The NED's opponents had aimed at eradicating the Endowment as a whole, not merely its funding for the party institutes. However, the parties proved to be the soft underbelly of the Endowment due to Congressional concerns about whether they would institute partisan programmes abroad. George Agree had been correct in arguing that a bipartisan party institute would be more acceptable to Congress. This decision cut the financial ground out from underneath the parties and strengthened the position of the AFL-CIO within the democracy promotion apparatus as the group with the largest amount of funding.

Conclusion

In broad perspective, the Democracy Program study group's negotiations with the Reagan administration and Congress had been successful. The democracy promoters had persuaded both to back the creation of an overt democracy promotion organisation, overcoming the obstacles that had blocked Project Democracy. The concept of democracy promotion itself helped to produce the necessary consensus between the non-state groups, the administration and Congress by subsuming the debate over how far to pursue democracy promotion within the USSR and in Third World dictatorships allied to the US, and replacing these with a global campaign to promote democracy with no clear strategic focus, while the fact that the study group had not generated specific programmes served to minimise areas of specific disagreement. This fuzziness over targeting allowed the democracy promoters to secure administration backing for their chosen organisation as a pragmatic alternative to Project Democracy and also de-emphasised the strategic debate in Congress.

More broadly, the creation of the NED allowed the reconstitution of the bipartisan consensus necessary to underpin US intervention in foreign political structures that had been missing since Vietnam and the collapse of the state–private

146 *The foundation of the National Endowment for Democracy*

network in 1967, and provided a vehicle for it to be implemented through. Although the new National Endowment for Democracy shared some features with the previous state–private network, in that both structures were backed by government funding and aimed at influencing non-state groups overseas in the US interest, the creation of the Endowment did not amount to a resurrection of previous CIA capabilities disguised by more appealing rhetoric. Neither did it represent the approval of a camouflaged Project Democracy. While the Endowment's operating methods were close to the CIA's state–private network in form, its goal of assisting in the creation of democratic systems overseas went far beyond the propaganda initiatives prosecuted before 1967 and which made up an integral part of Project Democracy. The advent of democracy promotion thus represented the harnessing of state–private network operating methods to the goal of promoting political reform overseas.

The Endowment also differed from the previous state–private network in its overt nature. The shift from a covert to an overt state–private relationship fundamentally changed the dynamic for the management of political operations overseas in two key ways. First, the decision to create a Congressionally-funded foundation brought the legislature into a new, more open process for the management of political action operations overseas and provided it with a share of the leverage over the funding of operations which had been exercised only by the state under the previous model of covert funding channelled through the CIA. Congress had already shown it could wield this power by deleting funds for the party institutes, and could use it in the future to police NED operations. Second, whereas in the pre-1967 network the national security bureaucracy had exercised the supervision necessary to harness private efforts into a coherent campaign in support of national security interests, political operations were now to be overseen by a semi-private body, the NED itself, which had extremely weak powers to carry out such a coordinating function. This weak command and control risked producing a disjointed campaign in which the core groups pursued their own interests in a way that did not accord with either US national security objectives, or the promotion of democracy. Thus, fundamental questions about the future shape of democracy promotion were still unanswered, providing opportunities for the state, Congress and the core groups to define its parameters through their actions as the Endowment began its operations.

Notes

1 Letter, L.E. Stanfield to George Agree, 'Grant No. OTR-0098-G-SS-3029–00', 1 December 1982, attached to APF, Minutes of 1982 Fourth Meeting Board of Directors American Political Foundation, 16 December 1982, Folder 3: APF Minutes, Box 1, George E. Agree Papers, LOC.
2 The Democracy Program, 'The Commitment to Democracy: A Bipartisan Approach', Appendix C: Democracy Program Staff and Consultants, 18 April 1983, *National Endowment for Democracy: Key NED Documents*, accessed 10 March 2010, http://ned.org/docs/democracyProgram.pdf.
3 Memo, Walter Raymond to William Clark, 21 January 1983, letter, Michael A. Samuels, to Dr Scott Thompson, 27 January 1983, and attached documents, 'The Role

The foundation of the National Endowment for Democracy   147

of American Business in Public Diplomacy', 'Support for Free Enterprise Development' and 'Project Democracy: An Inter-Agency Programme to foster the Growth of Democracy Worldwide: Statement of Purpose', Folder 1/83–6/83, Box OA91162, Walter Raymond Files, RL.

4 Michael A. Samuels, 'Project Proposal: A Comprehensive Policy Response to Expanding U.S. Interests in the Third World', 1980, 1, attached to Letter, George Agree to Mr Michael A. Samuels, 15 February 1980, Folder 1: APF Correspondence, Box 1, George E. Agree Papers, LOC, 2–3.

5 The Democracy Program, Appendix IV, 50.

6 Government Accountability Office, 'Events leading to the establishment of the National Endowment for Democracy', GAO/NSIAD-84–121, 6 July 1984, *US Government Accountability Office Electronic Records Archive*, accessed 19 December 2014. http://archive.gao.gov/d6t1/124606.pdf, 14.

7 Letter, L.E. Stanfield to George Agree.

8 Government Accountability Office, 12.

9 Ibid., 11–12.

10 The Democracy Program, 'The Commitment to Democracy: A Bipartisan Approach', Appendix C.

11 Ibid.

12 Government Accountability Office, 8. My italics.

13 Government Accountability Office, 13.

14 Memo, George Agree to William E. Brock, Charles T. Manatt, 22 February 1983, Folder 1: APF Correspondence, Box 1, George E. Agree Papers, LOC.

15 Memo, George Agree to the Board of Directors of the American Political Foundation, 30 August 1983, Folder 1: APF Correspondence, Box 1, George E. Agree Papers, LOC.

16 Ibid., 3.

17 Memo, George Agree, to William E. Brock, Charles T. Manatt.

18 Ibid., 3.

19 Letter, George Agree to William Brock, 10 March 1983, Folder 1: APF Correspondence, Box 1, George E. Agree Papers, LOC.

20 Memo, George Agree to William E. Brock, Charles T. Manatt.

21 Memo, George Agree to the Board of Directors, 3.

22 Ibid., 4.

23 Anonymous, 'A Critique of the proposal to give political parties Federal funds to promote democracy overseas', July 1983, Folder 6: Reports and Proposals, Box 1, George E. Agree Papers LOC, 1–2 and 4–5.

24 See section on 'The West German Analogy', 7, in Ibid.

25 Ibid., 2.

26 Ibid., 5.

27 Letter, William Clark to William Brock, 14 March 1983, The Democracy Program, Appendix D, 70.

28 'Project Democracy', *Washington Times*, 5 July 1983, Folder: Press, Box 1, George E. Agree Papers, LOC.

29 The Democracy Program, 'The Commitment to Democracy: A Bipartisan Approach', 14.

30 Ibid., 48.

31 Ibid., 49.

32 Ibid.

33 Ibid., 50.

34 Anonymous, Congressional Record – House, 9 June 1983, Folder: National Endowment for Democracy, Box 2, George E. Agree Papers, LOC, H3801.

35 Congressional Record – House, 9 June 1983, H3812.

36 Ibid., 2.

148 *The foundation of the National Endowment for Democracy*

37 Cable, George P. Shultz to all American Republic diplomatic posts, January 1984, Folder 9, Box OA91698, Walter Raymond Files, RL, 1.
38 Ibid., 1.
39 International Political Committee, 'Agenda and Summary of the International Political Committee (IPC) Meeting', 30 March 1983, DDRS, accessed 11 December 2006.
40 Cable, George P. Shultz to all American Republic diplomatic posts, 2.
41 Clifford P. Hackett, 'Endowing Democracy: An idea that came & went', *Commonweal*, 7 October 1983, attached to letter, Gary Hart to George Agree, 24 October 1983, Folder 1: APF Correspondence, Box 1, George E. Agree Papers, LOC, 522.
42 George Lardner, Jr, 'In Bid to Endow Democracy, Rep. Fascell Gathers Many Hats', *Washington Post*, 3 June 1983, Folder: Press, 1979–1984, Box 1, George E. Agree Papers, LOC.
43 The Democracy Program, 'The Commitment to Democracy', 5.
44 Ibid., 6.
45 Government Accountability Office, Appendix IV, 50.
46 Congressional Record – House, 9 June 1983, H3811.
47 The Democracy Program, 'The Commitment to Democracy', 14.
48 Hugh Wilford, *The Mighty Wurlitzer: How the CIA Played America* (Cambridge, Massachusetts and London, England: Harvard University Press, 2008), 86, 92–93, 125–126, 236.
49 The Democracy Program, 27–32.
50 Ibid., 1, 20–21.
51 Ibid., 33–34.
52 Ibid., 35–36.
53 Government Accountability Office, 9–10.
54 Ibid., 21.
55 Ibid., 20.
56 Ted Morgan, *A Covert Life: Jay Lovestone; Communist, Anti-communist, and Spymaster* (New York: Random House, 1999), 144, 197–202 and 213–225.
57 Government Accountability Office, 20.
58 The Democracy Program, 36.
59 Ibid., 20.
60 Barbara Conry, 'Cato Foreign Policy Briefing No. 27: Loose Cannon: The National Endowment for Democracy', 8 November 1993, *The Cato Institute*, accessed 10 October 2014, www.cato.org/pubs/fpbriefs/fpb-027.html.
61 Government Accountability Office, 40.
62 Democracy Program, 'The Commitment to Democracy: A Bipartisan Approach', 44.
63 *An Act To authorize appropriations for fiscal years 1984 and 1985 for the Department of State, the United States Information Agency, the Board for International Broadcasting, the Inter-American Foundation, and the Asia Foundation, to establish the National Endowment for Democracy, and for other purposes*, Public Law 98–164. 98th Congress, 22 November 1983, accessed 23 December 2014, www.gpo.gov/fdsys/pkg/STATUTE-97/pdf/STATUTE-97-Pg1017.pdf.
64 Congressional Record – House, 9 June 1983, H3812.
65 In order, from Congressional Record – House: Gilman, H3812; Zablocki, H3815; Hyde, H3820; Edwards, H3820; Lagomarsino, H3820; Burton, H3819.
66 Congressional Record – House, H3815.
67 Ibid., H3804.
68 Ibid., H3812.
69 Ibid., H3812.
70 Congressional Record – House, H3812.
71 Ibid., H3818.
72 Ibid., H3816.

73 Hackett, 'Endowing Democracy', 522.
74 Ibid.
75 Congressional Record – House, 9 June 1983, H3820.
76 Ibid., H3818.
77 Hackett, 'Endowing Democracy', 522–523.
78 George Lardner Jr, 'House Opposes Funding; Democracy Promotion Is Hit', *Washington Post*, 1 November 1983, Nexis UK, www.lexisnexis.com/uk/nexis.

6 Promoting democracy

The foundation of the NED in 1983 had created an organisation to conduct democracy promotion initiatives, but had not generated a strategic framework for them to be prosecuted within. This left unresolved the question of whether the targeting of these operations would be most influenced by the imperative of promoting democracy, national security objectives, or the partisan interests of the core groups within the Endowment. It also left open the larger question of whether democracy promotion operations would foster popular empowerment and development, or whether democratic change would be limited by the need to safeguard US interests in societies in which the Endowment chose to intervene. The record of the Endowment's initial operations from 1984 to 1986 indicates that while democratic ideology had an impact on the NED in terms of legitimating, limiting, and shaping its tactics, and while the core groups sometimes supported foreign civil society organisations based on partisan reasoning or ideological affinity,[1] the key driver behind its operations was national security.

The concept of democracy promotion had allowed the core groups, the administration and Congress to converge over the creation of an overt organisational structure for democracy promotion operations. The outcome was a new structure for the management of overt state–private operations in which Congress played a role, as the provider of funding, which it had not played in the pre-1967 covert organisational structure. This role gave Congress leverage which it could use to enforce its understanding of democracy promotion as the support of democratic forces in dictatorships through democratic methods. Elements of the NED coalition who had paid lip-service to democracy promotion to gain funding to pursue their own projects soon found that operations which were rooted in national security but lacked a clear democracy promotion rationale could result in Congressional sanctions. These sanctions constrained the NED within the pro-democratic framework that had legitimised its creation, as they laid down a marker that legitimising operations through an abstract democratic ideology was insufficient; such operations should genuinely aim at strengthening democratic forces through democratic methods.

However, Congressional sanctions did not lead to a policy of pursuing operations based solely on the imperative of promoting democracy overseas. Instead, the list of countries where the NED carried out politically significant interventions tallies with the national security concerns of the Reagan administration and points to a clear subordination of democracy promotion operations to US security interests. This subordination was partly due to the fact that, organisationally, the Endowment relied on support from the US state to secure funding from Congress and to conduct large-scale operations aimed at altering political structures. It was eased and rationalised by the fact that, rather than seeing democracy promotion and US national security as contradictory the Endowment's leadership conflated the universal ideology of democracy promotion with the particular national security interests of the United States and so tended to pursue their operations within the overall framework of national security priorities which had been set by the state.

The outcome of the double limitation of the Endowment's freedom of operation by Congress and the administration, and the ideological conflation of democracy and national security, was the pursuit of political operations overseas through democratic methods on a tactical basis in situations where the promotion of democracy was believed to enhance US national security. The effort to create democratic regimes in friendly dictatorships was driven by the perception that such regimes would be less vulnerable to anti-US revolutions and could provide the stability which US interests required. Similarly, the effort to build democratic movements in enemy dictatorships was driven by the perception that transitions to democracy would remove the threat to the US that such regimes posed. Thus, the extension of democracy and the interests of the United States were seen to be intertwined.

This conflation of the interests of the United States as a nation-state with those of democracy as a political philosophy and system also had an effect on the selection of foreign groups for NED support. In friendly dictatorships the overall goal of securing stability, coupled with the perception of the Endowment's leadership that groups focussed on radical restructuring of their societies were undemocratic and thus undeserving of support, meant that the groups supported were elite-led forces friendly to the United States. The outcome of the NED's actions was a form of democracy managed by pro-US elites who enacted surface reforms to dampen down popular unrest but did not embark on the fundamental restructuring of their societies required to resolve the injustices which had given rise to political instability in the first place. In enemy dictatorships such as Soviet bloc states, the Endowment supported groups who advocated the transformation of their societies in ways that followed Western political and economic models and meshed with US interests rather than challenging them. Democracy promotion was ultimately a tactic that allowed the United States to mould pro-US successor elites in both friendly and enemy states to preserve or extend its strategic position. In no case were these national security goals subordinated to the goal of promoting democratic revolutions, especially where change might damage US interests.

152 *Promoting democracy*

Democracy promotion and the national security bureaucracy

Although the administration had supported the creation of the NED in 1983 as the best possible organisation for implementing a campaign for democracy at that time, the Endowment's relationship with the national security bureaucracy was ill-defined. The question of control surfaced soon after the creation of the NED, in a struggle over the terms of the grant agreement that the Endowment needed to sign with the USIA to access the $18 million which Congress had appropriated for it. The grant agreement produced by USIA clearly aimed at tightening the agency's control over the NED. In January 1984, as grant negotiations between the Endowment and USIA were breaking down, NED's lawyers charged that the Agency's draft grant agreement 'contains at least 19 explicit instances of attempts to change the NED's independent, private-sector status through unauthorized governmental control'.[2] Among these 19 objectionable proposals were stipulations that the NED be subject to USIA's normal conditions for other private sector grantees, that the Agency have powers to oversee and inspect the Endowment, that the agreement of a USIA officer be required for funding transfers to other groups, and that USIA have the right to terminate any grants which it believed were not in the interests of the US government.[3]

These provisions were clearly aimed at circumscribing the independence of the Endowment. As the NED was effectively a pass-through taking money from USIA and then handing the bulk of it to four non-governmental organisations, who would then channel funding to other groups, who could then channel it to other groups if they wished, it was possible that the money would be diverted to groups which did not serve the interests of the United States as USIA saw them; these provisions for inspection and grant termination could be used to minimise such problems. The Endowment and its supporters within the administration recognised the agenda behind this manoeuvre, with the new organisation's Acting President, Allen Weinstein, noting that '[s]imply put, the issue is one of control'.[4] NSC Director of International Communications and member of the Project Democracy Working Group Walter Raymond echoed this analysis.[5] USIA's demands effectively usurped the freedom of the NED board to manage the Endowment, which posed a threat to the board's conception of how democracy promotion should work. This threatened to undo the work the Endowment's leaders had carried out to design a structure that could avoid such governmental management during the Democracy Program study, to maintain autonomy and to safeguard the credibility of democracy promotion operations by de-linking them from the state.

The Endowment and those administration officials who held to a wider vision of the burgeoning campaign for democracy moved swiftly to advance arguments for a more autonomous model of democracy promotion. More idealistic democracy promoters such as William Brock argued that too close a degree of government control would be damaging to both the US government and the Endowment, and recalled that

Promoting democracy 153

the National Endowment Board and its charter were structured to be independent of any government agency for the simple and obvious reason that those of us involved in its genesis felt an urgent need to insulate any Administration from its activities, and vice versa, in order that the larger goal of building democratic institutions could proceed as quickly and effectively as possible.[6]

The long-range effort to build democratic structures abroad would be more effective if it were de-linked from the immediate national security concerns and diplomatic considerations of the US government, which sometimes needed to co-operate with dictators or at least avoid offending them for pragmatic reasons.

This sophisticated argument was unlikely to impress national security officials working on a shorter time-scale. Instead, Weinstein chose to focus on an immediate national security concern, the upcoming Presidential elections in El Salvador, to break funding loose:

[t]ime is running out. Without a grant agreement in hand within the next few days, for example, it will be impossible for the Endowment and the four Institutes to send representatives to El Salvador ... to consider President Magana's request that we take a leading role in the observer process during the elections.[7]

According to the Acting President preparations for the mission would have to be at least put on hold, as the Board had ordered him to close down the Endowment within a few days if no satisfactory grant agreement were reached.[8] This programme was of key importance to all of the actors within the administration, as Reaganites, State Department pragmatists, more moderate NSC officials and the NED itself supported democratic reform in El Salvador. The certification of the upcoming elections as free and fair would remove an obstacle to moving military aid through a Congress that was concerned about the Human Rights situation in El Salvador. Furthermore, this certification would be far more credible if it were made by private observers rather than administration officials. This argument was successful in motivating sympathetic NSC officials to support the Endowment against USIA, and in resolving the larger question of relations between the Endowment and the administration. The NSC informed USIA that, 'This is a Presidential program which we must get implemented as soon as possible. We need it not only in Central America but elsewhere.' The organisation also stated that '[We] do not want the negotiations to break down over the question of control; that should not be the issue.'[9]

The course of this debate has several implications for understanding the NED's relationship with the Reagan administration and its national security objectives. First, although sections of the administration wished to secure a level of control over the Endowment that went beyond the 'light' control proposed by the State Department in April 1982, they were unable to do so. Second, Reaganite fears that the NED would pursue an ideological project that undermined

154 *Promoting democracy*

national security interests were clearly exaggerated. While idealistic democracy promoters such as Brock had advanced arguments for NED autonomy based on the organisation's long range mission, it was the arguments based on a short-term national security interest – El Salvador – which galvanised the Endowment's supporters within the administration. The fact that the NED and national security officials were able to agree over this immediate priority showed the importance of US national security considerations as a key driver of Endowment strategy.

There were both practical and ideological reasons for this. The Endowment's status as a government–backed organisation meant that it would be extremely difficult for it to take actions which contradicted the policies of those who made funding requests to Congress on its behalf. In addition, the fact that the NED was already working on a programme connected to one of the key national security difficulties faced by the administration showed that the Endowment's leaders identified democracy promotion and national security rather than seeing a conflict between them. Idealists who could have been expected to diverge further from US national security policy such as George Agree were no longer connected with the project at this point, having given way to former US government personnel such as NED treasurer John Richardson, a former President of Radio Free Europe and Nixon administration State Department Assistant Secretary for Educational and Cultural Affairs; or National Republican Institute Chairman Keith Schuette, a former aide to Alexander Haig. Thus, the chances of the Endowment launching a rogue action that would undermine national security policy to promote democracy were low. This is clearly the strategic calculation which the NSC had based its decision to support NED autonomy on. Government influence over the Endowment could be wielded, but it would be a subtle matter of assuring that leadership positions were held by those who could be trusted, rather than corralling the Endowment into a legal framework which would hamper its operational effectiveness on the ground by making it appear to be too close to the US government.

This did not mean that no further scope for conflict between the imperatives of democracy promotion and national security that could lead to disagreements between the Reagan administration and non-state democracy promoters existed. Rather, any conflicts which arose between these two groups would turn on discussion of whether promoting democracy in a particular case would serve to enhance US national security aims or detract from them, not on whether to prioritise one over the other. However, the question of whether covert or undemocratic methods were a permissible element of democracy promotion was still to be resolved.

National security versus democracy: the Endowment's early funding initiatives in Panama, the UK and France

Congress' power to approve or deny funding appropriations for the National Endowment for Democracy provided it with a degree of leverage over the new overt political operations that it had not possessed over the previous covert state–private network. The Endowment quickly discovered that Congress was prepared to use this power to ensure that it did not merely deploy democracy promotion as a legitimating concept for operations rooted in national security priorities with little democratic content. The limits of the NED's remit to act in support of national security objectives when these clashed with democracy promotion ideologically were illustrated by Congressional reaction to the Endowment's early operations in Panama, the UK and France. These operations were all funded by FTUI, the AFL-CIO's democracy promotion foundation, and in each case they appeared to be driven by national security concerns and anti-communism rather than the NED's mission to promote democracy.

The FTUI's early anti-communist operations

The first of these problematic cases involved FTUI funding in Panama, which was clearly motivated more by union and US interests than democracy promotion. In 1984 FTUI passed $20,000 of its Endowment funding to a Panamanian union which then used it to hold a rally in support of Nicolàs Ardito Barletta, one of the candidates in the Presidential election;[10] Panama's first since Omar Torrijos had seized power in 1968. Barletta was the favoured candidate of Colonel Noriega, Commander of the Panamanian National Guard and the country's de facto military dictator, who believed that Barletta would be a pliable front man for his continued rule behind the scenes. Barletta's main opponent in the elections was Arnulfo Arias, a charismatic conservative nationalist and populist who had been President on three previous occasions and had been overthrown by the army each time.[11]

There was a clear US national interest in an election victory by Barletta, a candidate who was seen as 'friendly to Washington'[12], as the CIA predicted that 'a Barletta victory would be characterized by continuing strong relations with the United States [and] support for US policy in Central America and the Caribbean ...'[13] US bases in the Canal Zone played a role in supporting US policy in El Salvador and in channelling aid and intelligence to the Contras,[14] although these actions were illegal under the terms of the Carter–Torrijos canal treaty.[15] This co-operation could be expected to continue under a President linked to Noriega, while Arias had built his political career on opposition to the US role in Panama[16] and was likely to take a different attitude. The AFL-CIO also strongly supported the Contras, funding speaking tours by Contra leaders to the US to drum up support for Contra aid.[17] Thus, the AFL-CIO's conception of US national interests and its ideological anti-communism led to support for Barletta, rather than a strictly pro-democratic policy. The National Guard made Barletta's victory certain by halting the counting of votes and then stuffing ballot boxes. Barletta was nicknamed 'Fraudito' by the opposition and removed from office by Noriega after announcing the formation of an enquiry into the murder of one of the Colonel's political opponents by National Guard officers in September 1985. He was replaced by a more pliable politician.[18] Although the Reagan

156 *Promoting democracy*

administration knew of this fraud almost immediately, it became publicly known in the US only two years later, and the administration made no protests at the time.[19]

The FTUI's funding operation in Britain was also based on anti-communism. Soon after the NED began to receive its grant money from USIA in March 1984, FTUI made a grant of $49,000 to the Labour Committee for Transatlantic Understanding in Britain, which was used to send a delegation to a NATO defence seminar in Brussels. The Committee was a section of the British Atlantic Committee, an organisation more concerned with lobbying for NATO positions in Europe than promoting the growth of democratic processes. The Committee had long-standing connections with both the US government and the AFL-CIO, having been founded in 1976 by Joseph Godson, a former US labour attaché to Britain with close connections to the AFL-CIO[20] and a senior consultant on the Democracy Program study that had recommended the creation of the NED.[21] The committee also had strong links to the AFL-CIO, as AFL-CIO President Lane Kirkland was one of its vice-presidents.[22] It had been funded secretly by NATO until 1980, when the British government admitted the source of the funding.[23] Godson's connections to both the AFL-CIO and the Democracy Program make it unlikely that he was unaware of the committee's new source of funding.

This programme was undoubtedly directed at the same ends as parallel but unconnected US government efforts, which included exchanges organised by the USIA and the State Department; to propagandise the British centre-left in favour of US nuclear policy in Western Europe, especially in the wake of the Labour Party's 1983 anti-nuclear manifesto commitments.[24] The Labour Committee for Transatlantic Understanding was mentioned in the Project Democracy programme list, under the heading 'Foreign and Defence Information', as one of a number of AFL-CIO-connected committees important in countries 'whose democratic labour movements and parties ... have drifted apart from the United States on security issues.'[25] This, coupled with the Committee's connections to the Labour Party's right-wing,[26] makes it likely that the aim of the programme was to generate Labour Party support for US strategic initiatives in Western Europe such as INF deployment. Although this programme was in line with US national security interests, it could not be justified as a contribution to the cause of democracy promotion.

FTUI's two grants in France followed a similar pattern of focussing on anti-communism rather than the promotion of democracy. These were on a much larger scale than the funding in Britain; taken together, they involved grants of more than $1 million over 1984–85. The first set of grants, totalling $830,000, went to the AFL-CIO's long-standing French ally, Force Ouvrière,[27] an anti-communist union which the AFL had helped to create and finance at the beginning of the Cold War. The fact that the purpose of the funding was uncertain made the operation seems even more questionable. Irving Brown, the AFL-CIO's foreign policy chief, was quoted in a French newspaper as saying that Force Ouvrière did not need the money for its domestic operations in France;

rather, 'The funds that we send are used outside the regular trade union work. Bergeron (FO leader) explained to me that it was used to help the refugees, the Polish trade unionists and the immigrants.'[28] However, in the same article Brown stated that Force Ouvière had to be supported '[b]ecause the apparatus of the CGT [a left-wing French trade union confederation] is still here and it can destroy France ...'[29] The funding was probably used to assist anti-communist exiles, but the secrecy surrounding it, coupled with Brown's comments, put the NED in the position of being seen to interfere in the domestic politics of an already-democratic US ally.

The destination of the second set of grants was even more problematic. Instead of being used to support a democratic organisation, this money went to a group that had questionable democratic credentials. The organisation, which received $575,000, was the Inter-University Union (UNI),[30] a small anti-communist sect of French university professors and students. The UNI had run propaganda campaigns highlighting Soviet forced labour and Human Rights violations and also published a magazine, *Solidarite Atlantique*, devoted to exposing Soviet disinformation and Human Rights abuses;[31] actions clearly in line with the US interest in waging anti-communist propaganda in Western Europe to increase support for its own political and military policies. Irving Brown was a keen supporter of the group; referring to an anti-Gorbachev rally the organisation had staged in Paris while the Soviet leader was visiting, he commented, 'I think that what UNI did in Paris against Gorbachev and the Gulag was a positive thing; we have to help democratic forces that are fighting against them.'[32] In terms of simple anti-communism support for the UNI may have represented a worthwhile investment. However, the organisation also had an anti-democratic reputation within France; it had dubious links to the Service d'Action Civique, a Gaullist paramilitary group that had been dissolved in 1982 by order of the French Parliament after a number of its activists had been killed during factional struggles within the organisation, and its leaders also had ties to the fascist Front National.[33]

The rationale for the grants: democracy promotion as anti-communism

FTUI's hard-line anti-communist approach was enabled by the NED's new President, Carl Gershman, who had replaced Allen Weinstein. The exact reason for Weinstein's removal from his position at the NED in February 1984 is not clear; however, the Reagan administration's patience with him may have been at an end after the drawn-out controversy with USIA over the grant negotiations. In addition, according to Madison he had 'reportedly alienated some board members'.[34] Gershman joined the NED from a position in the Reagan administration's mission to the United Nations under Jeane Kirkpatrick, which had become 'a centre for lots of these ideas on the ideological confrontation with communist totalitarianism'.[35] The new President was a neoconservative who espoused a tough anti-communist worldview and had been critical of the Carter

158 *Promoting democracy*

administration, and the liberal elite, for their weakness and naivety in the face of the Soviet threat.[36]

Gershman also had strong connections to the US labour movement through his membership of a small US political party, the Social Democrats USA, which had provided officials and leaders to the AFL-CIO's Department of International Affairs,[37] and through his personal friendship with AFL-CIO President Lane Kirkland.[38] Moreover, Gershman owed his position as NED President to Kirkland. According to Madison, the deletion of the earmarking of funding for the political parties by Congress in 1983 gave Kirkland a strong hold over the organisation, as the AFL-CIO now had the lion's share of the funding, while NDI and NRI had nothing. Kirkland proposed to divert some of labour's funding to the party institutes if they would allow him the final choice of President. The man he chose was Carl Gershman. While Dante Fascell and the AFL-CIO denied that such a deal had ever taken place, others connected with the NED confirmed it.[39] Kirkland's role in lobbying for Gershman's appointment is also confirmed by his biographer, Arch Puddington.[40]

Once in power the new President agreed not only to allow FTUI to pursue the anti-communist funding initiatives described above; he also agreed to allow the foundation to keep these operations secret from Congress.[41] The rationale for this secrecy, as explained by FTUI's Director, Eugenia Kemble, in a memo to Gershman, was that

> The beneficiaries of these funds would be in danger or in trouble if the financing was made public ... because repressive governments or groups of communists could use this information against the individuals or the unions that we want to help. [42]

Kemble also argued that some of the organisations FTUI intended to dispense funding to had already been promised secrecy by the AFL-CIO, which could not now go back on this agreement.[43] France was on the list of 13 countries where grants were to be kept secret, along with Poland and various Latin American countries.[44]

At first glance the nature of these operations – their support of non-democratic forces, in some instances, their focus on waging anti-communist propaganda and their covert nature – would seem to indicate hidden micro-management of Endowment operations by the Reagan administration. Indeed, the funding dispensed to British and French groups would have fitted comfortably into Project Truth, the administration's anti-Soviet propaganda campaign aimed at Western Europe, or the Western European initiatives proposed for Project Democracy. However, the fact that the funding for Force Ouvière and the UNI had been proposed by the AFL-CIO for inclusion in Project Democracy in August 1982 indicate that these actions were taken on the initiative of the union itself.[45]

What these problematic operations reveal is not close administration control of the Endowment, but the operationalisation by the AFL-CIO of a concept of democracy promotion in which the promotion of democracy was identified in an abstract fashion with the union's conception of American interests, which in these cases were defined narrowly in terms of anti-communism. Rather than generating a new strategy which embraced the concept of democracy promotion put forward by the APF and the intellectuals associated with it or redefining its existing interests to conform to such a concept, the union seemed to see democracy promotion as a convenient ideal, and the Endowment as a convenient structure, for it to extract funding from Congress. This money came with fewer strings than its AID funding and could be used to pursue anti-communist covert operations, just as the union had done in partnership with the CIA in the 1950s and 1960s.

The AFL-CIO's failure to fold its own interests into a coherent programme to promote democracy was a result of the flawed process and dynamics of the Democracy Program study, during which the participants had not so much subsumed their existing interests and perspectives into an overarching concept of democracy promotion, as allied their political resources to create an instrument which would provide them with the funding they required to pursue these interests. Kemble's demand for secrecy, in particular, made a mockery of the idea of democracy promotion as a transparent alternative to the covert operations of the past and indicated that the AFL-CIO had not integrated the concept of democracy promotion into the conduct of its foreign operations.

Congressional reaction

The union soon discovered that the new, more open management of state–private operations, in which Congress played a key role, effectively ruled out the pursuit of such narrowly anti-communist actions. The legislature's role in appropriating funding for the NED provided it with influence that it had lacked under the previous Executive-managed covert framework, and when these operations became public the Congressional response was swift and punitive. Details of the Panama operation were the first to leak out when US ambassador to Panama, Everett Briggs, sent a cable to the State Department accusing the AFL-CIO of meddling in the 1984 election. 'The embassy,' he wrote, 'requests that this harebrained [sic] project be abandoned before it hits the fan.'[46] This cable was leaked to Congress, triggering a funding crisis for the Endowment.[47] On 31 May 1984, the House voted to remove all Congressional funding from the NED,[48] resulting in a fevered attempt by both the Endowment and the Reagan administration to lobby senators to block this change.[49] This effort included direct intervention from the President, who wrote to key senators that 'At a time when the opponents of democracy lavishly support their allies, we cannot abandon the field of political competition. The cause is too important. The stakes are too great.'[50]

The Senate restored the NED's funding; however, it was clear that a catastrophe had been narrowly averted. This danger was underlined by the exposure of the grants made to French organisations by the French daily *Liberation* in November 1985. Although the general problem was that Congress could not understand why the NED was promoting democracy in a country that was

160 *Promoting democracy*

already democratic,[51] it was the funding of the UNI, which was perceived as an extremist neo-fascist group, which particularly harmed the Endowment's credibility as a supporter of democracy. This event forced a reassessment of the secrecy policy by Gershman, who ruled that the practice of making secret payments had to be abandoned.[52] However, by this point the damage had been done, as Congress had already voted to reduce the AFL-CIO's disproportionate share of the NED's funding due to its 'uncertainty about Endowment operations'.[53] In late 1985, the Endowment limited the amount of funding any NED grantee could receive to 25 per cent of the total in response to Congressional action, ending the disproportionate influence the AFL-CIO had wielded within the organisation.[54] Congress also ruled that USIA had the right to audit the Endowment; that the NED should be subject to the Freedom of Information Act; and that copies of all funding proposals put before the Board should also be sent to the Deputy Secretary of State for Political Affairs.[55]

Congressional anger resulted from the fact that the operations in Panama, the UK and France strayed outside the consensus position that had allowed the NED to be created in 1983. This consensus position, which had allowed the administration, Congress and the core groups to converge, was that while democracy promotion would enhance the long-term national security of the US, it would do so through democratic methods aimed at building democratic movements and governments abroad. In contrast, the AFL-CIO's actions were based on the idea that democracy promotion was primarily a battle against Soviet communism and that programmes and funding initiatives could and should be prosecuted covertly. Congress had dismissed this framework for democracy promotion when it favoured the NED over Project Democracy. It was only by appealing to Congress using arguments based on democracy rather than anti-communism that the administration was able to avoid the complete de-funding of the Endowment. Even so, the most anti-communist component of the NED – the AFL-CIO – emerged from these controversies with its power reduced.

Congress' response to these operations laid down a clear marker that future operations would need to be pro-democratic not only in terms of rhetoric but also in terms of intent and form. The legislature had also proven that while it was unwilling to remove funding from the NED as a whole, it was willing to punish individual foundations that did not follow this line. In this way it set out clear limits to NED operations and showed that it had the power to enforce these limits. Thus, while the Reagan administration and elements within the Endowment such as the AFL-CIO prioritised national security over democracy, the influence of Congress reinforced the idea that democracy promotion should attempt to achieve national security objectives through democratic methods.

Operating within the consensus: the Caribbean, Central America and the Soviet bloc

While a strategy blending political operations framed as democracy promotion with national security considerations was ideologically unjustifiable in Western

Promoting democracy   161

Europe, key democracy promotion operations in Central America and the Caribbean, and those directed against the Soviet Empire, proved to be relatively uncontroversial. In both of these theatres, democracy promotion and national security were seen to be mutually reinforcing frameworks for policy rather than antagonistic ones. In addition, there was a degree of consensus between the administration, Congress and the NED over strategy and tactics that translated into a lack of friction between these actors.

Restoring democracy in Grenada

Grenada' Marxist government was a long-standing target of the Reagan administration, which had drawn up plans to destabilise it in 1981,[56] and the 1983 US invasion of the island was a response to a perceived opportunity to remove a Marxist government in the Western Hemisphere. Relations between the US and Grenada had been poor since the former Crown Colony's first elected Prime Minister, the authoritarian Eric Gairy, had been overthrown by the Marxist New Jewel Movement, led by Maurice Bishop, in 1979. Bishop had then instituted a dictatorship and formed an alliance with Cuba. However, in 1983 he was in turn overthrown and then executed by more hard-line figures within the NJM. The Reagan administration took advantage of the political confusion and instability this caused on the island to launch an invasion that removed the NJM from power, rolling back communism in the Caribbean. While a small number of US troops continued to occupy the island after the initial victory, plans were laid by the Reagan administration for elections that would result in a pro-US democratic government. The danger in pursuing this course was that an election could be won by the corrupt and unstable Gairy, who had returned from exile. National security officials believed that a Gairy victory might then trigger a leftist coup attempt by remaining elements of the NJM.[57]

Rather than being at loggerheads over the priority to accord national security objectives versus democracy promotion in this situation, the NED and the US government co-operated; in fact, plans to create a stable pro-US democratic government with a role for the AFL-CIO and the NED envisaged had been floated by Reaganite NSC staffer Constantine Menges even before the invasion.[58] Both the state and democracy promotion groups then participated in an effort to produce a pre-determined outcome by supporting the campaign of New National Party leader Herbert Blaize, a candidate thought to be moderate and pro-US. Two NED foundations, the NRI and FTUI, which channelled funding to AIFLD, the AFL-CIO's Latin American labour foundation, acted as part of a political programme coordinated by the State Department and the NSC which included US government agencies, other US private groups and political consultants from other Caribbean nations, worked successfully to influence achieve this outcome.[59] The US Government clearly supported Blaize's party, the NNP. An NSC memo written in the run-up to the December 1984 election notes that 'Careful coordination and selective polling is underway to ensure that the best NNP candidate is selected for each of the 15 [electoral] districts',[60] with the

162   *Promoting democracy*

'political operation' being coordinated with the NNP's Jamaican political consultants, and predicted that 'a coordinated, well managed and effectively funded political campaign can be successful in Grenada.' The NRI and AIFLD were key players in the political process and were linked to the Reagan administration through an additional State Department officer who had been sent to Grenada 'with the explicit purpose of facilitating co-ordination' of the political programme.[61] The NSC also brought in Republican private citizens such as Clifford White, a former Republican campaign manager, and Joe Canzeri, a former White House aide, to raise further election funds for the NNP.[62] Although sections of the NED coalition had a pre-existing commitment to political action in Grenada, as the AFL-CIO had proposed operations in support of anti-communist Grenadian unions to the administration in August 1982, in 1984 the two NED foundations involved were clearly acting as a part of a wider effort coordinated by the administration.

Congress raised few objections to these NED programmes, which seemed to aim at the creation of a democratic government through democratic processes. This was complacent, as rather than acting in an even-handed manner to ensure that democratic processes were observed by all sides in the election, the NRI and AIFLD carried out a 'get-out-the-vote' campaign that benefitted only Blaize. The two foundations ran programmes to encourage a heavy turnout in the election, with NRI granting $20,000 to a supposedly non-partisan organisation, the Grenada Civic Awareness Organisation,[63] and AIFLD disbursing $80,000 to the Grenadian labour movement.[64] The AIFLD money was spent on 'get-out-the-vote' publicity, posters and bumper stickers,[65] while the NRI-funded Grenada Civic Awareness Organisation ferried potential NNP voters to the polls in taxis.[66] This campaign worked against the other serious contender, Gairy, who was more likely to win if turnout was low. Although Gairy's potential support base was small, it was extremely loyal and more likely to vote on Election Day.[67] The actions of the two NED foundations, and of the US effort of which they formed a component, were aimed at securing victory for Blaize rather than Gairy, thus securing US national security objectives in Grenada, not at ensuring an electoral process in which all groups had an equal chance to compete. These NED programmes were criticised by ever-persistent Congressional critic Hank Brown, who charged that the NED foundations had carried out 'a "get-out-the-vote" effort on behalf of one side in Grenada', '... in spite of a NED policy prohibiting funds from going to election campaigns in other countries.'[68] However, the fact that this effort had been carried out within a framework of democratic processes muted Congressional criticism, in contrast to the serious disagreements over operations in Panama and in Western Europe.

Supporting transition elections in Guatemala

The following year the NED carried out an important electoral programme in Guatemala that also had a direct bearing on US national security interests. The political and military situation shaping policy towards Guatemala was similar to that of El Salvador; a civil war between a military junta and a Marxist insurgency was raging, while the Reagan administration pushed for greater support for the military and Congress held up aid due to concerns about Human Rights abuses by the Guatemalan army and death squads linked to it.[69] As in El Salvador, the Guatemalan junta decided to engineer a transition to civilian rule as part of its counter-insurgency campaign, an effort that the US government supported.[70] US policy towards democratisation in Guatemala fitted into the consensus which had emerged from debates between the administration factions and Congress over El Salvador and then generalised into a framework for Central America in early 1982. The State Department saw such transitions as strengthening containment by replacing unpopular and therefore possibly unstable dictatorships with democratic governments that would have more internal legitimacy. Reaganites calculated that the problems they had experienced getting military aid through Congress would disappear once democratic governments acceptable to the legislature had been installed.

There was little need to support a specific candidate, as in contrast to Grenada there was little chance that anti-US forces would triumph. None of the guerrilla parties or organisations were allowed to take part in the elections, with the Socialist Democratic Party (PSD) being the most leftist party allowed to field a candidate.[71] The State Department described both of the front-runners, Vinicio Cerezo of the Christian Democrats and Jorge Carpio of the Union of the Center (UCN), as 'political moderates with whom we could work.'[72] An electoral victory by either would not threaten US objectives. However, the US government did require the elections to be, and to be seen to be, as legitimate as possible to guarantee Congressional approval of aid for the Guatemalan government. This calculation was highlighted in a July 1985 State Department paper that stated that 'our ability to get Congress to accept increased economic and military aid levels depends on successful elections.'[73] The same argument was made in other policy memoranda and in a letter from President Reagan to Guatemalan President General Oscar Mejia, which had been prepared by the National Security Council staff.[74] Robert McFarlane also reminded Reagan in October 1985 that 'the successful conduct of the elections is vital for the credibility of our policy of supporting democratic governments in Central America.'[75] The NED also had its own reasons for becoming involved in Guatemala, as the country had been listed by Michael Samuels and William Douglas in their 1981 article, 'Promoting Democracy', as a country where a transition from a right-wing military junta to a democratic regime would serve US national security interests by creating a more stable government.

NED programmes were used in Guatemala as part of a wider US government effort to ensure that the elections were procedurally clean and technically well-organised in order to elect a government which would be acceptable to Congress. The administration requested NED assistance in July 1985, with the NSC proposing that 'The State Department and AID should encourage the National Endowment for Democracy to fund projects related to the upcoming elections' such as the training of poll watchers.[76] Several weeks later the State Department

164   *Promoting democracy*

reported that the Endowment was to disburse $152,450 to Caribbean/Central American Action, a private organisation founded at President Carter's request to combat revolution in the region, to be spent on polls and get-out-the-vote activities.[77] A grant of $100,000 in NED funding was also channelled through FTUI to AIFLD and then to the Study Centre of the CUSG, a key Guatemalan union, for get-out-the-vote and voter mobilisation activities in the run-up to the 1985 election.[78] These NED projects meshed with US government initiatives such as the provision of ballot paper and the training of Electoral Tribunal officials and poll-watchers through US and Latin American organisations financed by AID, as well as a raft of economic support measures designed to keep the Guatemalan government afloat during the elections.[79]

While the NED programmes served US national security interests, they also served to safeguard the interests of the AFL-CIO. AIFLD's funding of the CUSG allowed the AFL-CIO to channel support to a client union. The CUSG had strong links to the American trade union confederation; it had been set up by AIFLD before the creation of the NED[80] with a portion of the $300,000, which the organisation received annually for operations in the country from AID.[81] The CUSG had been initially set up as a pro-government union; both the US ambassador and the Guatemalan President at that time, Efrain Rios Montt, spoke at its inaugural conference in 1983.[82] Thus, while supporting broad US national security objectives in the country, FTUI was also able to channel its funding in such a way as to increase the influence of its Guatemalan partner organisation and to preserve it during the political transition.

These expenditures prompted little Congressional criticism, and the elections were seen in the US as legitimate. After Cerezo's election victory in 1986, NED President Carl Gershman proclaimed that 'Guatemala has moved from a transitional to a post-transitional situation of democracy ...'[83] However, there were several problems with portraying the Guatemalan elections as fully democratic. First, the elections were not aimed at empowering the population. Instead, they constituted a phase in the army's counter-insurgency strategy[84] and had been carried out to stabilise the country politically and increase the government's international legitimacy so as to secure economic and military aid from the US and other potential donors.[85] The 1985 constitution, under which the elections were conducted, enshrined into law the military's powers to run the self-defence patrols and model villages which had allowed the army to regiment rural populations and led to Human Rights abuses.[86] Second, important issues were excluded from the political agenda. No candidate in the election criticised the military for Human Rights abuses, suggested investigations of such abuses, advocated reducing the power of the military or called for negotiations with the insurgents,[87] placing important issues outside the scope of the political debate. Third, the elections did not address the socioeconomic inequalities which had first given rise to both the power of the oligarchy and the insurgency; all candidates pledged not to pursue socioeconomic reforms, such as land reform.[88] Finally, the fact that participation in the elections was restricted to forces within a political range which included the extreme right but excluded the extreme left, coupled with the fact

Promoting democracy 165

that political executions and disappearances continued throughout the process,[89] meant that the range of political options on offer was limited and undoubtedly contributed to the candidates' compliant attitude towards the military and the oligarchy.

The transition left the military with substantial powers to prosecute the war against the insurgents and did not end Human Rights abuses by the army, which continued under the elected Cerezo government, and even increased after its first year in power.[90] Thus, while an important goal of supporting the electoral process for the Guatemalan military and for sections of the Reagan administration was to increase political stability, the process also functioned as a 'demonstration election', defined by Herman and Brodhead as an election 'organized and staged by a foreign power primarily to pacify a restive home population, reassuring it that ongoing interventionary processes are legitimate and appreciated by their foreign subjects.'[91] The election was supported to increase the legitimacy of the Guatemalan government and thus the administration's ability to expedite aid through Congress. The NED programmes associated with the election fitted into this framework, rather than challenging it. However, outwardly the NED had acted to support a democratic transition away from a military government.

Democracy promotion in the Soviet bloc

This equation of democracy promotion with national security also characterised the anti-Soviet democracy promotion operations carried out in this period. In terms of democratic ideology, there was little ambiguity to negotiate in the targeting of the Soviet Empire, where the enemies of democracy were also America's enemies, and America's friends were generally democrats. The NED pursued operations within the tactical consensus that had been generated by the Conference on the Democratization of Communist Countries, held by the administration in October 1982 and attended by AFL-CIO representatives and by John Richardson, now NED Chairman. This approach differentiated between communist countries based on their degree of openness to Western influence and consisted of a dual policy of launching propaganda measures against the USSR to increase the flow of information to Soviet citizens while using private groups to support movements in the more vulnerable countries such as Poland. In line with this approach, the NED pursued the political/ideological offensive aimed at the Soviet bloc called for in NSDD-75 to promote gradual democratisation, in concert with propaganda campaigns by semi-autonomous instrumentalities such as Radio Liberty and Radio Free Europe, and a US government policy of conditioning aid for Eastern bloc countries on their willingness to protect and implement political and economic reforms.[92]

NED funding directed at the Soviet Union was mainly aimed at supporting émigré groups based in other countries and assisting them to smuggle written propaganda into the USSR. One of the NED's first grants was made to the Sakharov Institute, an organisation largely staffed by Soviet émigrés based at the

166 *Promoting democracy*

Hoover Institution at Stanford University. The Institute was named after Andrei Sakharov, the dissident Soviet physicist who had helped to found the Moscow Human Rights Committee, although Sakharov had no connection with it. The Institute held a conference in September 1984 aimed at generating support for the establishment of a 'Center for the Democratization of the Soviet Union'.[93] The NED sent a representative to the conference, which was also attended by Richard Pipes, then retired from the NSC, and Soviet émigré Vladimir Bukovsky, who had also spoken at the Conference for the Democratization of Communist countries.[94] The Sakharov Institute conference discussed ways to democratise the USSR, with Pipes commenting that 'Radio broadcasting is the most obvious vehicle, as well as smuggling in books to Soviet citizens'.[95] The Institute subsequently received NED funding.[96]

The Endowment also put this plan directly into operation itself by channelling funds to US private groups that used them to finance the publication of books and journals by émigrés based in the West which were then smuggled into the USSR. These materials were concerned with history, politics and culture and many were targeted at the Soviet elite. One example of this type of material was *Syntaxis*, a Russian language quarterly edited by the dissident Andrei Sinyavsky and funded by grants passed through a group called The American Friends of Free Speech Abroad. *Syntaxis* 'seeks to encourage alternative political, social and economic thought in the Soviet Union' and was distributed there through unofficial channels.[97] Another such journal was *Internal Contradictions in the USSR*, a quarterly published by émigrés using funding passed through Freedom House which was aimed at 'higher levels of the Soviet bureaucracy'.[98] The Endowment even financed the publication of a new Russian translation of *Animal Farm*.[99]

The NED also financed propaganda projects targeted at specific demographic groups within the USSR, consistent with Alexander Haig's original vision of sending aid to nationalist groups within the Soviet Union to create instability and disruption. Money was passed to the Joint Baltic American National Committee, an umbrella organisation for Latvian, Lithuanian and Estonian émigrés based in the US, which passed the money on to groups based in Sweden, which then distributed books and films on the period of Estonian independence and current news to young Estonians.[100] The Baltic States had a stronger sense of nationalism than some of the other Soviet republics, so feeding nationalist feeling there might have served to aggravate centripetal tendencies within the USSR. Soviet workers were also not neglected; a grant of $129,000 was made to finance the publication of *Soviet Labour Review*, an anti-communist newsletter containing information on Soviet labour law and working conditions. The newsletter was published in London by the National Alliance of Russian Solidarists (NTS),[101] a right-wing émigré organisation that had previously participated in some of the CIA's operations at the beginning of the Cold War.[102] Thus, the goals and tools which had been agreed at the state–private conference in 1982 to be carried out by Project Democracy and codified in NSDD-75, after an interagency struggle which left their parameters vague, were now transferred to the NED, which used

Promoting democracy 167

them to pursue an evolutionary approach to democratisation of the USSR acceptable to all political factions in the US.

In the Soviet satellite states of Eastern Europe, the Endowment's programs went beyond distributing propaganda to include the support of dissident groups. This was particularly true of Poland, which had been a Reaganite priority for several years. From 1981 onwards, the President and hard-line policymakers such as William Casey had seen Poland as the weak link in the chain of Soviet satellites in Eastern Europe, and Solidarity as a movement capable not only of destabilising the Polish communist regime but also of spurring the growth of similar movements in other Eastern European countries. The NED soon began channelling aid to Solidarity so as to allow the organisation to continue to operate in the repressive political conditions existing in Poland. To do this, NED funding was channelled through the AFL-CIO to the Solidarity Co-ordinating Office Abroad in Brussels. This funding was used to fund regional union structures inside Poland itself,[103] and to buy printing equipment and computers in order to allow the union to spread its message.[104] According to Domber, by 1986 the FTUI was paying roughly two-thirds of the coordinating Committee's annual budget.[105]

The Endowment also passed money to other US private groups such as Freedom House to be spent on publications to be distributed within Poland[106] and also carried out programmes aimed at publicising Solidarity and Human Rights violations by the Polish government in the West through grants from FTUI to the Committee in Support of Solidarity,[107] a US organisation which had been set up by the AFL-CIO in 1981 to propagandise in favour of the Polish union. Grants to the CSS also empowered Solidarity to spread its message within the Soviet bloc, as the Committee translated many of its proclamations into Czech, Ukrainian and Russian.[108] In addition, the NED provided legal and material assistance to Polish political prisoners through the Aurora Foundation and the Polish American Congress Charitable Foundation,[109] with the clear political rationale that if activists knew that they or their families would be supported in the event of imprisonment, the deterrent effect of repression on the movement would be lessened. According to a US House Intelligence Committee Member speaking after the end of the Cold War:

> In Poland we did all of the things that are done in countries where you want to destabilize a communist government and strengthen resistance to that. We provided the supplies and technical assistance in terms of clandestine newspapers, broadcasting, propaganda, money, organizational help and advice.[110]

The Endowment's actions in Eastern Europe and the Soviet Union represented political and propaganda initiatives waged to gradually loosen the CPSU's grip on its satellites and on power within the USSR, prosecuted through an organisation which was far more plausibly deniable, and credible to dissidents than the CIA.

In Grenada, Guatemala, Poland and the USSR, programmes carried out by the NED remained within the consensus negotiated by the NED groups, Congress

168 *Promoting democracy*

and the administration. All occurred in dictatorships or countries emerging from dictatorship, none were kept secret from Congress, and none gave aid to overtly anti-democratic forces. In addition, none caused damage to a regime allied with the US, while the Soviet bloc programmes helped to undermine enemy states. On the surface, the national security interests of the United States and the promotion of democracy meshed perfectly. This was not necessarily the case in Grenada, where the US interest in supporting the election of a pro-US candidate led to a partisan campaign of support for that candidate, or in Guatemala, where the imperatives of legitimating and stabilising the regime led to support of a democratic process which was flawed and limited. These facts indicate that at bottom the process was being driven by national security, not democratic imperatives. However, there was wide agreement on the operations within the US elite. This was not to be the case with the NED's next significant programme.

Democracy promotion versus the Kirkpatrick Doctrine: the Philippines

In contrast to the consensus displayed over the previous operations, US policy towards the Philippines was riven by disagreement over whether the promotion of democracy would enhance or undermine US national security interests. In this case the US elite confronted one of the most important foreign policy issues of the Carter and Reagan Presidencies: the question of what policy to follow towards a pro-US dictator whose misrule was damaging US national security interests. This debate pitted proponents of the Kirkpatrick Doctrine – the idea that pro-US authoritarians should be supported against Marxist rebels in order to prevent a communist victory – against others who supported the view set out by Douglas and Samuels that a transition to democracy in such threatened states was the key to creating political stability and preventing radical forces from coming to power. The substantive issue was not democratic idealism or hostility to democracy; but how to most effectively safeguard existing US geopolitical interests in the Philippines.

The Philippines: another Nicaragua in the making?

The Philippines was ruled at that time by Ferdinand Marcos, who had come to power in a democratic election in 1965, had subsequently declared martial law in 1972, and had governed as dictator since. Like its predecessors, the Reagan administration initially embraced Marcos in order to safeguard US interests in the Philippines. The most important of these were the US naval base at Subic Bay and air base at Clark Field. Clark was the headquarters of the 13th US Air Force and also provided airlift capacity to transport US troops to Diego Garcia in the Indian Ocean, for ultimate deployment in the Persian Gulf. Subic Bay was an integral element of the US' Asia-Pacific base network, which embraced Japan, Micronesia and Hawaii. The base was a logistics and intelligence hub for the US 7th Fleet, and had grown in importance since the USSR had gained access to the Cam Ranh Bay naval base in Vietnam after the US withdrawal.[111] However, the political landscape in the Philippines was changing, as Marcos faced a growing challenge to his rule from a Marxist insurgency spearheaded by the New People's Army (NPA) and from a democratic opposition movement. A regime change which empowered Marxists or nationalistic Filipino democrats could threaten US access to the bases.

In 1983, political stability in the Philippines began to deteriorate noticeably after the assassination of Marcos' most popular and threatening political opponent, Benigno Aquino, mere moments after his return to the Philippines from exile in the US. This event and its aftermath had a significant impact on the policy of US support for Marcos. The Marcos regime was already facing a well-organised and dynamic insurgency prosecuted by the New People's Army, and faring poorly against it. However, Aquino's death was followed by popular protests against the regime that extended far beyond the alienated urban and rural poor to sectors which the administration had considered loyal to Marcos. The following month saw an anti-regime march through Makati, the financial district of Manila, by 100,000 businessmen and office workers.[112] This opposition from the general public and the business community, coupled with the expanding NPA insurgency in the countryside and the fact that around 20 per cent of the population already supported the National Democratic Front, the left's political umbrella group, conjured up fears in the State Department that a centre-left revolutionary alliance of the same type as that which had toppled the Somoza regime in Nicaragua in 1979 could be formed.[113]

Fear that the Philippines was in a pre-revolutionary situation prompted a reassessment of the policy of uncritical support for Marcos by embassy personnel on the ground in Manila and mid-level officials in Washington. In Manila the US ambassador, Michael Armacost, began to meet with representatives of the opposition and in November 1983 gave a speech at the Makati Rotary Club praising the assassinated Aquino's commitment to free elections.[114] In Washington the administration created an interagency group to monitor the situation in the Philippines. This group was dominated by mid-level officials such as the Assistant Secretary for East Asian and Pacific Affairs, Paul Wolfowitz, the Assistant Secretary for International Security Affairs, Richard Armitage, and mid-level conservative NSC Asian specialists such as Gaston Sigur and Richard Childress. Although this did not represent a removal of US government support for Marcos, it did indicate that officials were now carefully considering the US' options and waiting to see how the situation developed.

In addition to this subtle shift in attitude in the bureaucracy, more liberal Congressmen also began to query the basic assumptions of US policy towards the Philippines; in October 1983 Congressman Stephen Solarz, who had proposed greater US support for democratisation in the Philippines and other friendly dictatorships during the Project Democracy hearings, shepherded a non-binding resolution through the House which called for an investigation of Aquino's killing and 'genuine, free and fair elections to the National Assembly'.[115] However, the upper level of the administration maintained its support for the

170 *Promoting democracy*

Marcos regime. On 6 October Vice-President George Bush stated that the US would not 'cut away from a person who, imperfect though he may be on human rights, has worked with us.'[116]

The NED became involved in this situation in 1984 due to a request from ambassador Armacost for political aid to Filipino civil society groups. Armacost proposed that the NED provide $1 million to a Filipino citizen organisation, NAMFREL, which trained and organised poll-watchers, to guarantee a 'fairly-conducted Philippine parliamentary election' in May 1984. When proposing this programme, Armacost asked a careful question:

> Is the Endowment likely to look with favor upon a proposal for financial support to a non-partisan civic effort to ensure free and fair elections in a *friendly/allied* country?[117]

This was hardly the first US electoral intervention in the Philippines. The poll-watching organisation which Armacost wanted the NED to fund had first been formed by the CIA in the 1950s to prevent the corrupt and ineffective President Quirino from stealing the 1953 elections and to secure the election of the pro-US Defense Minister Ramon Magsaysay, who Washington believed would be more effective at combatting the Marxist Huk insurgency then raging. The CIA had dispatched New York lawyer Robert Kaplan to Manila in 1953 with instructions to make sure Magsaysay won the election. Kaplan's solution was to set up NAMFREL, a supposedly neutral civil society organisation that in fact supported Magsaysay against the incumbent.[118] The organisation was now being reactivated. Armacost feared that if steps were not taken to ensure a fair election, there was a possibility of a 'widespread election boycott and then increased confrontation and polarisation.'[119] If the population believed there was no way to change the government through the political system, they might abandon this system completely, which would only benefit the NPA. The idea of channelling electoral aid to opposition elements through the non-governmental NED fit in with Armacost's developing policy of keeping US government action off-stage in order to avoid provoking nationalist feeling among Filipinos.[120]

The Endowment accepted Armacost's invitation.[121] This was unsurprising, as the Philippines had been listed as an authoritarian regime that would benefit from democracy promotion programmes in Douglas and Samuels' article of 1981. The AFL-CIO was already involved in giving aid to the Trade Union Congress of the Philippines (TUCP),[122] a conservative union which had originally been set up by the Marcos regime,[123] and the Endowment as a whole began to broaden its political work in the Philippines beyond trade unionism by beginning to focus on election monitoring. The subsequent legislative elections may be counted as a defeat for Marcos, due to the fact that despite serious fraud around 60 opposition delegates were elected to the National Assembly.

Neither mid-level officials nor the NED were at this point committed to removing Marcos from power; however, the growing disquiet over the policy of supporting Marcos in the bureaucracy, Congress and now the NED was given a

Promoting democracy 171

boost in June 1984 by further evidence of the threat posed by the Filipino Left. According to a report written by Manila embassy political officer James Nach, the NPA was becoming a serious threat; in fact, in some areas of the Philippines the communists had effectively replaced the central government. Nach argued that the insurgency was being fuelled by social and economic inequalities that the Marcos regime had done little to address and much to exacerbate[124] and so serious reforms were needed to win civilian support away from the NPA. Without these reforms, 'ultimate defeat and a communist takeover of the Philippines' was 'a very possible scenario'.[125] However, he had little confidence that the corrupt and ineffective Marcos regime would implement the necessary reforms.[126] Nach's conclusions were supported by Admiral Crowe, Chairman of the Joint Chiefs of Staff, who visited the Philippines and reached the same assessment of the situation, and by two staffers attached to the Senate Foreign Relations Committee, who returned from a visit convinced that a dangerous communist insurgency was underway.[127]

Although the picture of growing communist strength was alarming, the administration, and the elite as a whole, was divided over what action to take to remedy the situation. Mid-level officials such as Armitage and Wolfowitz, Michael Armacost, who had been recalled from Manila to become the State Department's Undersecretary for Political and Military Affairs, and US embassy personnel in Manila, believed that democratic reform was necessary now to ward off revolution later.[128] Additional pressure came from Congress. During hearings on the Philippines in Congress in September 1984, Stephen Solarz argued that a communist victory in the Philippines, by cutting off US access to the bases at Clark Field and Subic Bay, would make it impossible for the US to manage the balance of power in Asia.[129] Armacost's replacement as ambassador, Stephen Bosworth, signalled his support for reform by stating to the Makati Rotary Club in October 1984 that 'it is not a question of how to avoid change; it is rather a question of how change can be managed.'[130]

In contrast, high level officials such as Casey, Weinberger and the President himself believed that the safest course of action was to stand by Marcos.[131] Weinberger was reluctant to embrace political change in the islands, while the CIA Director supported Marcos solidly.[132] The President, speaking in October 1984, argued that 'there are things [in the Philippines] ... that do not look good to us from the standpoint ... of democratic rights ... what is the alternative? It is a large Communist movement to take over the Philippines.'[133] Most of the administration's high-level policymakers still believed that stability in the Philippines could best be achieved through support for Marcos.

Political action supported by a fragile consensus

Attempts to resolve this split led to the adoption of a compromise position put forward by State Department officials and set out in NSDD-163 in February 1985. The document called for political, economic and military reform in the Philippines, but stated that it should be implemented by and through the Marcos

172   *Promoting democracy*

regime. The goal was the 'revitalization of democratic institutions to assure both a smooth transition when President Marcos does pass from the scene and longer-term stability'.[134] However, no timetable for Marcos to leave power was given. The policy was clearly informed by policymakers' perceptions of what had occurred in Nicaragua in 1979, as it stated that 'Our goal is *not* to replace the current leadership of the Philippines' and that 'We are *not* promoting the dismantling of institutions that support stability – as occurred in Nicaragua during the collapse of the Somoza regime'.[135] In order to overcome the divisions within the administration, the NSDD was 'designed to be all things to all people';[136] a compromise between those who feared that Marcos was exacerbating an insurgency he could not defeat and thus should be replaced, and those who feared a repetition of the Sandinista triumph in Nicaragua if the US pressured him too strongly. This stalemate continued throughout the first half of 1985, with US officials descending on Marcos to urge serious reforms, which he ignored.[137]

However, this compromise policy was elastic enough to permit the funding of civil society groups within the Philippines, especially by non-governmental organisations such as the National Endowment for Democracy. The Endowment implemented the stance towards pro-US dictatorships outlined in the original proposals for democracy promotion made by Samuels in 1980 and Douglas and Samuels in 1981, which had argued that the best policy in such cases was to pursue a long-range strategy of fostering the growth of democratic successor groups who could be prepared to compete for power with radical opposition groups after a regime breakdown. This stance was compatible with the administration's compromise policy of fostering a degree of reform while not pressuring Marcos to step down. During this period of stalemate within the administration, the NED continued to expand its political operations on the ground, allocating $3.2 million for the Asian-American Free Labor Institute (AAFLI), an AFL-CIO labour centre focussed on training friendly unionists in Asia, to fund programs in the Philippines in 1985.[138] These funds went to the TUCP,[139] and were aimed primarily at combatting the influence of the left and the NPA in Filipino civil society, not the Marcos government. The Executive Director of AAFLI, Charles Gray, made this clear in 1985, stating: 'The political opposition to Marcos is not well organized, so the only alternative social program is that of the communists. We're trying to develop the TUCP to fill the void if Marcos goes.'[140] If this occurred, it was hoped that the TUCP would act as a bulwark against the leftist KMU union federation, which the Americans believed was connected with the communist party and the NPA guerrillas.[141]

To this end, the NED allocated funding aimed at increasing the union's capacity to wage the internal political battle against the Filipino Left. Endowment funding helped to finance a TUCP information center to combat 'left-wing propaganda',[142] and also radio programming by the union.[143] It also provided the support for the TUCP to expand its political reach into the countryside,[144] where support for the NPA was stronger. According to the Endowment, this support strengthened the union movement and the democratic center as a whole.[145] The fact that radical unions rather than the Marcos regime were the targets of this

Promoting democracy 173

program is given further backing by the comments of an AAFLI administrator in the Philippines, who stated:

> Some of the regional labour leaders receiving AAFLI money are becoming powerful politically. Imagine if you have $100,000 to give out to families in $500 chunks. Your stock goes way up, faster than the stock of any of the militant labour groups.[146]

Thus, the NED was building up a 'Third Force' of 'democratic successors' who would be able to compete politically with the Filipino Left if Marcos fell from power.

Other organisations within the US foreign policy apparatus were also forging links with key sectors where opposition to Marcos was growing. In March 1985 Filipino officers who were disaffected with the Armed Forces of the Philippines' performance against the NPA guerrillas formed the Reform the Armed Forces Movement (RAM), a network of officers committed outwardly to improving the army's combat capability through increasing its professionalism and the removal of politically loyal but inept senior officers, and more covertly to the removal of the regime if necessary to win the war.[147] The Embassy in Manila and the Department of Defence encouraged the formation of the group and provided it with support;[148] a move that could be interpreted as support for RAM's ideas on military reform within the framework of a continuing Marcos regime, as the organisation did not broadcast its political goals.

The growth of left-wing power and intra-administration divisions

The fragile consensus within the administration ended in mid-1985, again due to increased fears of leftist/communist political strength in the Philippines rather than increasing ideological fervour for democracy. In July a joint study on the Philippines carried out by the CIA, DIA and State Department predicted a growth of left-wing military and political power over the next 18 months if the Marcos dictatorship remained in power until the next national elections, scheduled for 1987.[149] The time frame for resolving the crisis and building up a possible successor regime was narrowing.

The situation led to a meeting of officials from the State Department, CIA, DIA and independent academics and businessmen at the National War College in August to discuss policy options. Pragmatic conservatives such as Wolfowitz, Armitage and Armacost called for US covert funding for key opposition organisations such as NAMFREL and RAM. Armacost even attempted to promote the idea of launching a coup against Marcos; however, this proved to be unpopular, as policymakers remembered the chaos caused by the coup against President Diem in South Vietnam in 1963.[150] Congress also intervened in the form of a Senate amendment to the foreign aid bill linking aid to the Philippines to progress on Human Rights and democracy,[151] much as the legislature had demanded certification of such progress before aid would be released to El Salvador in the early 1980s.

174   *Promoting democracy*

However, although pressure was growing within and outside the administration for the removal of Marcos there was still no policy consensus, as high-level Reaganite policy-makers such as Casey, Weinberger, White House Chief of Staff Donald Regan and the President believed that the most prudent course to follow was to provide Marcos with US backing to defeat the NPA.[152] These conservatives feared a repeat of Nicaragua, where they believed the Carter administration had undermined the friendly Somoza dictatorship and opened the way to a Marxist seizure of power.[153] To these policymakers the moderate opposition beginning to cluster around Corazon Aquino, Benigno Aquino's widow, was an unknown quantity which might prove unable to stand up to the communists or might call for the US to vacate its geopolitically-important bases at Subic Bay and Clark Field.[154]

The struggle between the ideologues in the upper reaches of the administration and mid-level pragmatists remained unresolved.[155] However, key proponents of reform such as Wolfowitz and Armitage blitzed the regime with demands for reform in public testimony to Congress in late October 1985, repeating the core points of their basic message: that Marcos' misrule was fostering the growth of the insurgency and putting the US bases in danger, and that the way out of the crisis was reform.[156]

Marcos' own attempt to resolve the crisis was the announcement of 'snap elections' in November 1985, a decision which pleased the Reaganites and alarmed the State Department and its allies. The Reaganites believed that 'snap elections' would end the political crisis, as a Marcos victory would give the Filipino President the stability he needed to deal strongly with the NPA.[157] This group was more interested in such stability than the integrity of the election process. Two weeks before voting Donald Regan stated that even if Marcos were re-elected through fraud the administration would have to do business with him, pointing out that '[t]here are a lot of governments elected by fraud'.[158] For this reason the Reaganites were lukewarm on the idea of a Congressional observer mission, as it would be easier to maintain support for Marcos if Americans did not witness the massive fraud the regime would need to survive.[159] Although the White House eventually agreed to a 20-person Congressional observer mission to be headed by Senator Richard Lugar, it attempted to pack the delegation with reliable conservatives.[160] In contrast, the State Department believed that if Marcos won through fraud only the NPA would benefit, as the elimination of the possibility of peaceful change would swell its ranks with disaffected moderates.[161] It also feared that the moderate opposition would not be organised enough to mount a serious electoral challenge to Marcos in the time available; this was also Marcos' calculation.[162] However, this turn of events also gave the Department and the NED an opportunity to foster the democratic transition which they believed would stabilise the Philippines, if it could be managed.

Promoting democracy 175

Fostering a democratic transition

To capitalise on this opportunity the US embassy in Manila and the NED both increased their support for the opposition on the ground, going beyond a long-term policy of preparing democratic successor organisations to supporting a transfer of power to opposition groups in the near future. US Charge d'Affaires Philip Kaplan spurred the opposition on in its preparations for the elections, emphasising to a gathering of key leaders 'the need for the opposition to get its act together given the limited time left before a campaign starts.'[163] At the same time, the embassy pushed Aquino to nominate a conservative and former Marcos loyalist, Salvador 'Doy' Laurel, as her running-mate,[164] with the final negotiations on unifying the opposition coalition being conducted under the auspices of Cardinal Sin, the head of the Catholic Church in the Philippines.[165] Doy was trusted by the Americans and had much more reliable instincts on the issues of anti-communism and US access to the bases than Aquino.[166] This alliance forged a centre-right opposition ticket and warded off a key danger – that Aquino would shift to the left and take up positions that did not conform to US national security interests. Aquino's shift on anti-communism and the bases, under the guidance of Laurel and the embassy, lessened this danger.[167]

The NED supplemented the embassy's exhortation of the opposition to campaign seriously by funding NAMFREL to reprise its poll-watching role in the elections. Although NAMFREL was legally a non-partisan organisation it was no more neutral than was COMELEC, the Marcos regimes' election commission. Any step towards effective monitoring of electoral fraud was implicitly a step away from Marcos and US funding for NAMFREL represented another facet of a State Department strategy described by Armacost after the elections as 'encourage[ing] the constraints' on Marcos, which also included the US government observer mission.[168] In total, NAMFREL received funding of $1 million through the NED and also through AID.[169] This funding had to be passed through smaller Filipino civil society organisations which made up the NAMFREL coalition to conceal it.[170] NED money was channelled through FTUI, then AAFLI, then the TUCP, whose Secretary General, Ernesto Herrera, was a member of NAMFREL's Executive Council.[171] NAMFREL's poll-watchers operated a 'Quick Count' system which would enable them to keep their own tally of votes cast for each party in the elections;[172] thus, if the Marcos regime slowed or stopped the count to falsify results, NAMFREL or the Endowment's official observer delegation, sponsored by NRI and NDI,[173] would be able to present accurate figures to the US government.

The administration as a whole accepted this funding initiative. Paul Wolfowitz was vocal in his demand for the Marcos regime to restore official accreditation to NAMFREL, withdrawn after the elections of 1984.[174] Reagan administration hard-liners accepted the funding of NAMFREL because they believed Marcos would win the elections, and having this victory confirmed by a watchdog not linked to the regime would increase its credibility.[175] In addition, the NED had assisted in and certified elections in line with the conservative

176   *Promoting democracy*

foreign policy viewpoint previously in Grenada and Guatemala, so hard-liners had little reason to believe it would diverge from their policy.

This calculation proved to be flawed. It was the alternative vote tabulation system operated by NAMFREL, which produced different results to those announced by the regime,[176] together with the electoral irregularities and intimidation of voters reported by the organisation throughout the election,[177] which allowed the opposition to convincingly demonstrate the high levels of fraud which had occurred on Election Day.[178] Based on this information, Lugar's election observation team concluded that widespread fraud had occurred, with Lugar calling NAMFREL 'our eyes and ears.'[179] The NDI/NRI sponsored observer mission also released a report citing fraud and intimidation by pro-Marcos forces during the election.[180]

The public nature of this fraud created a crisis for Reaganite policy from which the only exit was acceptance of a democratic transition. The fact that the elections had been stolen in the glare of US media attention gave pro-democracy forces the opportunity to put pressure on the Reaganites to live up to their democratic rhetoric. In Washington, Congress threatened a cut-off of all aid to the Philippines unless Aquino was recognised as the new President.[181] In the Philippines, Aquino called on the Reagan administration to support her, stating that 'Those who are prepared to support armed struggles for liberation elsewhere discredit themselves if they obscure the nature of what we are doing peacefully here'.[182] The Secretary of State, George Shultz also swung definitively into the anti-Marcos camp for pragmatic reasons after deciding that 'The protection of our strategic interest lies in the fostering of a transition to a more democratic government.'[183]

This pressure was given force by massive street demonstrations in favour of Aquino and a mutiny by RAM, the anti-Marcos officers' organisation. There is no hard evidence that US personnel on the ground suggested or encouraged this mutiny; however, rebel military helicopters were allowed to refuel at Clark Field.[184] In Washington, the NSC remained briefly uncertain about what course of action to follow, with Donald Regan, Reagan's Chief of Staff, invoking the spectre of Khomeini's seizure of power in Iran to argue that the US should continue to support Marcos, as the administration could not be certain that any successor government would be a better option, and change might benefit the communists.[185] However, the game was clearly up, and Marcos' strongest supporters, Casey and Weinberger, changed their position, albeit reluctantly.[186] Reagan was persuaded to withdraw all US support from the Marcos regime, and the democratic transition which the NED, Congress and the State Department had been pushing for followed quickly.

As in Grenada and Guatemala, this democratic transition had been carried out for reasons of national security, not an ideological commitment to democracy. The anti-Marcos faction within the US elite had fostered a transition because they believed it was the most effective way to achieve the primary US national security goal; a stable and anti-communist Philippines. Each progressive hardening of this faction's position, from a policy of pressuring Marcos to reform while building up anti-communist civil society organisations to one of supporting

Aquino politically against the dictator, had been prompted by a growing fear of the military and political strength of leftist Filipino groups who, if they took power, could be expected to put pressure on the US to vacate the bases at Clark Field and Subic Bay and to pursue an anti-American foreign policy. This faction's nightmare was a cross-class opposition alliance linking moderates and leftists such as had occurred in Nicaragua in 1979, and it acted at crucial junctures to ward off this possibility. Armacost commented several weeks after Aquino's victory:

> Our objective was to capture ... to encourage the democratic forces of the centre, then consolidate control by the middle and also win away the soft support of the NPA. So far, so good.[187]

It is unlikely that these officials would have become so hostile to Marcos in the absence of the threat they perceived from the NPA.

Containing change

Although this transition was described by the NED as a 'dramatic triumph of democracy' in its 1986 report, its depth was limited.[188] The opposition forces which the State Department and the NED supported aimed at a conservative democracy, a restoration of the institutions which had existed before Marcos gutted them, rather than a radical transformation. Indeed, Paul Wolfowitz had argued in the run-up to the elections that, 'reform in the Philippines has a certain conservative character to it, because one is talking about restoring military professionalism, one is talking about a free market economy, and one is talking about going back to certain democratic traditions.'[189] This restoration was accomplished successfully: five years after the fall of Marcos, 85 per cent of the 200-member House of Representatives consisted of the political clans who had traditionally governed the Philippines under the period of corrupt, oligarchic democracy from 1946–72.[190] US pressure on Marcos to step down had been aimed at containing the popular mobilisation then taking place on the streets, which the policy of fostering a democratic transition had been designed to avoid. RAM's eleventh-hour rebellion against Marcos, which the US had helped to succeed within the wider context of the democratic transition, distanced the military from the Marcos regime and preserved it as a repressive force to be used later if necessary, rather than allowing it to be weakened by the fall of the dictatorship. Aquino's government remained under the shadow of this military after the transition as recurrent coup attempts, some led by former RAM officers,[191] led it to remove more liberal officials unacceptable to the military.[192]

While many of these limiting factors were a product of Filipino political culture and US policy in general, the NED also acted after the transition to contain the mobilisation of popular forces that could have pressed for more radical socioeconomic reforms, rather than to empower them. It did this by funding more conservative Filipino civil society groups to allow them to combat

178 *Promoting democracy*

groups that it saw as dangerously radical or leftist. The FTUI continued its funding of the TUCP, which received the second largest total of NED funding allocated to a trade union organisation during the 1980s; only Poland's Solidarity received more.[193] This funding was disbursed to 'strengthen pro-democratic unions in the Philippines so that they will become the pre-eminent representatives of workers under the umbrella of the TUCP'[194] and to 'allow the TUCP to supplant the [leftist trade union federation] KMU as the spokesman for working men and women in the Philippines.'[195] This was significant because the KMU wanted the US to leave its bases and Clark Field and Subic Bay, and also supported stronger land reform measures than the TUCP.[196] The issue of land reform was linked to the security situation, as the fact that in the mid-80s 20 per cent of the population owned 80 per cent of the land[197] was a clear cause of the NPA insurgency. Aquino's land reform bill, drafted with the backing of a Congress controlled by the landed oligarchy and businessmen, exempted 75 per cent of all land from redistribution. In the first three years of the campaign only 7 per cent of this eligible land was redistributed, with agrarian reform subsequently grinding to a halt.[198] Thus, the accession of a populist but conservative President, a conservative legislature and action in civil society to combat radical forces acted to block a key reform.

The NED also funded other conservative civil society groups to shape the transition and maintain the elite in power. It combatted GABRIELA, a left-wing feminist organisation by funding KABATID, a conservative women's group dominated by members of the elite that it hoped would act as a counter-weight.[199] CIPE began funding the Philippines Chamber of Commerce (PCCI), to help it to create a nationwide organisation[200] that would unify it as an interest group sector and convert it away from the 'crony capitalism' of the Marcos era and towards 'private enterprise values'.[201] Thus, rather than aiding popular forces the NED and the US government acted to contain them, easing Marcos out of power to preserve a state and military apparatus which served US interests from the threat of revolution. The strategy of creating stability through a democratic transition in pro-US authoritarian states had been proven effective, while the threat of more radical change from below had been warded off.

Conclusion

The NED's operations under the Reagan administration were not conducted in accordance with an overarching strategic framework that prioritised democracy promotion over short-term national security objectives. Instead, democracy promotion was deployed as a political/organisational tool to achieve pre-existing US national security objectives in specific cases. This double character of the NED's political operations, democratic in form but oriented towards security concerns, is partly attributable to the fact that its leaders conflated the spread of democracy with US national security, an orientation that was reinforced after the Endowment was created by the appointment of NED officials who had previously held positions within the national security bureaucracy.

Promoting democracy 179

The melding of democracy promotion and national security in the NED's practice was also a product of the limitations on the Endowment's freedom of action produced by the management model for democracy promotion operations, which provided both Congress and the administration with leverage over the NED. While the Endowment was formally autonomous, this organisational framework constrained it in two ways. First, Congress' leverage as the provider of funding ensured that operations would aim at the support of democratic forces, rather than groups that were simply pro-US or anti-communist. Congress had not hesitated to threaten the funding of individual foundations that gave support to foreign groups it disapproved of. Second, the fact that the NED needed support from the administration to operate, secure funding and conduct large-scale operations aimed at altering political structures led to the Endowment targeting countries where US national security priorities were at stake and could be achieved through the use of democracy promotion.

These ideological and organisational factors resulted in the subordination of democracy promotion to national security objectives and its use as a tool to achieve these objectives, rather than an independent strategy or element of policy. National security objectives were the deciding factor in the choice of which specific countries would be targeted for large-scale operations aimed at altering political structures. In these cases, democracy promotion was used as a tactic to preserve or extend strategic positions important to the US. NED actions in the Soviet bloc served to delegitimise enemy governments and foster the growth of dissident movements, weakening Soviet power and control. In Latin America and Asia, democracy promotion was deployed in pro-US dictatorships suffering from the threat of radical revolutions as a tool for generating consent among the masses of the population for political arrangements shaped by domestic elites, action by the US state and the NED itself. Successful transitions to democracy legitimised new pro-US regimes that were less vulnerable to revolution and would act in US interests. While this tactic was contentious in the Philippines, it proved to be a more effective approach to securing US interests than the Kirkpatrick Doctrine.

Although these political outcomes were achieved through democratic methods, the depth of reform that was pursued in these new democracies was limited by the subordination of democracy promotion to national security imperatives. The practical effect of democracy promotion programmes was to entrench pro-US elites in power rather than to promote democratic transitions that could have resulted in far-reaching socioeconomic change. Instead, popular empowerment was limited through US and NED support of forces that could be relied on to act in ways consistent with enduring US interests and who would not upset the political, economic and social structures that preserved stability and US access to strategic positions.

180 *Promoting democracy*

Notes

1 Joshua Muravchik, 'US Political Parties Abroad', *The Washington Quarterly* 12, no. 3 (1989): 93–94, accessed 10 March 2011, DOI: 10.1080/01636608909477518.
2 Memo, Stuart Philip Ross and Buel White to Allen Weinstein, 10 January 1984, Folder 14, Box OA91698, Walter Raymond Files, RL, 3.
3 Ibid.
4 Letter, Allen Weinstein to Robert McFarlane, 25 January 1984, Folder 14, Box OA91698, Walter Raymond Files, RL, 1.
5 Memo, Walter Raymond to Robert McFarlane, 25 January 1984, Folder 14, Box OA91698, Walter Raymond Files, RL.
6 Letter, William E. Brock to Charles Wick, 26 January 1984, Jan. 25, 1984, Folder 14, Box OA91698, Walter Raymond Files, RL.
7 Letter, Weinstein to McFarlane, 2.
8 Ibid.
9 'Talking Points for USIA', attached to memo, Walter Raymond to Robert McFarlane, 28 January 1984, Folder 14 Box OA91698 Walter Raymond Files, RL.
10 Aaron Bernstein, 'Is Big Labor Playing Global Vigilante?' *Business Week*, 4 November 1985, Nexis UK, www.lexisnexis.com/uk/nexis.
11 Margot Hornblower, 'Panamanians Vote in Peaceful Election', *Washington Post*, 7 May 1984, Nexis UK, www.lexisnexis.com/uk/nexis.
12 CIA, 'SNIE 84/2–84: Panama: Prospects for the Election', 1 April 1984, *CIA Freedom of Information Act Electronic Reading Room*, accessed 25 August 2012, www.foia.cia.gov/sites/default/files/document_conversions/89801/DOC_0000434242. pdf, 5.
13 Ibid.
14 John Weeks and Andrew Zimbalist, 'The Failure of Intervention in Panama: Humiliation in the Backyard', *Third World Quarterly* 11, no. 1 (1989): 5, 10, accessed 10 September, 2012, DOI:10.1080/01436598908420137; Richard Millett, 'Looking Beyond Noriega', *Foreign Policy*, 71 (Summer 1988): 49, accessed 10 September 2012, www.jstor.org/stable/1148903, and Thomas Carothers, *In The Name of Democracy: US Policy toward Latin America in the Reagan Years* (Berkeley and Los Angeles, California: University of California Press, 1991), 169.
15 Weeks and Zimbalist, 'The Failure of Intervention in Panama', 4.
16 John Weeks, 'Panama: The Roots of Current Political Instability', Third World Quarterly, 9 no. 3 (July, 1987): 770–771, accessed 10 September 2012, DOI:10. 1080/01436598708420000.
17 Tom Barry and Deb Preusch, *AIFLD in Central America: Agents as Organizers* (Albuquerque: The Inter-Hemispheric Education Resource Centre, 1990), 51 and 25–30.
18 Everett Ellis Briggs, 'The Noriega Fiasco: Our Man in Panama', *New York Times*, 10 September 2007, accessed 10 October 2014, www.nytimes.com/2007/09/10/ opinion/10ihtedbriggs.1.7448826.html?pagewanted=1&_r=0.
19 Carothers, *In The Name of Democracy*, 168.
20 Hugh Wilford, *The CIA, the British Left and the Cold War: Calling the Tune?* (London and Portland Oregon: Frank Cass, 2003), 176–181.
21 The Democracy Program, 'The Commitment to Democracy: A Bipartisan Approach', Appendix C: Democracy Program Staff and Consultants, 18 April 1983, National Endowment for Democracy, accessed 10 March 2010 www.ned.org/ documents.
22 Britons get cash from US 'slush fund'/British organisations receiving money from US sources to "promote democracy"', *Guardian*, 9 December 1985, Nexis UK, www.lexisnexis.com/uk/nexis.
23 Ibid.

Promoting democracy 181

24 Giles Scott-Smith, 'Searching for the Successor Generation: Public Diplomacy, the US Embassy's International Visitor Program and the Labour Party in the 1980s', *British Journal of Politics and International Relations* 8 no. 2 (2006): 214–237, accessed 10 July 2012, DOI: 10.1111/j.1467–856X.2006.00221.x..

25 'Democracy and Public Diplomacy: An Inter-Agency Program', 12, attached to memo, Steve Steiner to Robert Blackwill, Acting, Folder: Democracy Initiative (2), Box 91753, Steve Steiner Files, RL.

26 'Britons get cash from US "slush fund"'.

27 'Union receiving secret US funds', *Guardian*, 8 December 1985, Nexis UK, www.lexisnexis.com/uk/nexis, 1.

28 Translation of Liberation article, Wednesday, 27 November 1985, 3, attached to letter, Irving Brown to Vice Admiral John M. Poindexter, 6 December 1985, Folder 3, Box OA91698, Walter Raymond Files, RL.

29 Ibid., 4.

30 'Union receiving secret US funds', 2.

31 Ibid.

32 Brown, 4–5.

33 Cable, American Embassy Paris to the Secretary of State, November 1985, Folder 3, Box OA91698, Walter Raymond Files, RL, 3.

34 Christopher Madison, 'Selling Democracy', *The National Journal*, 28 June 1986, Nexis UK, www.lexisnexis.com/uk/nexis, 7.

35 Gershman, quoted from Nicolas Guilhot, *The Democracy Makers: Human Rights and International Order* (New York, Chichester: Columbia University Press, 2005), 90.

36 Carl Gershman, 'The Rise and Fall of the New Foreign Policy Establishment', *Commentary*, accessed 1 November 2014, www.commentarymagazine.com/article/the-rise-fall-of-the-new-foreign-policy-establishment/.

37 Beth Sims, *Workers of the World Undermined: American Labor's Role in US Foreign Policy* (Boston, MA: South End Press, 1992), 34–35 and 46–47.

38 Arch Puddington, *Lane Kirkland: Champion of American Labor* (New Jersey: John Wiley and Sons, Inc., 2005), 223–224.

39 Madison, 'Selling Democracy', Ibid.

40 Puddington, *Lane Kirkland*, 223–224.

41 Ben A. Franklin, 'Democracy Project Facing New Criticisms', *New York Times*, 4 December 1985, Nexis UK, www.lexisnexis.com/uk/nexis, 1.

42 Quoted from 'Agency Suspends Grant To Right-Wing Student Group', The Associated Press, 27 November 1985, Nexis UK, www.lexisnexis.com/uk/nexis, 2.

43 Franklin, 2.

44 'Agency Suspends Grant to Right-Wing Student Group', 2.

45 Anonymous, Document beginning 'In response to request ...', August 1982, Folder 11/82, Box OA91162, Walter Raymond Files, RL, 1.

46 Quoted from Bernstein, 'Is Big Labor Playing Global Vigilante?'; see also 'Exporting democracy; Crusaders fall out', *The Economist*, 16 June 1984, Nexis UK, www.lexisnexis.com/uk/nexis

47 'Exporting democracy; Crusaders fall out'.

48 Ibid.

49 Memo, Robert McFarlane to the President, 12 June 1984, Folder 1 (NED 1984–85), Box OA91698, Walter Raymond Files, RL, for details of the NSC lobbying campaign.

50 Letter, Ronald Reagan to Senator Mark Hatfield, 12 June 1984, Folder 1 (NED 1984–5), Box OA91698, Walter Raymond Files, RL, RL.

51 Franklin, 'Democracy Project Facing New Criticisms'.

52 Ibid.

182 *Promoting democracy*

53 Ibid.; and William Safire, 'Finders' Keeper', *New York Times*, 22 December 1985, Nexis UK, www.lexisnexis.com/uk/nexis, 2.
54 Government Accountability Office, 'Promoting Democracy: The National Endowment for Democracy's Management of Grants Overseas,' September 1986, *US Government Accountability Office Electronic Records Archive*, accessed 16 August 2012, http://archive.gao.gov/f0302/131416.pdf.
55 Government Accountability Office, 'Statement of John M. McCabe, General Accounting Office, Before the Committee on Foreign Affairs, Subcommittee on International Relations, House of Representatives, on the National Endowment for Democracy's administration of its grants program', 14 May 1986, *US Government Accountability Office Electronic Records Archive*, accessed 2 December 2014, www.gao.gov/products/129867.
56 Patrick E. Tyler, 'U.S. Tracks Cuban Aid to Grenada; In '81, Senate Unit Nixed CIA Plan To Destabilize Isle', *Washington Post*, 27 February 1983, Nexis UK, www.lexisnexis.com/uk/nexis.
57 'Centrist candidate elected Premier', Facts on File World News Digest, 7 December 1984, Nexis UK, www.lexisnexis.com/uk/nexis.
58 Constantine C. Menges, *Inside the National Security Council: The True Story of the Making and Unmaking of Reagan's Foreign Policy* (New York: Simon and Schuster, 1988), 65, 81.
59 Memo, Walter Raymond, Constantine Menges and Raymond Burghardt to Robert McFarlane, 5 October 1984, Folder 8, Box 30, Executive Secretariat, NSC: Country Files, Latin America, Grenada, RL, 2.
60 Ibid.
61 Ibid.
62 Memo, Walter Raymond to Robert McFarlane, 16 October 1984, Folder 8, Box 8, Executive Secretariat, NSC: Country Files, Latin America, Grenada, RL, 2.
63 Edward Cody, 'US-backed coalition wins big in Grenada', *Washington Post*, 4 December 1982, Nexis UK, www.lexisnexis.com/uk/nexis, 2.
64 Joseph B. Treaster, 'US groups helping get out the vote in Grenada', *New York Times*, 2 December 1984, Nexis UK, www.lexisnexis.com/uk/nexis, 2.
65 Ibid.
66 Cody, 2.
67 Ibid.
68 Hank Brown, 'Statement before the Subcommittee on International Operations, Committee on Foreign Affairs', 12 March 1985, Folder 7, Box OA91698, Walter Raymond Files, RL, RL, 4.
69 Carothers, *In the Name of Democracy*, 61–63.
70 Richard Wilson, 'Continued Counterinsurgency: Civilian Rule in Guatemala', in *Low Intensity Democracy: Political Power in the New World Order*, ed. Barry Gills, Joel Rocamora and Richard Wilson (London: Pluto Press, 1993), 131–132.
71 Susanne Jonas, 'Elections and Transitions: Guatemala and Nicaragua', in *Elections and Democracy in Central America*, ed. John A. Booth and Mitchell A. Seligson (Chapel Hill and London: The University of North Carolina Press, 1989), 136.
72 Memo, Nicholas Platt to Robert McFarlane, 7 June 1985, DDRS, accessed 14 September 2012, 11.
73 Memo, Nicholas Platt to Robert McFarlane, 18 July 1985, DDRS, accessed 16 July 2012, 2.
74 Memo, Nicholas Platt to Robert McFarlane and Robert H. Tuttle, 7 October 1985, DDRS; Letter, Ronald Reagan to General Mejia, 30 October 1985, DDRS, accessed 27 August 2012.
75 Memo, Robert McFarlane to the President, 29 October 1985, DDRS, accessed 16 July 2007.

Promoting democracy 183

76 Memo, Robert McFarlane to George P. Schultz, James A. Baker, Casper W. Weinberger, John R. Block and William J. Casey, 10 July 1985, DDRS, accessed 16 July 2007.
77 Memo, Nicholas Platt to Robert McFarlane, 23 July 1985, DDRS, accessed 16 July 2007, 1. For more information on the C/CAA, see John A. Soares Jr., 'Strategy, Ideology, and Human Rights: Jimmy Carter Confronts the Left in Central America, 1979–1981', *Journal of Cold War Studies* 8, no. 4 (2006): 63, accessed 16 May 2014, EBSCO Host.
78 Barry and Preusch, *AIFLD*, 23.
79 Memo, Platt to McFarlane, 23 July 1985.
80 Barry and Preusch, *AIFLD*, 21.
81 Ibid., 22.
82 Ibid.
83 Quoted from Jonas, 'Elections and Transitions', 133.
84 See Robert H. Trudeau, 'The Guatemalan Election of 1985: Prospects for Democracy', 106; Jonas, 'Elections and Transitions,' 136–137; in *Elections and Democracy in Central America*, ed. John A. Booth and Mitchell A. Seligson (Chapel Hill and London: The University of North Carolina Press, 1989).
85 Jonas, 'Elections and Transitions', 139.
86 Ibid., 135.
87 Trudeau, 'The Guatemalan Election of 1985', 106; Jonas, 'Elections and Transitions,' 136–137.
88 Trudeau, 106; he further comments, 'meaningful land reform remains an illusion'; Jonas, 135.
89 Jonas, 138.
90 Jonas, 140; Aryeh Neier, 'Human Rights in the Reagan Era: Acceptance in Principle', *Annals of the American Academy of Political and Social Science* 506 (November 1989): 37, accessed 10 May 2011, www.jstor.org/stable/1046652; and Wilson, 'Continued Counterinsurgency', 134.
91 Edward S. Herman and Frank Brodhead, *Demonstration Elections: US-Staged Elections in The Dominican Republic, Vietnam and El Salvador* (Boston: South End Press, 1984), 5.
92 Carl Bernstein, 'The Holy Alliance', *Time Magazine*, 24 February 1992, accessed 27 August 2012, http://carlbernstein.com/magazine_holy_alliance.php.
93 The Associated Press, 'Stanford President Opposes Plan to Smuggle Books into Soviet Union', The Associated Press, 5 November 1984, Nexis UK, www.lexis nexis.com/uk/nexis.
94 George P. Schultz, cable to all diplomatic posts, Folder 9/82–10/82, Box OA91162, Walter Raymond Files, RL.
95 'Sakharov Institute Plans "Smuggle" Books to USSR', 4 November 1984, The Associated Press, http://web.lexis-nexis.com/executive.
96 National Endowment for Democracy, 'Annual Report, 1986', Folder: National Endowment for Democracy, Box OA92014, Alison B. Fortier Files, RL, 23.
97 Ibid., 21.
98 Ibid., 22.
99 Ibid., 23.
100 Ibid.
101 Britons get cash from US 'slush fund'/British organisations receiving money from US sources to "promote democracy"'.
102 Peter Grose, *Operation Rollback: America's Secret War behind the Iron Curtain* (Boston and New York: Houghton Mifflin Company, 2000), 48–49, 183–185.
103 Gregory F. Domber, 'The AFL-CIO, the Reagan Administration and Solidarnosc', *The Polish Review* 52, no. 3 (2007): 297, accessed 10 November 2014, www.jstor. org./stable/25779685.

184 *Promoting democracy*

104 Lorrie McHugh, 'AFL-CIO gives support to Solidarity', PR Newswire, 10 November 1989, Nexis UK, www.lexisnexis.com/uk/nexis.
105 Domber, 'The AFL-CIO, the Reagan Administration and Solidarnosc', 297.
106 National Endowment for Democracy, 'Annual Report, 1986', 19.
107 Ibid., 18–19.
108 Ibid.
109 National Endowment for Democracy 'Annual Report, 1986', 18–20.
110 Quoted from Gerald Sussman, *Branding Democracy: US Regime Change in Post-Soviet Eastern Europe* (New York: Peter Lang Publishing, Inc, 2010), 128.
111 Gregory Corning, 'The Philippine Bases and US Pacific Strategy', *Pacific Affairs* 63 no. 1 (1990): 10–13, accessed 5 September 2014, www.jstor.org/stable/2759811.
112 Amy Blitz, *the Contested State: American Foreign Policy and Regime Change in the Philippines* (Oxford: Rowman and Littlefield Publishers Inc, 2000), 158–159.
113 Ibid., 160.
114 Raymond Bonner, *Waltzing with a Dictator: The Marcoses and the Making of American Foreign Policy* (New York: Vintage Books, 1988), 357.
115 Blitz, *the Contested State*, 160–161.
116 Quoted from Ibid., 160.
117 Cable, Michael Armacost to George P. Schultz, 25 February 1984, Box OA91698, Folder 9, Box OA91698, Walter Raymond Files, RL.
118 Bonner, *Waltzing with a Dictator*, 39–42; Nick Cullather, 'America's Boy? Ramon Magsaysay and the Illusion of Influence', *The Pacific Historical Review* 62 no. 3 (1993): 326, accessed 30 September 2009, www.jstor.org/stable/3640933. See Jonathan Nashel, *Edward Lansdale's Cold War* (Amherst and Boston: University of Massachusetts Press, 2005), 32–37 for CIA support of Magsaysay during the 1953 election campaign.
119 Cable, Armacost to Schultz.
120 Sandra Burton, *Impossible Dream: The Marcoses, the Aquinos and the Unfinished Revolution* (New York: Warner Books, Inc., 1989), 243–244.
121 William I. Robinson, *Promoting Polyarchy: Globalization, US Intervention, and Hegemony* (Cambridge; Cambridge University Press, 1996), 130.
122 Bernstein, 'Is Big Labour playing global vigilante?'
123 Tim Shorrock and Kathy Selvaggio, 'Which side are you on AAFLI?' *The Nation*, 15 February 1986, accessed 28 August 2012, www.highbeam.com/doc/1G1-4136171.html.
124 Bonner, *Waltzing with a Dictator*, 360–363.
125 Quoted from Ibid., 360.
126 Blitz, 163.
127 Ibid.
128 Ibid., 165
129 Stanley Karnow, *In Our Image: America's Empire in the Philippines* (New York: Random House, Inc., 1989), 406–407.
130 Quoted from Robinson, *Promoting Polyarchy*, 124.
131 Blitz, *The Contested State*, 163.
132 Karnow, *In Our Image*, 408.
133 Quoted from Blitz, *The Contested State*, 164.
134 White House, 'NSDD 163: US policy towards the Philippines', 20 February 1985, FAS, accessed 21 June 2007, www.fas.org/irp/offdocs/nsdd/nsdd-163.htm, 1.
135 Ibid., 1–2.
136 Burton, *Impossible Dream*, 253.
137 Bonner, *Waltzing with a Dictator*, 368.
138 Shorrock and Selvaggio, 'Which side are you on AAFLI?'
139 Robinson, *Promoting Polyarchy*, 135.
140 Bernstein, 'Is Big Labour Playing Global Vigilante?' 5.

Promoting democracy 185

141 Shorrock and Selvaggio.
142 National Endowment for Democracy, 'Annual Report, 1984', *National Endowment for Democracy: Annual Reports*, accessed 27 May 2014. www.ned.org/docs/annual/1984Report.pdf, 20.
143 National Endowment for Democracy, 'Annual Report, 1985', *National Endowment for Democracy: Annual Reports*, accessed 27 May 2014. www.ned.org/docs/annual/1985%20NED%20Annual%20Report.pdf, 23.
144 'Annual Report, 1984', 20 and 'Annual Report, 1985', 23.
145 'Annual Report, 1985', 22.
146 Shorrock and Selvaggio.
147 Burton, *Impossible Dream*, 265–267.
148 Bruce W. Jentleson, 'Discrepant Responses to Falling Dictators: Presidential Belief Systems and the Mediating Effects of the Senior Advisory System', *Political Psychology* 11, no. 2 (1990): 375, accessed 5 April 2014, www.jstor.org/stable/3791694.
149 Robinson, 125.
150 Bonner, *Waltzing with a Dictator*, 379–380.
151 Blitz, *The Contested State*, 169.
152 Ibid., 168–169.
153 Bonner, 384.
154 Stephen Bosworth interviewed by Michael Mahoney for *The Foreign Affairs Oral History Collection of the Association for Diplomatic Studies and Training*, 24 February 2003, accessed 20 July 2013, www.adst.org/OH%20TOCs/Bosworth,%20Stephen.toc.pdf, 84.
155 Bonner, *Waltzing with a Dictator*, 383–384.
156 Bill Keller, 'US Says it Fears Philippines Faces a Wide Civil War', *New York Times*, 30 October 1985, Nexis UK, www.lexisnexis.com/uk/nexis; Gene Kramer, 'Possible Communist Victory Seen', The Associated Press, 31 October 1985, Nexis UK, www.lexisnexis.com/uk/nexis.
157 Bonner, *Waltzing with a Dictator*, 393.
158 Quoted from David F. Schmitz, *The United States and Right-wing Dictatorships 1965–1989* (Cambridge: Cambridge University Press, 2006), 237.
159 Bonner, *Waltzing with a Dictator*, 416.
160 Ibid., 417.
161 Bud Newman, 'State Indicates Apprehension about Philippine Elections', United Press International, 12 November 1985, Nexis UK, www.lexisnexis.com/uk/nexis.
162 Burton, *Impossible Dream*, 297.
163 Quoted from Walden Bello, 'Counterinsurgency's Proving Ground: Low-Intensity Warfare in the Philippines', in *Low Intensity Warfare: How the USA Fights Wars without Declaring Them*, ed. Michael T. Klare and Peter Kornbluh (London: Methuen, 1989), 169.
164 Ibid.; Bonner, *Waltzing with a Dictator*, 396–397.
165 Burton, *Impossible Dream*, 314–316.
166 Robinson, *Promoting Polyarchy*, 127.
167 Blitz, *The Contested State*, 172.
168 Quoted from Walden Bello, 'From Dictatorship to Elite Populism: The United States and the Philippine Crisis', in *Crisis and Confrontation: Ronald Reagan's Foreign Policy*, ed. Morris H. Morley (New Jersey: Rowman and Littlefield, 1988), 241.
169 Bonner, *Waltzing with a Dictator*, 414.
170 Ibid., 413; Schmitz, *The United States and Right-wing Dictatorships*, 175.
171 National Endowment for Democracy, 'Annual Report, 1986', 2
172 Bonner, *Waltzing with a Dictator*, 412–413.
173 National Endowment for Democracy, 'Annual Report, 1986', 2 and 13.
174 David B. Ottaway, 'U.S. Puts Marcos on Notice; Election Must Be "Free and Fair"', *Washington Post*, 13 November 1985, Nexis UK, www.lexisnexis.com/uk/nexis.

186 *Promoting democracy*

175 Bonner, *Waltzing with a Dictator*, 415.
176 Seth Mydans, 'Observers of vote cite wide fraud by Marcos party', *New York Times*, 10 February 1986, Nexis UK.
177 Blitz, 175.
178 Seth Mydans, 'Turnout Heavy in Philippine Voting amid Reports of Widespread Abuses', *New York Times*, 7 February 1986, Nexis UK, www.lexisnexis.com/uk/nexis.
179 Fernando Del Mundo, 'untitled', United Press International, 7 February 1986, Nexis UK, www.lexisnexis.com/uk/nexis.
180 National Endowment for Democracy, 'Annual Report, 1986', *National Endowment for Democracy: Annual Reports* accessed 27 May 2014, www.ned.org/docs/annual/1986%20NED%20Annual%20Report.pdf, 13.
181 Blitz, 177.
182 Quoted in Bonner, *Waltzing*, 437.
183 George P. Schultz, *Turmoil and Triumph: My Years as Secretary of State* (New York: Charles Scribner's Son, 1993), 628.
184 Jentleson, 'Discrepant Responses', 377; Karnow, *In Our Image*, 417.
185 Burton, *Impossible Dream*, 396; Karnow, *In Our Image*, 420–421.
186 Jentleson, 'Discrepant Responses', 379.
187 Quoted in Robinson, *Promoting Polyarchy*, 139.
188 'Annual Report, 1986', 3.
189 Quoted from Steve Coll, 'Paul Wolfowitz, Devising U.S. Policy in a Turbulent Time', *Washington Post*, 7 February 1986, Nexis UK, www.lexisnexis.com/uk/nexis.
190 Sheila S. Coronel, 'Dateline Philippines: The Lost Revolution', *Foreign Policy* 84 (1991): 167, accessed 20 April 2010, www.jstor.org/stable/1148789.
191 Karnow, *In Our Image*, 424.
192 Joel Rocamora, 'Lost Opportunities, Deepening Crisis: The Philippines under Cory Aquino', in *Low Intensity Democracy: Political Power in the New World Order*, ed. Barry Gills, Joel Rocamora and Richard Wilson (London: Pluto Press, 1993), 199–200.
193 Robinson, *Promoting Polyarchy*, 137.
194 Ibid., 136.
195 Ibid., 137.
196 Lois A. West, 'US Foreign Labor Policy and the Case of Militant Political Unionism in the Philippines', *Labor Studies Journal* 16, no. 4 (1991): 51, 69, accessed 10 November 2014, EBSCO Host.
197 Robinson, *Promoting Polyarchy*, 142.
198 Ibid., 143.
199 Ibid., 131–134.
200 Ibid., 131. See also 'Annual Report, 1986', 12–13.
201 Ibid.

Conclusion

US democracy promotion during the final phase of the Cold War and beyond

This study has examined the strategic and organisational factors that shaped the rise of democracy promotion under the Reagan administration. This process was both an episode in the longer history of the relationship between the export of democracy and US national security, and a key turning point which led to a reassessment of this relationship at the strategic level by the US elite, and to the generation of new organisational structures and tactics aimed more directly than previous policies at the creation of functioning democratic systems overseas.

The debates of the 1980s did not generate an overarching strategic framework that meshed democracy promotion and US national security, as the elite was divided into contending factions that proposed different strategic objectives and targets for democracy promotion. These divisions could not be overcome, only de-escalated. The outcome was a privately-managed but government-linked institution, the National Endowment for Democracy, which pursued projects of democratisation consistent with US national security objectives in both friendly and hostile dictatorships on a tactical basis. This was a compromise solution, which left tensions between democracy and US national security unresolved systematically at the strategic level, at the level of organisation, and at the level of programmes.

This conclusion examines the results of the rise of democracy promotion during the final phase of the Cold War in three areas: the strategic framework; the relationship between the state and non-state actors in the implementation of democracy promotion; and the relationship between democratic reform overseas and US national security. It then briefly discusses the development of democracy promotion after the Cold War and the tensions that have continued to characterise it.

The strategic framework

Individuals and groups outside the national security apparatus took the lead role in generating a strategic framework, separated from short-term state actions and priorities, for democracy promotion, and the tactics and organisational structure to pursue it. This framework was not constructed purely to pursue democratic reform overseas in line with US domestic values, but because these actors believed the promotion of democracy could be used as a vehicle to create more security for the US. However, in their attempt to realise their vision, these non-state actors encountered pre-existing attitudes and agendas in other sections of the elite.

The process of generating a strategic framework reconciling democracy promotion and national security led to disagreements between factions with differing conceptions of the relationship between democracy and national security objectives located within the administration, in Congress, and within the private sphere. Reaganite policymakers, motivated chiefly by anti-communism, advocated a narrow democracy campaign aimed at the promotion of reform within the Soviet Empire and efforts to combat communist groups. In contrast, officials in the State Department favoured a more expansive campaign aimed at containing Soviet expansion by preparing democratic successor groups in pro-US dictatorships while containing the USSR through support for dissident and nationalist groups. Each group feared that pursuit of its opponents' strategy could harm US interests, either by provoking rifts with pro-US dictators or crackdowns in enemy states, which could destroy friendly groups the US sought to empower. However, debate could not be limited to these groups of policymakers, as the requirement that democracy promotion be overt, a legacy of the covert state–private network's implosion in 1967, provided avenues for Congressional Democrats, who favoured an even-handed campaign against dictatorships of the left and right, and the non-state democracy promoters themselves, to influence the process.

The concept of democracy promotion proved to be capable of generating a consensus among this fragmented elite which allowed political operations to be pursued such as the support of Solidarity in Poland, dissident groups within the USSR, and friendly democratic forces in the Philippines. This shift in the rationale for US political intervention overseas from the anti-communist conception that had characterised the pre-1967 period of the Cold War to a conception focussed explicitly on concrete support for democracy and democratic forces provided an ideational grounding for these activities which was far more enduring and far more rooted in US political culture. However, this accommodation over democracy promotion actively led to failure to resolve the strategic question. A policy conceived and articulated in terms of this vision of democracy promotion could not be limited either to a focus solely on building democracy in the USSR rather than friendly dictatorships, or to pursuing operations to create political difficulties for the Soviet regime while failing to push for more wide-ranging democratic reforms when opportunities to do so arose. Instead, the concept included both containment through the creation of democratic systems in friendly dictatorships and attempts to transform enemy regimes, while prioritising neither goal and subsuming both under the concept of democracy promotion.

The lack of strategic debate within the network of non-state democracy promoters who engineered the creation of the NED, as opposed to the rifts within and between the administration and Congress, indicates that this strategic fuzziness was intrinsic to the concept of democracy promotion, rather than being imposed by factions in the Reagan administration or Congress in an attempt to

Conclusion: US democracy promotion   189

engineer consensus. Instead of being used to support a clear strategic option, the concept superseded differing agendas and so transcended the strategic issues. This convergence led the state and private groups to focus on the creation of the NED as a pragmatic solution to the problem of how to carry out political operations abroad rather than on resolving their differences over strategic agendas. This focus on organisational problems de-escalated policy conflicts within the elite over democracy promotion but blocked the formation of a strategic consensus. The result was a compromise which led to the creation of an organisation which could pursue democracy promotion on a case-by-case basis, not a coherent strategic framework.

The relationship between state and non-state actors in Cold War US democracy promotion

Although the fact that the NED received government funding invites parallels with the pre-1967 CIA-guided state–private network, the shift from a set of covert relationships based on a shared anti-communism to an overt relationship aimed at the promotion of democracy created a new dynamic for the management of political operations overseas. Congress' rejection of a supervisory role for the International Political Committee, necessary to secure the credibility of the NED under the new overt funding relationship, removed one possible mechanism for resolving the tensions between national security and democracy that remained due to the failure to generate a strategic framework. Instead, these tensions were resolved on a case-by-case basis through an overt management structure for political operations, which provided the Executive and Congress with different methods of influence over the Endowment.

The Endowment's double dependency on Congress and the Executive acted to contain its operations to cases where US national security interests could be pursued through democratic tactics. The NED's financial dependency on Congressional appropriations provided the legislature with leverage which it used to ensure that the NED foundations did not deploy democracy promotion merely as a concept to legitimate anti-communist operations with little or no democratic content. In contrast, the administration strengthened the NED's orientation towards national security due to the fact that it generated the foreign policy framework that the NED pursued its operations within and provided the pressure on other states and support for NED actions on the ground needed to carry out large-scale political projects. This double dependency on the Executive and Congress acted to more clearly define and institutionalise the new mode of political intervention pursued by the NED as being aimed at the fostering of democratic groups and systems compatible with US national security interests, rather than as a resurrection of previous CIA capabilities. The shift from a covert to an overt operating structure helped to lock in this change.

These arrangements meant that on a day-to-day basis the Endowment had a measure of autonomy to direct funding to democratic groups without micromanagement from the national security bureaucracy, giving it the flexibility to

190   *Conclusion: US democracy promotion*

pursue a double mission of transforming enemy states and fostering democratic transitions in friendly dictatorships. Some disjuncture between the groups the NED supported overseas and day-to-day US foreign policy was permissible, allowing the US to pursue diplomatic relations with key dictatorships while simultaneously preparing more suitable successor elites. However, this autonomy functioned within the limits set by the national security bureaucracy and Congress, and it was unlikely that the NED would give aid to foreign groups whose objectives were irreconcilable with US national security interests and so place its funding in danger.

In cases where support for democratic groups or political transitions could secure US national security interests, Congress and administration used the leverage they possessed to influence the NED's actions. In the cases of Grenada and Guatemala, the NED functioned within a framework set by the Reagan administration without substantial dissent from Congress. In the case of the Philippines, the NED, pragmatic administration officials and Congressional Democrats supported a transition that all believed to be in the US interest, despite uncertainty over the benefits of such a political transition in the top levels of the Reagan administration. However, pressure from top-tier policymakers was necessary to convince Marcos to leave power so that the democratic transition could unfold.

In later Cold War cases of democratisation, such as the 1988 referendum which led to subsequent democratic elections and the removal of the Pinochet dictatorship in Chile, the 1990 Nicaraguan elections which removed the FSLN from power, and the collapse of communism in Eastern Europe, coordination between the actors involved in democracy promotion was stronger. In these cases the NED was an actor within a larger US policy framework that also included the use of diplomacy or economic pressure by the US state to foster democratic transitions consistent with US interests. In Chile, Reagan administration policy had shifted towards support for a transition to democracy by the mid-80s,[1] and the US state used diplomatic and economic pressures to facilitate this.[2] Similarly, in Nicaragua the US government applied economic, military and diplomatic pressures to the Sandinista regime which acted alongside democracy promotion funding to remove the FSLN from power.[3] Furthermore, much of the funding the Endowment used to run programmes in these cases took the form of special grants provided by Congress or government agencies such as AID for these specific countries. Of the $2,010,000 that the Endowment disbursed in 1988 for democracy promotion in Eastern Europe, $1 million in funding for Solidarity originated from a special Congressional appropriation. In 1989, the year of the Polish elections that established Solidarity as a political force, the amount was approximately doubled to $4,065,826, with $2,000,000 of this being channelled to the Polish opposition from special Congressional appropriations and $308,868 from AID. In 1990, the total amount for Eastern Europe was $11,365,720; $995,700 from Congress and $8,467,462 from AID.[4] The NED also received an extra $1 million through a special Congressional appropriation for political work connected to Chile's 1988 plebiscite.[5] Extra funding spent on

Conclusion: US democracy promotion   191

NED programmes related to Nicaragua's 1990 election amounted to $7,143,525 from AID and $235,000 from a special Congressional appropriation.[6]

These links had the effect of making the NED an actor in US foreign policy that used its unique organisational status and political skills to conduct policies in line with goals agreed with Congress and the national security bureaucracy. Thus, effective action to support democratic forces in line with US national security interests required a consensus between the Endowment, administration officials and Congress, the three main actors in the new management structure for political operations overseas, which was forged on a case-by-case basis when these forces were able to agree that support for democratic reform could defend or extend US power. However, an unresolved tension inherent in the new structure for the implementation of political operations was that while a private group had been preferred due to the plausible deniability and credibility which it could bring to democracy promotion operations, neither the Executive nor Congress proved willing to provide the NED with complete autonomy. The ambiguous position of the NED as a privately-managed institution linked to and funded by the state constituted a threat to its credibility as an independent actor which all groups involved in the generation of democracy promotion failed to resolve at the moment of its creation.

National security and democratic reform

At the level of programmes, democracy promotion did not serve merely as a rhetorical justification for the continuation of covert operations aimed only at securing US national security interests in an overt form. Instead, the Endowment aimed at the promotion of democratic forms and institutions. However, democracy is a contested political concept, and democratic theory recognises a number of different models of democracy that vary from a narrow definition focussed on procedures and institutions to forms which emphasise higher degrees of direct participation and redistributive reform.[7] During the Cold War, the US and the NED promoted a form of liberal democracy based on the US model which did not embrace deeper levels of redistributive reform, or the welfarism associated with post-war models of liberal democracy.[8]

This outcome was partly a result of an ideological identification of democracy by policymakers and private democracy promoters with the particular system that developed in the United States. However, it was also a result of the limitation of the NED's autonomy through its dependence on and ideological congruence with the state, which resulted in the use of democracy promotion on a tactical basis to achieve pre-existing US national security interests by supporting transitions to a form of democracy which was compatible with US interests. This form emphasised the procedural features of democracy but did not embrace the social and economic reforms called for by previous concepts of reform and development in the Third World such as Human Rights or Modernisation.

Democracy promotion's focus on political liberty and its de-emphasis of social and economic development made it a more effective tool against

192 *Conclusion: US democracy promotion*

communism than the Human Rights campaign waged under Carter. Whereas communist states such as the Soviet Union could argue that they were in compliance with the social and economic aspects of Human Rights, the narrowing of the concept to political liberties delegitimised these regimes and served as a more effective weapon of ideological warfare. This shift provided both an ideological rationale for the dismantling of these regimes and an end-goal to be achieved. This goal was pursued through the support of anti-communist dissident forces such as Solidarity and, as political space in Eastern Europe opened up, other political groups across the region.[9] The political and economic dismantling of the communist systems these groups conducted brought the Cold War to an end, not merely as a geopolitical competition but as an ideological one, as the successor elites supported by the US reformed their societies in line with Western political and economic models.

In Third World dictatorships the US supported the construction of 'low intensity' democratic or polyarchic systems characterised by political contestation between elites, rather than a more populist political dynamic and redistributive socioeconomic reforms.[10] While this de-emphasis of socioeconomic change was ideologically consistent with the promotion of liberal democracy, it was also a result of a shift in the concept of democracy promotion. The original vision put forward by Douglas in 1972 represented a continuation of the Modernisation paradigm of conducting socioeconomic reform, implemented through the construction of mass democratic parties to carry out such deeper reform measures when in power.[11] However, the concept was narrowed by Michael Samuels and then government officials such as Alexander Haig into a political tool for aiding pro-US groups in order to block the growth of radical forces and to create stability in the national security interests of the United States. This shift had practical consequences. It resulted in US and NED support for transitions which occurred within restrictive parameters set by undemocratic forces, such as the Guatemalan military, or which favoured right or centre-right forces uncommitted to wider social and economic reforms, as in the Philippines. In addition the civil society groups supported by the NED also played a role in limiting the wider impact of such transitions by opposing other groups advocating more radical reform, as NED grantees such as the TUCP did in the Philippines.

There was little attempt to support forces aiming to accomplish tasks which academic theorists of democracy promotion such as Carothers consider to be important in creating a substantively democratic system, such as 'breaking down ... entrenched antidemocratic power structures' or 'reducing entrenched concentrations of economic power'.[12] The focus of US policy was not to empower forces aiming at social and economic restructuring of foreign societies, but to defuse such movements through the promotion of a form of change that focussed narrowly on the creation of political structures and procedures which would be seen as sufficiently legitimate to win the acceptance, active or passive, of the populations of target states. This tactic was less risky than the pursuit of the deep socioeconomic reforms which Modernisation called for, which had the potential to destabilise the target society and give rise to unexpected outcomes incompatible

Conclusion: US democracy promotion   193

with US interests, or the Carter administration's Human Rights policy of reducing US support for dictatorships to pressure them to liberalise, which could destabilise the sitting regimes but did not provide an acceptable political alternative which the US could support to block seizures of power by radical movements. In contrast, the narrower process of political reform which democracy promotion constituted enabled the US to support political change from decaying authoritarian regimes to more stable electoral democracies without destabilising the wider society or opening political systems to forces likely to challenge US interests.

Democracy promotion provided a way in which two different projects, the undermining of enemy regimes and the stabilisation of friendly states through political reform, could be integrated conceptually as aspects of one global liberal democratic revolution. However, the channelling of funding and support to pro-US groups which constituted democracy promotion in practice tended to favour types of reform which were consistent with US national security interests.

Democracy promotion and US foreign policy after the Cold War

The rise of democracy promotion under the Reagan administration has had an impact on the foreign policy of all subsequent administrations. The debates of the 1980s left behind them a set of ideas on the relationship between democracy and national security and the beginnings of an institutional framework for democracy promotion programmes which were expanded upon in the post-Cold War world, as well as a series of tensions which have continued and intensified.

The collapse of the Soviet system, widely interpreted as a victory for liberal democracy, together with the rise to prominence of Democratic Peace Theory, the idea that a democratic world will be more peaceful because democracies do not go to war with one another, further boosted the popularity of democracy promotion within the US elite and resulted in its increased deployment both as an ideological anchor of US foreign policy and a vehicle for pursuing US goals in the post-Cold War period. The Clinton administration decided on 'Democratic Enlargement' as the key US foreign policy goal to replace containment and expounded this in speeches by National Security Advisor Anthony Lake, by the President, and in its national security strategy.[13] The 9/11 attacks then increased the importance of democracy promotion as a national security goal by pointing to the existence of a threat which policymakers believed could be combatted through the promotion of democratic reform overseas. The George W. Bush administration deployed democracy promotion as a key element of US foreign policy in the Middle East[14] in order to remove or reform the dictatorships which, the President argued, gave rise to terrorist movements by closing off opportunities for non-violent political change.[15] This argument was based on similar premises to the idea put forward by non-state democracy promoters and some State Department officials under Reagan that democratic reform could be used to defuse Marxist movements. Although democracy promotion has been

194 *Conclusion: US democracy promotion*

rhetorically de-emphasised under the Obama administration, it has continued to be an element of US foreign policy.[16]

The institutionalisation of US democracy promotion has also expanded. The Endowment continues to operate, and continues to be influenced by the Executive through instructions and negotiations regarding the use of extra funding, and by Congress through earmarking of funding for specific countries, instructions and suggestions attached to its appropriations.[17] The US state has also taken up a major direct role in democracy promotion, as the Endowment has been joined by agencies and offices created after the Cold War and during the War on Terror, such as AID's Bureau of Democracy, Conflict and Humanitarian Assistance, the State Department's Bureau of Democracy, Human Rights and Labor, and the Middle East Partnership Initiative, all of which provide funding for civil society groups overseas and attempt to encourage democratic reform.[18] US government spending on democracy promotion has also increased exponentially. The Obama administration's budget request for democracy promotion in 2012 was $2.8 billion,[19] compared to the budget for the Endowment in its first year, which was under $20 million.

This degree of institutionalisation has created a permanent constituency of support for and bureaucratic interest in democracy promotion as a policy. While the creation of the Endowment provided a focal point for non-state democracy promoters to coalesce around and to communicate with and lobby Congress through, the greater embedding of democracy promotion in government agencies after the Cold War has created a democracy promotion lobby within the national security bureaucracy itself. These private and state lobbies do not necessarily have the decisive voice in policymaking on democracy promotion in each contingency. However, their existence means that a return to a Nixonian-style foreign policy which eschews democracy promotion completely is not possible without major restructuring within the national security bureaucracy and a widespread devaluing of the idea of democracy promotion in US political culture; neither of which seems likely.

Alongside these developments, however, the strategic and organisational incoherence at the heart of democracy promotion has continued. Democracy promotion, when pursued seriously, has remained a case-by-case or regional enterprise focussed on those areas where it can be used as a vehicle for achieving US national security interests. Even the Bush administration, which sometimes couched its foreign policy in extremely universalistic democratic rhetoric, targeted its democracy promotion activities on the Middle Eastern states seen as threatening to the United States, either because their regimes were hostile to the United States or because they were seen as incubators of further terrorist threats, while maintaining alliances with dictatorships in South and Central Asia.[20] Organisationally, the US government 'democracy bureaucracy' is riven by departmental rivalries, differing priorities, overlapping programmes, and even lacks a common definition of democracy promotion.[21] An important reason for this is that the national security bureaucracy lacks a command centre for democracy promotion initiatives tasked with developing and coordinating an overall

Conclusion: US democracy promotion 195

democracy strategy[22] similar to the Reagan administration's International Political Committee or Special Planning Group. This means that coordination between government agencies, and with non-state groups, is likely to continue to emerge in relation to specific countries on a case-by-case basis, due to the imperfect fit between democracy promotion and US national security interests.

A further issue is that the credibility problem originally created by the NED's links to the state has been exacerbated by the institutionalisation of democracy promotion within government agencies, the higher rhetorical profile given to democracy promotion under the Bush administration, and the involvement or perceived involvement of the NED and the US in highly public attempted and successful regime changes in Serbia in 2000,[23] Venezuela in 2002,[24] Georgia in 2003,[25] Haiti[26] in 2004 and the Ukraine in 2005.[27] Due to these developments many authoritarian governments have become deeply suspicious of democracy promotion, leading to legal restrictions on foreign funding for NGOs in Russia and a number of authoritarian states in the former Soviet Union, Latin America and Africa.[28] These restrictions create a more hostile environment for the Endowment and other organisations, both state and private, to operate in. Furthermore, some democracy activists in areas such as the Middle East have perceived democracy promotion as a tool of or smokescreen for the pursuit of US geopolitical interests.[29] One of the original rationales behind vesting democracy promotion activities in a non-governmental organisation was to safeguard the credibility of such programmes by maintaining a separation between them and the national security bureaucracy. However, the forces involved in the creation of the NED failed to solve the obvious credibility problem created by the organisation's receipt of government funds, and the increasingly important profile of democracy promotion in the US' national security strategy and organisational infrastructure has only worsened the problem.

Finally, the clash between democracy promotion and short-term national security objectives continues at the level of individual cases. This was particularly apparent in the Bush administration's policy towards the reform of authoritarian allies in the Middle East, which was torn between the competing imperatives of fostering democratisation over the long term to remove the terrorist threat to the US and blocking the accession to power of Islamist movements.[30] This often led to inconsistent pressure on allied authoritarian Arab states to reform.[31] This was clear in the case of US policy towards Egypt, where the US' fear of growing Islamist political power resulted in the reduction of pressure on the Mubarak administration to reform by the Bush and Obama administrations.[32] Far from representing a triumph for US democracy promotion, the outbreak of the 2011 revolution in Egypt, and the Arab Spring Uprisings in general, resulted in the uncontrolled popular mobilisations that democracy promotion seeks to avoid through fostering orderly and limited political change to decompress potentially explosive political conflicts. It may well have been beyond the power of the US to alter this outcome. However, in Egypt the limitation of democracy promotion by competing security interests meant that when the Mubarak regime began to lose control the US had no clear policy towards

196 *Conclusion: US democracy promotion*

political change and no chosen successor group to support. This resulted in a lack of US influence over Egypt's transition, which led in turn to political instability and renewed authoritarianism.

Conclusion

The policy debates over the role of democracy in US foreign policy of the early 1980s produced a rationale for US political intervention overseas which transcended previous conceptions rooted in anti-communism. However, they did not produce a coherent strategy which meshed democracy and national security, but a compromise between the two imperatives at an organisational and tactical levels. At the organisational level, the NED was largely autonomous on a day-to-day basis; however, the orientation of its senior officials towards US national security goals and institutional constraints on full autonomy ensured that its actions, especially those aimed at large-scale political change, were compatible with US national security interests. At the tactical level, the NED supported democratic groups committed to a type of liberal democracy consistent with US interests rather than wider or differing reform projects which might clash with such interests. The final result was a new method for undermining enemy regimes and stabilising friendly states by fostering the growth of pro-US successor elites. After the Cold War democracy promotion was further institutionalised in policy declarations and in the organisational machinery of the national security bureaucracy; however, the legacy of strategic incoherence, lack of formal organisational coordination, and the damage to the credibility of US democracy promotion caused by state involvement, have intensified.

This outcome reflects the persistence of the clash between the two imperatives of exporting democracy and pursuing national security interests at the operational, as opposed to conceptual and rhetorical, level of US foreign policy. This tension leads to conflicts over the relationship of democracy to US national security, as some policymakers prioritise the democratisation of particular countries or regions, while believing that democratisation projects in other areas are compatible with US interests but of lesser importance, and that in still other areas democratisation may actively threaten US interests by opening up the political systems of key states to hostile forces. These calculations are not fixed but are altered by changes in external geopolitical conditions, by changes in the balance of political forces within possible target states, and by shifting balances of power within the national security bureaucracy or other institutions, which are sometimes linked to these geopolitical shifts. Due to this there can be no fixed overarching strategy that fuses democracy and US national security. In place of a strategic approach, there has been a constantly evolving process of negotiation between different factions of policymakers and other interested parties, in which accommodation over specific countries on a case-by-case basis is the only realistic outcome.

This process of calculation and negotiation means that efforts to promote democratic reform have not occurred on a global scale with the same level of

Conclusion: US democracy promotion   197

intensity; nor have specific areas been targeted in line with a grand strategy or commensurate with their need for assistance to build democratic structures. Instead, US democratisation programmes and policies have been concentrated in states where the US has key national security objectives that can be safeguarded or accomplished through such efforts. Democracy has been a policy goal in enemy states where policymakers believe that the national security threat posed by the state is traceable to the dictatorial nature of its domestic system, and that there is a good prospect of altering this system through pressure for democracy. In allied dictatorships, a transition to democracy has been pursued when the current government is believed to be in danger of collapsing and where there is a good prospect that strengthening a political movement compatible with US interests can pre-empt a seizure of power by forces hostile to the US. In these circumstances the US support of democracy is a concrete policy goal, not merely a rhetorical trope. However, the fact that democracy is used as a tool for the pursuit of US interests means that US support is distributed only to political groups with reform projects consistent with these interests, reproducing the strategic clash between democracy and US interests at the level of cases and countries.

Beyond any surface reconciliation of democracy and national security in US foreign policy which occurs, the deeper tensions involved in the pursuit of both of these imperatives continue and cannot be resolved, despite arguments put forward by policymakers or neoconservative commentators that such a resolution has been or can be achieved to yield a coherent policy of promoting democracy on a global basis.[33] Democracy cannot be abandoned as a component of foreign policy and replaced with a focus on pure realpolitik in terms of national security or economic interest, as this would be unpalatable in terms of domestic politics and would dissipate the advantages that the US gains from its disjointed support for democracy at the rhetorical level and in specific cases where concrete support for political reform can defend or extend US power. Equally, a policy focussed on the unqualified promotion of democracy as the highest and most constant of goal of US policy would soon encounter the reality that US national security in some cases or regions is dependent on relations with dictatorial regimes, and that not all foreign populations, if given full political autonomy, would make choices consistent with US interests. The tension between democracy and US national security is not one that is susceptible to resolution, but a recurring feature of America's engagement with the world.

Notes

1 Morris Morley and Chris McGillion, 'Soldiering On: The Reagan Administration and Redemocratisation in Chile, 1983–1986', *Bulletin of Latin American Research* 25, no. 1 (2006): 1–22, accessed 19 August 2014, DOI: 10.1111/j.0261–3050.2006.00150.x.
2 William Robinson, *Promoting Polyarchy: Globalization, US Intervention & Hegemony* (Cambridge: Cambridge University Press, 1996), 167–175.
3 Ibid., 235–239.
4 National Endowment for Democracy, 'Annual Report 1988', *National Endowment*

198 *Conclusion: US democracy promotion*

  for Democracy: Annual Reports, accessed 27 July 2013. www.ned.org/docs/annual/1988%20NED%20Annual%20Report.pdf, 21–25, 'Annual Report 1989', 19–24, and 'Annual Report 1990,' 23–30, accessed 27 July 2013.

5 National Endowment for Democracy, 'Annual Report 1988', 33–35.

6 NED, 'Annual Report 1990', 42–43.

7 Christopher Hobson, 'The Limits of Liberal-Democracy Promotion', *Alternatives* 34 (2009): 399, accessed 10 May 2013, doi: 10.1177/030437540903400402; Milja Kurki, 'Democracy and Conceptual Contestability: Reconsidering Conceptions of Democracy in Democracy Promotion', *International Studies Review* 12 (2010): 372–376, accessed 10 May 2013, doi: 10.1111/j.1468–2486.2010.00943.x; and David Held, *Models of Democracy* (Cambridge: Polity, 2006).

8 Hobson, 386 and 399; Kurki, 365; and Steve Smith, 'US Democracy Promotion: Critical Questions', in *American Democracy Promotion: Impulses, Strategies, Impacts*, ed. Michael Cox, G. John Ikenberry and Takashi Inoguchi (Oxford: Oxford University Press, 2000); 70.

9 'Annual Report 1990', 23–30.

10 Barry Gills, Joel Rocamora, Joel and Richard Wilson, 'Low Intensity Democracy', in *Low Intensity Democracy: Political Power in the New World Order*, ed. Barry Gills, Joel Rocamora and Richard Wilson (London: Pluto Press, 1993), 3–34, Hobson, 393 and Robinson, 49.

11 William A. Douglas, *Developing Democracy* (Washington DC: Heldref Publications, 1972), 119–121.

12 Thomas Carothers, *Critical Mission: Essays on Democracy Promotion* (Washington DC: Carnegie Endowment for International Peace, 2004), 166, 263.

13 Anthony Lake, 'From Containment to Enlargement', 21 September, *FAS*, accessed 27 January 2012, http://fas.org/news/usa/1993/usa-930921.htm, Douglas Brinkley, 'Democratic Enlargement: The Clinton Doctrine', *Foreign Affairs* 97, no. 106 (1997): 110–117 and White House, 'A National Security Strategy of Engagement and Enlargement', 1 February 1995, *National Security Strategy Archive*, accessed 19 December 2014. http://nssarchive.us/NSSR/1995.pdf, 2.

14 White House. 'The National Security Strategy of the United States of America', 17 September 2002, *National Security Strategy Archive*, accessed 3 December 2014, http://nssarchive.us/NSSR/2002.pdf, 6 and White House, 'The National Security Strategy of the United States of America', 16 March 2006. *National Security Strategy Archive*, accessed 19 December 2014, http://nssarchive.us/NSSR/2006.pdf, 4–7, 33.

15 See George W. Bush, 'Remarks Given at the 20th Anniversary of the National Endowment for Democracy', 6 November 2003, accessed 3 May 2014, www.ned.org/george-w-bush/remarks-by-president-george-w-bush-at-the-20th-anniversary.

16 Nicolas Bouchet, 'The democracy tradition in US foreign policy and the Obama presidency', *International Affairs* 89 no. 1 (2013): 48–51, accessed 9 June 2014, DOI: 10.1111/1468–2346.12003.

17 Thomas O. Melia, 'The Democracy Bureaucracy: The Infrastructure of American Democracy Promotion, Appendix 1: Being A Taxonomy of the Democracy Promotion Infrastructure', (Discussion paper prepared for the Princeton Project on National Security Working Group on Global Institutions and Foreign Policy Infrastructure, September, 2005), accessed 14 September 2012, www.princeton.edu/~ppns/papers/democracy_bureaucracy.pdf, 3–4, footnote 38 and Ibid., 'Appendix 2: Excerpts from Senate report 109–096 Department of State, Foreign Operations, and related programs Appropriations Bill FY 2006 (reported June 30, 2005)'.

18 Melia, 5–6, 10.

19 Figure taken from Bouchet, 48.

20 Thomas Carothers, 'Promoting Democracy and Fighting Terror', *Foreign Affairs* 82, no. 1 (2003): 85–91, accessed 6 December 2014, www.jstor.org/stable/20033430.

21 Melia, 12.

Conclusion: US democracy promotion   199

22 Ibid., 2.
23 Michael J. Barker, 'Taking the risk out of civil society: harnessing social movements and regulating revolutions', (refereed paper presented to the Australasian Political Studies Association Conference, University of Newcastle, 2006), 6–7, accessed 10 July 2014, www.newcastle.edu.au/Resources/Schools/Newcastle%20Business%20School/APSA/INTLREL/Barker-Michael.pdf, and Gerald Sussman, *Branding Democracy: US Regime Change in Post-Soviet Eastern Europe* (New York: Peter Lang, 2010), 140–147.
24 Eva Golinger (2007), *The Chavez Code: Cracking US Intervention in Venezuela* (London: Pluto Press, 2007).
25 Barker, 8–10 and Sussman, 147–162.
26 Max Blumenthal, 'The Other Regime Change', *Salon.com*, 17 July 2004, accessed 4 February 2012, www.salon.com/2004/07/17/haiti_coup/.
27 Sussman, 155–163.
28 National Endowment for Democracy, 'The Backlash against Democracy Assistance', 8 June 2006, *National Endowment for Democracy: Key NED Documents*, accessed 29 January 2012, www.ned.org/docs/backlash06.pdf, 24, 40–50.
29 Erin A. Snider and David M. Faris, 'The Arab Spring: US Democracy Promotion in Egypt', *Middle East Policy* 18, no. 3 (2011): 55, accessed 3 December 2014, DOI: 10. 1111/j.1475–4967.2011.00497.x.
30 David Hastings Dunn, 'Bush, 11 September and the Conflicting Strategies of the "War on Terrorism"', *Irish Studies in International Affairs* 16 (2005): 30, 32, accessed 5 September 2013, www.jstor.org/stable/30001932; Katerina Dalacoura, 'US Democracy Promotion in the Arab Middle East since 11 September 2001: A Critique,' *International Affairs* 85, no. 1 (2005): 972, accessed 27 April 2014, www.jstor.org/stable/3569070.
31 Ibid., 968.
32 Fawaz A. Gerges, *Obama and the Middle East: The End of America's Moment?* (New York: Palgrave Macmillan, 2012), 162–165.
33 George W. Bush 'Second Inaugural Address', 20 January 2005, *Project Gutenberg: Inaugural Addresses of the Presidents of the United States*, accessed 4 December 2014, www.gutenberg.org/files/925/925-h/925-h.htm#link2H_4_0056; Mark Palmer, *Breaking the Real Axis of Evil: How to Oust the World's Last Dictators by 2025* (Lanham, Maryland: Rowman and Littlefield Publishers Inc, 2005); Joshua Muravchik, *Exporting Democracy: Fulfilling America's Destiny* (Washington DC: American Enterprise Institute, 1991).

Bibliography

Archives

Library of Congress

George E. Agree Papers

Ronald Reagan Presidential Library

Staff Member and Office Files

Alison B. Fortier
Executive Secretariat, NSC
Robert Kimmitt
Walter Raymond
Steve Steiner

Online resources

Central Intelligence Agency Freedom Of Information Act Electronic Reading Room, Special Collections, *Ronald Reagan, Intelligence and the End of the Cold War*, www.foia.cia.gov/Reagan.asp [last accessed 26 September 2014]

Declassified Documents Reference System [last accessed 14 September 2012]

DISAM: Defense Institute of Security Assistance Management, *Readings in Security Assistance: A selected bibliography of articles of current interest*, www.disam.dsca.mil/pubs/Indexes/Vol%204 [last accessed 16 March 2011]

Federation of American Scientists, *National Security Decision Directives* – Reagan, www.fas.org/irp/offdocs/nsdd/index.html [last accessed 20 April 2012]

Foreign Affairs Oral History Collection, Association for Diplomatic Studies and Training, Arlington, VA, www.adst.org. [last accessed 30 September 2014]

US Government Accountability Office Electronic Records Archive, www.gao.gov/ [last accessed 19 December 2014]

National Endowment for Democracy, http://ned.org/publications [last accessed 27 May 2014]

National Security Strategy Archive, http://nssarchive.us/ [last accessed 19 December 2014]

US Department of State Office of the Historian, *Foreign Relations of the United States 1945–50: Retrospective Volume, Emergence of the Intelligence Establishment.* http://history.state.gov/historicaldocuments/frus1945-50Intel/d269. [last accessed 19 December 2014]

US Department of State Office of the Historian, *Foreign Relations of the United States 1964–1968, Volume X, National Security Policy.* http://history.state.gov/historicaldocuments/frus1964-68v10/d134. [last accessed 19 December 2014]

US Department of State Office of the Historian, *Foreign Relations of the United States 1977–1980, Volume II, Human Rights and Humanitarian Affairs.* http://static.history.state.gov/frus/frus1977-80v02/pdf/frus1977-80v02.pdf. [last accessed 27 November 2014]

US Department of State Freedom of Information Act Electronic Reading Room. www.state.gov/m/a/ips/c22798.htm [last accessed 24 April 2006]

Newspapers and news magazines

Business Week
Newsweek
The Boston Globe
The Christian Science Monitor
The Economist
Guardian
International Herald Tribune
The Nation
The National Journal
New York Times
Washington Post
Washington Times
Wall Street Journal
Time Magazine

Newswires

The Associated Press
Facts on File
United Press International

Memoirs and biographies

Carter, James Earl. *Keeping Faith: Memoirs of a President.* Fayetteville, Arkansas: University of Arkansas Press, 1982.

Haig, Alexander M. *Caveat: Realism, Reagan and Foreign Policy.* New York: Macmillan Publishing Company, 1984.

Helms, Richard with Hood, William. *A look over my shoulder: a life in the Central Intelligence Agency.* New York: Random House, 2003.

Menges, Constantine C. *Inside the National Security Council: The true story of the making and unmaking of Reagan's foreign policy.* New York: Simon and Schuster, 1988.

202   *Bibliography*

Meyer, Cord. *Facing Reality: From World Federalism to the CIA*. Lanham: University Press of America, 1980.

Pipes, Richard. *Vixi: Memoirs of a Non-Belonger*. New Haven and London: Yale University Press, 2003.

Reagan, Ronald. *An American Life*. London: Hutchinson, 1990.

Schultz, George P. *Turmoil and Triumph: My Years as Secretary of State*. New York: Charles Scribner's Son, 1993.

Thatcher, Margaret. *The Downing Street Years*. London: HarperCollins, 1993.

Books

Abrahamian, Ervand. *The Coup: 1953, the CIA and the Roots of Modern US-Iranian Relations*. New York and London: The New Press, 2013.

Alexandre, Laurien. *The Voice of America: From Détente to the Reagan Doctrine*. Norwood; New Jersey: Ablex Publishing Corporation, 1988.

Andrew, Christopher. *For the President's Eyes Only: Secret Intelligence and the American Presidency from Washington to Bush*. London: Harper Collins Publishers, 1996.

Barry, Tom, and Preusch, Deb. *AIFLD in Central America: Agents as Organizers*. Albuquerque, NM: Inter-Hemispheric Education Center, 1990.

Blitz, Amy. *The Contested State: American Foreign Policy and Regime Change in the Philippines*. Oxford: Rowman and Littlefield Publishers Inc, 2000.

Bonner, Raymond. *Waltzing with a Dictator: The Marcoses and the Making of American Policy*. New York: Vintage Books, 1988.

Brands, H.W. *The Wages of Globalism: Lyndon Johnson and the Limits of American Power*. Oxford: Oxford University Press, 1995.

Burton, Sandra. *Impossible Dream: The Marcoses, the Aquinos, and the Unfinished Revolution*. New York: Warner Books, 1989.

Cammack, Paul. *Capitalism and Democracy in the Third World: The Doctrine for Political Development*. London: Leicester University Press, 1997.

Cannon, Lou. *President Reagan: The Role of a Lifetime*. New York: Simon and Schuster, 1991.

Carothers, Thomas. *In the Name of Democracy: US policy towards Latin America in the Reagan Years*. Berkeley and Los Angeles, California: University of California Press, 1991.

Carothers, Thomas. *Critical Mission: Essay on Democracy Promotion*. Washington DC: Carnegie Endowment for International Peace, 2004.

Carter, James M. *Inventing Vietnam: The United States and State Building in Southeast Asia 1954–1968*. Cambridge: Cambridge University Press, 2008.

Chomsky, Noam. *Deterring Democracy*. London: Verso, 1991.

Douglas, William A. *Developing Democracy*. Washington DC: Heldref Publications, 1972.

Dueck, Colin. *Reluctant Crusaders: Power, Culture, and Change in American Grand Strategy*. Princeton and Oxford: Princeton University Press, 2006.

Dumbrell, John. *The Carter Presidency: A Re-evaluation*. Manchester: Manchester University Press, 1995.

Dumbrell, John. *American Foreign Policy: Carter to Clinton*. Basingstoke: Macmillan, 1997.

Evans, Tony. *US Hegemony and the Project of Universal Human Rights*. Basingstoke: Macmillan Press, 1996.

Bibliography 203

Fischer, Beth A. *The Reagan Reversal: Foreign Policy and the End of the Cold War*. Columbia; London: University of Missouri Press, 1997.

Friedman, Murray. *The Neoconservative Revolution: Jewish Intellectuals and the Shaping of Public Policy*. New York: Cambridge University Press, 2005.

Funigiello, Philip J. *American–Soviet Trade in the Cold War*. Chapel Hill: University of North Carolina Press, 1988.

Gaddis, John Lewis. *Strategies of Containment: A Critical Appraisal of American National Security Policy During the Cold War*. Revised and Expanded Edition. New York: Oxford University Press, 2005.

Garthoff, Raymond L. *Détente and Confrontation: American–Soviet Relations from Nixon to Reagan*. Washington DC: The Brookings Institute, 1985.

Garthoff, Raymond L. *The Great Transition: American–Soviet relations and the End of the Cold War*. Washington DC: The Brookings Institute, 1994.

Garton Ash, Timothy. *The Polish Revolution: Solidarity*. London: Penguin Books, 1999.

Gerges, Fawaz A. *Obama and the Middle East: The End of America's Moment?* New York: Palgrave Macmillan, 2012.

Gerson, Mark. *The Neoconservative Vision: From the Cold War to the Culture Wars*. Oxford: Madison Books, 1997.

Golinger, Eva. *The Chavez Code: Cracking US Intervention in Venezuela*. London: Pluto Press, 2007.

Grose, Peter. *Operation Rollback: America's Secret War Behind the Iron Curtain*. Boston; New York: Houghton Mifflin Company, 2000.

Guilhot, Nicolas. *The Democracy Makers: Human Rights and International Order*. New York, Chichester: Columbia University Press, 2005.

Gutman, Roy. *Banana Diplomacy: The Making of American Policy in Nicaragua 1981–1987*. New York: Simon and Schuster, 1988.

Halliday, Fred. *The Making of the Second Cold War*. London: Verso, 1984.

Halperin, Morton H. *Bureaucratic Politics and Foreign Policy*. Washington DC: The Brookings Institute, 1974.

Held, David. *Models of Democracy*. Cambridge: Polity, 2006.

Herman, Edward S. and Brodhead, Frank. *Demonstration Elections: US-Staged Elections in The Dominican Republic, Vietnam and El Salvador*. Boston: South End Press, 1984.

Hunt, Michael. *Ideology and US Foreign Policy*. New Haven and London: Yale University Press, 1987.

Johnson, Loch K. *A Season of Inquiry: The Senate Intelligence Investigation*. Lexington, Kentucky: The University Press of Kentucky, 1985.

Karnow, Stanley. *In Our Image: America's Empire in the Philippines*. New York: Random House, 1989.

Kaufman, Burton I. and Kaufman, Scott. *The Presidency of James Earl Carter*. Second Edition, Revised. Lawrence, Kansas: University Press of Kansas, 2006.

Kinzer, Stephen. *Overthrow: America's Century of Regime Change from Hawaii to Iraq*. New York: Time Books, 2006.

Kolko, Gabriel. *Confronting the Third World: United States Foreign Policy, 1945–1980*. New York: Pantheon Books, 1988.

Kovrig, Bennett. *Of Walls and Bridges: The United States and Eastern Europe*. New York and London: New York University Press, 1991.

LaFeber, Walter. *Inevitable Revolutions: The United States in Central America*. New York and London: W.W. Norton & Company, 1984.

204   Bibliography

Lettow, Paul. *Ronald Reagan's Quest to Abolish Nuclear Weapons*. New York: Random House, 2005.

Lucas, Scott. *Freedom's War: The US Crusade against the Soviet Union 1945–56*. Manchester: Manchester University Press, 1999.

Melanson, Richard. *American Foreign Policy since the Vietnam War: the Search for Consensus from Nixon to Clinton*. Armonk, New York: M.E. Sharpe, 2000.

Mickelson, Sig. *America's Other Voice: the story of Radio Free Europe and Radio Liberty*. New York: Praeger, 1983.

Montgomery, Tommie Sue. *Revolution in El Salvador: From Civil Strife to Civil Peace*. Boulder, San Francisco and Oxford: Westview Press, 1995.

Morgan, Ted. *A Covert Life: Jay Lovestone; Communist, Anti-communist, and Spymaster*. New York: Random House, 1999.

Morley, Morris H. *Washington, Somoza and the Sandinistas: State and Regime in US Policy towards Nicaragua 1969–1981*. Cambridge: Cambridge University Press, 1994.

Muravchik, Joshua. *The Uncertain Crusade: Jimmy Carter and the Dilemmas of Human Rights Policy*. Washington DC: American Enterprise Institute for Public Policy, 1986.

Muravchik, Joshua. *Exporting Democracy: Fulfilling America's Destiny*. Washington DC: American Enterprise Institute, 1991.

Nashel, Jonathan. *Edward Lansdale's Cold War*. Amherst and Boston: University of Massachusetts Press, 2005.

Ninkovich, Frank. *The Diplomacy of Ideas: US foreign policy and cultural relations, 1938–1950*. Cambridge: Cambridge University Press, 1981.

Packenham, Robert A. *Liberal America and the Third World: Political Development Ideas in Foreign Aid and Political Science*. Princeton, New Jersey: Princeton University Press, 1973.

Palmer, Mark. *Breaking the Real Axis of Evil: How to Oust the World's Last Dictators by 2025*. Lanham, Maryland: Rowman and Littlefield Publishers Inc, 2005.

Pastor, Robert A. *Not Condemned to Repetition: the United States and Nicaragua*. Boulder, Colorado: Westview, 2002.

Perlmutter, Amos. *Making the World Safe for Democracy: a Century of Wilsonianism and its Totalitarian Challengers*. Chapel Hill: University of North Carolina Press, 1997.

Puddington, Arch. *Broadcasting Freedom: the Cold War triumph of Radio Free Europe and Radio Liberty*. Lexington, Kentucky: University Press of Kentucky, 2000.

Puddington, Arch. *Lane Kirkland: Champion of American Labor*. New Jersey: John Wiley and Sons, Inc., 2005.

Quinn, Adam. *US Foreign Policy in Context: National Ideology from the Founders to the Bush Doctrine*. London and New York: Routledge, 2010.

Rabe, Stephen G. *The Killing Zone: The United States Wages Cold War in Latin America*. Oxford: Oxford University Press, 2012.

Rachwald, Arthur. *In Search of Poland: The Superpowers' Response to Solidarity, 1980–1989*. Stanford, California: Hoover Press, 1990.

Robinson, William I. *Promoting Polyarchy: Globalization, US Intervention and Hegemony*. Cambridge: Cambridge University Press, 1996.

Rostow, W.W. *The Stages of Economic Growth: A Non-communist Manifesto*. Third Edition. Cambridge: Cambridge University Press, 1990.

Rowland, Robert C. and Jones, John M. *Reagan at Westminster: Foreshadowing the End of the Cold War*. Texas A & M University Press: United States of America, 2010.

Ryan, David. *US Foreign Policy in World History*. London and New York: Routledge, 2000.

Bibliography 205

Sanders, Jerry W. *Peddlers of Crisis: The Committee on the Present Danger and the Politics of Containment.* Boston: South End Press, 1983.

Saull, Richard. *The Cold War and After: Capitalism, Revolution and Superpower Politics.* London, Pluto Press, 2007.

Scheer, Robert. *With Enough Shovels: Reagan, Bush and Nuclear War.* New York: Random House, 1982.

Schmitz, David F. *Thank God They're On Our Side: The United States & Right-wing Dictatorships 1921–1965.* Chapel Hill and London: The University of North Carolina Press, 1999.

Schmitz, David F. *The United States and Right-wing Dictatorships, 1965–1989.* Cambridge: Cambridge University Press, 2006.

Schlesinger, Stephen and Kinzer, Stephen. *Bitter Fruit: The Story of the American Coup in Guatemala.* Expanded Edition. Cambridge, Massachusetts and London, England: Harvard University Press, 1999.

Schweizer, Peter. *Victory: The Reagan Administration's Secret Strategy that Hastened the Collapse of the Soviet Union.* New York: The Atlantic Monthly Press, 1994.

Scott, James M. *Deciding to Intervene: The Reagan Doctrine and American Foreign Policy.* Durham and London: Duke University Press, 1996.

Sims, Beth. *Workers of the World Undermined: American Labor's Role in US Foreign Policy.* Boston, MA: South End Press, 1992.

Smith, Tony. *America's Mission: the United States and the Worldwide Struggle for Democracy in the Twentieth Century.* Princeton New Jersey: Princeton University Press, 1994.

Snyder, Sarah B. *Human Rights Activism and the End of the Cold War: A Transnational History of the Helsinki Network.* Cambridge: Cambridge University Press, 2011.

Stonor Saunders, Frances. *Who Paid the Piper?: The CIA and the Cultural Cold War.* London: Granta Books, 1999.

Sussman, Gerald. *Branding Democracy: US Regime Change in Post-Soviet Eastern Europe.* New York: Peter Lang Publishing, Inc, 2010.

Taffet, Jeffrey E. *Foreign Aid as Foreign Policy: The Alliance for Progress in Latin America.* Abingdon: Routledge, 2007.

Westad, Odd Arne. *The Global Cold War: Third World Interventions and the Making of Our Times.* Cambridge: Cambridge University Press, 2005.

Williams, William A. *The Tragedy of American Diplomacy.* New York: Dell, 1972.

Wilford, Hugh. *The CIA, the British Left and the Cold War: Calling the Tune?* London, Portland Oregon: Frank Cass, 2003.

Wilford, Hugh. *The Mighty Wurlitzer: How the CIA Played America.* Cambridge Mass and London: Harvard University Press, 2008.

Book chapters

Bello, Walden. 'From Dictatorship to Elite Populism: The United States and the Philippine Crisis', in *Crisis and Confrontation: Ronald Reagan's Foreign Policy*, edited by Morris H. Morley, 214–251. New Jersey: Rowman and Littlefield, 1988.

Bello, Walden. 'Counterinsurgency's Proving Ground: Low-Intensity Warfare in the Philippines', in *Low Intensity Warfare: How the USA Fights Wars Without Declaring Them*, edited by Michael T. Klare and Peter Kornbluh, 158–183. London: Methuen, 1989.

Gendzier, Irene L. 'Play it Again Sam: The Practice and Apology of Development', in

206   *Bibliography*

Universities and Empire: Money and Politics in the Social Sciences During the Cold War, edited by Christopher Simpson, 57–97. New York: The New Press, 1998.

Gilman, Nils. 'Modernization Theory, the Highest Stage of American Intellectual History', in *Staging Growth: Modernization, Development and the Cold War*, edited by David C. Engerman, Nils Gilman, Mark H. Haefele and Michael E. Latham, 47–81. US: University of Massachusetts Press, 2003.

Gills, Barry. 'American Power, Neo-Liberal Economic Globalization and "Low Intensity Democracy": An Unstable Trinity', in *American Democracy Promotion: Impulses, Strategies and Impacts*, edited by Michael Cox, G. John Ikenberry & Takashi Inoguchi, 326–344. Oxford: Oxford University Press, 2000.

Gills, Barry, Rocamora, Joel and Wilson, Richard. 'Low Intensity Democracy', in *Low Intensity Democracy: Political Power in the New World Order*, edited by Barry Gills, Joel Rocamora and Richard Wilson, 3–35. London: Pluto Press, 1993.

Goldman, Ralph M. 'The Emerging Transnational Party System and the Future of American Parties', in *Political Parties: Development and Decay*, edited by Joseph Cooper and Louis Maisel, 59–99. Beverley Hills/London: Sage Publications, 1978.

Ikenberry, G. John. 'America's Liberal Grand Strategy: Democracy and National Security in the Post-War Era', in *American Democracy Promotion: Impulses, Strategies and Impacts*, edited by Michael Cox, John G. Ikenberry and Takashi Inoguchi, 103–127. Oxford: Oxford University Press, 2000.

Jonas, Susanne. 'Elections and Transitions: Guatemala and Nicaragua', in *Elections and Democracy in Central America*, edited by John A. Booth and Mitchell A. Seligson, 126–158. Chapel Hill and London: The University of North Carolina Press, 1989.

Kahler, Miles. 'The United States and Western Europe: the Diplomatic Consequences of Mr Reagan', in *Eagle Resurgent? The Reagan Era in American Foreign Policy*, edited by Kenneth A. Oye, Robert J. Lieber and Donald Rothschild, 297–335. Boston and Toronto: Little, Brown and Company Limited, 1987.

Lucas, W.S. 'Revealing the Parameters of Opinion: An interview with Frances Stonor Saunders', in *The Cultural Cold War in Western Europe 1945–60*, edited by Hans Krabbendam and Giles Scott-Smith, 12–31. London: Frank Cass, 2003.

Macdonald, Douglas J. 'Formal Ideologies in the Cold War: Toward a Framework for Empirical Analysis', in *Reviewing the Cold War: Approaches, Interpretations, Theory*, edited by Odd Arne Westad, 180–207. London: Frank Cass, 2000.

Nau, Henry. 'America's Identity, Democracy Promotion and National Interests: Beyond Realism, Beyond Idealism', in *American Democracy Promotion: Impulses, Strategies and Impacts*, edited by Michael Cox, John G. Ikenberry and Takashi Inoguchi, 127–151. Oxford: Oxford University Press, 2000.

Paget, Karen M. 'From Stockholm to Leiden: The CIA's role in the formation of the International Student Conference', in *The Cultural Cold War in Western Europe 1945–60*, edited by Hans Krabbendam and Giles Scott-Smith, 138–159. London: Frank Cass, 2003.

Paget, Karen M. 'From co-operation to covert action: the United States Government and students, 1940–52', in *The US Government, Citizen Groups and the Cold War: the State–Private Network*, edited by Helen Laville and Hugh Wilford, 66–83. London: Routledge, 2006.

Pastor, Robert A. 'The Reagan Administration and Latin America: Eagle Insurgent', in *Eagle Resurgent? The Reagan Era in American Foreign Policy*, edited by Kenneth A. Oye, Robert J. Lieber and Donald Rothschild, 359–392. Boston and Toronto: Little, Brown and Company Limited, 1987.

Bibliography 207

Pipes, Richard. 'Peace with Freedom', in *Alerting America: The Papers of the Committee on the Present Danger*, edited by Charles Tyroler, 22–36. Washington DC: Pergamon-Brassey's International Defence Publishers, 1984.

Posen, Barry R., and Van Evera, Stephen W. 'Reagan Administration Defense Policy: Departure from Containment', in *Eagle Defiant: United States Foreign Policy in the 1980s*, edited by Kenneth A. Oye, Robert J. Lieber and Donald Rothschild, 67–105. Boston and Toronto: Little, Brown and Company Limited, 1983.

Ralph, Jason G. ' "High Stakes" and "Low-Intensity Democracy": Understanding America's Policy of Promoting Democracy', in *American Democracy Promotion: Impulses, Strategies and Impacts*, edited by Michael Cox, G. John Ikenberry and Takashi Inoguchi, 200–218. Oxford: Oxford University Press, 2000.

Rocamora, Joel. 'Lost Opportunities, Deepening Crisis: The Philippines under Cory Aquino', in *Low Intensity Democracy: Political Power in the New World Order*, edited by Barry Gills, Joel Rocamora and Richard Wilson, 195–226. London: Pluto Press, 1993.

Smith, Steve. 'Democracy Promotion: Critical Questions', in *American Democracy Promotion: Impulses, Strategies and Impacts*, edited by Michael Cox, G. John Ikenberry and Takashi Inoguchi, 63–85. Oxford: Oxford University Press, 2000.

Trudeau, Robert H. 'The Guatemalan Election of 1985: Prospects for Democracy', in *Elections and Democracy in Central America*, edited by John A. Booth and Mitchell A. Seligson, 93–125. Chapel Hill and London: The University of North Carolina Press, 1989.

Wilson, Richard. 'Continued Counterinsurgency: Civilian Rule in Guatemala', in *Low Intensity Democracy: Political Power in the New World Order*, edited by Barry Gills, Joel Rocamora and Richard Wilson, 127–161. London: Pluto Press, 1993.

Journal articles

Barnes, Trevor. 'The Secret Cold War: The C.I.A. and American Foreign Policy in Europe, 1946–1956: Part I', *The Historical Journal* 24, no. 2 (1981): 399–415. Accessed 29 October 2005. www.jstor.org/stable/2638793.

Berger, Mark T. 'From Nation-Building to State-Building: The Geopolitics of Development, the Nation-State System and the Changing Global Order', *Third World Quarterly* 27, no. 1 (2006): 5–25. Accessed 12 March 2012. www.jstor.org/stable/4017656.

Blachman, Morris J. and Sharpe, Kenneth. 'De-Democratising American Foreign Policy: Dismantling the Post-Vietnam Formula', *Third World Quarterly* 8, no. 4 (1986): 1271–1308. Accessed 7 August 2009. www.jstor.org/stable/3991715.

Borhi, Laszlo. 'Rollback, Liberation, Containment, or Inaction?: US Policy and Eastern Europe in the 1950s', *Journal of Cold War Studies* 1, no. 3 (1999): 67–110. Accessed 9 September 2014. EBSCO Host.

Bouchet, Nicholas. 'The democracy tradition in US foreign policy and the Obama presidency', *International Affairs* 89 no. 1 (2013): 31–51. Accessed 9 June 2014. DOI: 10.1111/1468-2346.12003.

Carew, Anthony. 'The American Labor Movement in Fizzland: The Free Trade Union Committee and the CIA', *Labor History* 39 no. 1 (1998): 25–42. Accessed 16 May 2014. DOI: 10.1080/00236679812331387276.

Carothers, Thomas. 'Promoting Democracy and Fighting Terror', *Foreign Affairs* 82, no. 1 (2003): 84–97. Accessed 6 December 2014. www.jstor.org/stable/20033430.

Cmiel, Kenneth. 'The Emergence of Human Rights Politics in the United States', *The*

208 Bibliography

Journal of American History 86, no. 3 (1999): 1231–1250. Accessed 10 April 2013. www.jstor.org/stable/2568613.

Coronel, Sheila S. 'Dateline Philippines: The Lost Revolution', *Foreign Policy*, No. 84 (1991): 166–185. Accessed 20 April 2010. www.jstor.org/stable/1148789.

Corning, Gregory. 'The Philippine Bases and US Pacific Strategy', *Pacific Affairs* 63 no. 1 (1990): 6–23. Accessed 5 September 2014. www.jstor.org/stable/2759811.

Cottam, Martha L. 'The Carter Administration's Policy towards Nicaragua: Images, Goals and Tactics', *Political Science Quarterly* 107, no. 1 (1992): 123–146. Accessed 10 December 2010. www.jstor.org/stable/2152137.

Cullather, Nick. 'America's Boy? Ramon Magsaysay and the Illusion of Influence', *The Pacific Historical Review*, 62, no. 3 (1993): 305–338. Accessed 20 September 2009. www.jstor.org/stable/3640933.

Dalacoura, Katerina. 'US Democracy Promotion in the Arab Middle East since 11 September 2001: A Critique', *International Affairs* 85, no. 1 (2005): 964–966. Accessed 27 April 2014, www.jstor.org/stable/3569070.

de Vries, Tity. 'The 1967 Central Intelligence Agency Scandal: Catalyst in a Transforming Relationship between State and People.' *Journal of American History* 98, no. 4 (2012): 1075–1092. Accessed 16 May 2014. DOI: 10.1093/jahist/jar563.

Dobson, Alan P. 'The Reagan Administration, Economic Warfare, and Starting to Close Down the Cold War', *Diplomatic History*, 29, no. 3 (2005): 531–556. Accessed 3 August 2012. DOI: 10.1111/j.1467-7709.2005.00502.x.

Domber, Gregory F. 'The AFL-CIO, the Reagan Administration and Solidarnosc', *The Polish Review* 52, no. 3 (2007): 277–304. Accessed 10 November 2014. www.jstor. org./stable/25779685.

Fascell, Dante B. 'The Helsinki Accord: A Case Study', *Annals of the American Academy of Political and Social Science* 442 (March, 1979): 69–76. Accessed 15 April 2013. www.jstor.org/stable/1043482

Fisher, Christopher T. 'The Illusion of Progress: CORDS and the Crisis of Modernization in South Vietnam, 1965–1968', *Pacific Historical Review* 75, no. 1 (2006): 25–51. Accessed 12 March 2012. www.jstor.org/stable/10.1525/phr.2006.75.1.25.

Gershman, Carl. 'The Rise and Fall of the New Foreign-Policy Establishment', *Commentary* 70, no. 1 (1980): 13–24. Accessed 1 November 2014. www.commentarymagazine. com/article/the-rise-fall-of-the-new-foreign-policy-establishment/.

Glazer, Nathan. 'American Values & American Foreign Policy', *Commentary* 62, no. 1 (1976): 32–37.

Goddeeris, Idesbald. 'Lobbying Allies? The NSZZ Co-ordinating Office Abroad, 1982–1989', *Journal of Cold War Studies* 13, no. 3 (2011): 83–125. Accessed 26 October 2014. DOI:10.1162/JCWS_a_00143.

Hartmann, Hauke. 'US Human Rights Policy under Carter and Reagan, 1977–1981', *Human Rights Quarterly* 23, no. 2 (2001): 402–430. Accessed 5 April 2012. www. jstor.org/stable/4489339.

Hastings Dunn, David. 'Bush, 11 September and the Conflicting Strategies of the "War on Terrorism"', *Irish Studies in International Affairs* 16 (2005): 11–33. Accessed 5 September 2013. www.jstor.org/stable/30001932.

Hobson, Christopher. 'The limits of Liberal-Democracy Promotion', *Alternatives* 34 (2009): 383–405. Accessed 10 May 2013. DOI: 10.1177/030437540903400402.

Ish-Shalom, Piki. 'Theory Gets Real, and the Case for a Normative Ethic: Rostow, Modernization Theory, and the Alliance for Progress', *International Studies Quarterly* 50, no. 2 (2006): 287–311. Accessed 13 February 2013. www.jstor.org/stable/3693612.

Bibliography 209

Jacoby, Tamar. 'The Reagan Turnaround on Human Rights', *Foreign Affairs* 64, no. 5 (1986): 1066–1086. Accessed 7 March 2014. EBSCO Host.

Jentleson, Bruce W. 'Discrepant Responses to Falling Dictators: Presidential Belief Systems and the Mediating Effects of the Senior Advisory System', *Political Psychology* 11, no. 2 (1990): 353–384. Accessed 5 April 2014. www.jstor.org/stable/3791694.

Kaufman, Victor. 'The Bureau of Human Rights during the Carter Administration', *The Historian* 61, no. 1 (1998): 51–66. Accessed 16 May 2014. DOI: 10.1111/j.1540–6563.1998.tb01423.x.

Kennan, George F. 'The Sources of Soviet Conduct', *Foreign Affairs* 25, no. 4 (1947), reprinted in *Foreign Affairs* 65, no. 4 (1987): 852–868. Accessed 23 November 2014. EBSCO Host.

Kirkpatrick, Jeane. 'Dictatorships and Double Standards', *Commentary* 68, no. 5 (1979): 34–45.

Kirkpatrick, Jeane. 'US security and Latin America', *Commentary* 71, no. 1 (1981): 29–40.

Kurki, Milja. 'Democracy and Conceptual Contestability: reconsidering Conceptions of Democracy Promotion', *International Studies Review* 12 (2010): 362–386. Accessed 10 May 2013. DOI: 10.1111/j.1468–2486.2010.00943.x

Laqueur, Walter. 'The Issue of Human Rights', *Commentary*, 63, no. 5 (1977): 29–35.

LeoGrande, William M. 'A Splendid Little War: Drawing the Line in El Salvador', *International Security* 6, no. 1 (1981): 27–52. Accessed 12 February 2009. www.jstor.org/stable/2538528.

Lobe, Jim. 'The Bush Team Reloaded', *Middle East Report* no. 234 (2005): 10–16. Accessed 10 June 2012. DOI: 10.2307/1559363.

Lucas, Scott W. 'Beyond freedom, beyond control, beyond the Cold War: approaches to American culture and the State–Private Network', *Intelligence and National Security* 18, no. 2 (2003): 53–72. Accessed 15 January 2010. http://dx.doi.org/10.1080/0268452 0412331306740.

Manroop, Laxmikant and Singh, Parbudyal. 'The Role of the AFL-CIO in Regime Change: The Case of Guyana', *British Journal of Industrial Relations* 50, no. 2 (2012): 308–328. Accessed 30 November 2014. DOI: 10.1111/j.1467–8543.2011.00854.x

Maynard, Edwin S. 'The Bureaucracy and Implementation of US Human Rights Policy', *Human Rights Quarterly*, 11, no. 2 (1989): 175–248. Accessed 28 November 2009. www.jstor.org/stable/761957.

Millett, Richard. 'Looking Beyond Noriega', *Foreign Policy*, 71 (Summer 1988): 46–63. Accessed 10 September 2012. www.jstor.org/stable/1148903.

Mistry, Kaeten. 'The Case for Political Warfare: Strategy, Organisation and US Involvement in the 1948 Italian Election', *Cold War History* 6 no. 3 (2006): 301–329. Accessed 30 September 2014. DOI: 10.1080/14682740600795451.

Monten, Jonathan. 'The Roots of the Bush Doctrine: Power, Nationalism and Democracy Promotion in US Strategy', *International Security* 29, No. 4 (2005): 112–156. Accessed 8 November 2014. DOI:10.1162/isec.2005.29.4.112.

Morley, Morris and McGillion, Chris. 'Soldiering On: The Reagan Administration and Redemocratisation in Chile, 1983–1986', *Bulletin of Latin American Research* 25, no. 1 (2006): 1–22. Accessed 19 August 2014. DOI: 10.1111/j.0261–3050.2006.00150.x.

Moynihan, Daniel Patrick. 'The Politics of Human Rights', *Commentary* 64, no. 2 (1977): 19–26.

Muravchik, Joshua. 'US Political Parties Abroad', *The Washington Quarterly* 12, no. 3 (1989): 91–100. Accessed 10 March 2011. DOI: 10.1080/01636608909477518.

Neier, Aryeh. 'Human Rights in the Reagan Era: Acceptance in Principle', *Annals of the*

210 Bibliography

American Academy of Political and Social Science 506 (November 1989): 30–41. Accessed 10 May 2011. www.jstor.org/stable/1046652.

Pastor, Robert. 'Continuity and Change in US Foreign Policy: Carter and Reagan on El Salvador', *Journal of Policy Analysis and Management* 3, no. 2 (1984): 175–190. Accessed 10 February 2010. EBSCO Host.

Peceny, Mark and Stanley, William D. 'Counterinsurgency in El Salvador', *Politics & Society* 38, no. 67 (2010): 67–94. Accessed 26 November 2014. DOI: 10.1177/0032329 209357884.

Pinto-Duschinsky, Michael. 'Foreign Political Aid: The German Foundations and their US Counterparts', *International Affairs* 67, no. 1 (1991): 33–63. Accessed 16 May 2014. www.jstor.org/stable/2621218.

Podhoretz, Norman. 'Making the World Safe for Communism', *Commentary*, 61, no. 4 (1976): 31–41.

Samuels, Michael A. and Douglas, William A. 'Promoting Democracy', *The Washington Quarterly* 4, no. 3 (1981): 52–65. Accessed 30 May 2012. http://dx.doi.org/10.1080/01636608109451791.

Samuels, Michael A. and Sullivan, John D. 'Democratic Development: A New Role for US Business', *Washington Quarterly* 9, no. 3 (1986): 161–181. Accessed 10 June 2012. DOI: 10.1080/01636608609450839.

Saull, Richard. 'Locating the Global South in the Theorisation of the Cold War: Capitalist Development, Social Revolution and Geopolitical Conflict', *Third World Quarterly* 26, no. 2 (2005): 253–280. Accessed 16 May 2014. DOI: 10.1080/0143659042000 339119.

Schmitz, David F. and Walker, Vanessa. 'Jimmy Carter and the Foreign Policy of Human Rights: The Development of a Post-Cold War Foreign Policy', *Diplomatic History* 28, no. 1 (2004): 113–144. Accessed 10 April 2013. DOI: 10.1111/j.1467–7709.2004. 00400.x.

Scipes, Kim. 'Why Labor Imperialism? AFL-CIO's leaders and the developing world', *WorkingUSA: The Journal of Labor and Society* 13 (2010): 465–479. Accessed 10 November 2014. DOI: 10.1111/j.1743–4580.2010.00306.x

Scott-Smith, Giles. 'Searching for the Successor Generation: Public Diplomacy, the US Embassy's International Visitor Program and the Labour Party in the 1980s', *British Journal of Politics and International Relations* 8, no. 2 (2006): 214–237. Accessed 10 July 2012. DOI: 10.1111/j.1467–856X.2006.00221.x.

Scott-Smith, Giles. 'The Free Europe University in Strasbourg: U.S. State–Private Networks and Academic "Rollback"', *Journal of Cold War Studies* 16 no. 2 (2014): 77–107. Accessed 22 June 2014. DOI: 10.1162/JCWS_a_00452.

Shimko, Keith L. 'Reagan on the Soviet Union and the Nature of International Conflict', *Political Psychology* 13, no. 3 (1992): 353–377. Accessed 15 September 2014. www. jstor.org/stable/3791603.

Snider, Erin A. and Faris, David M. 'The Arab Spring: US Democracy Promotion in Egypt', *Middle East Policy* 18, no. 3 (2011): 49–62. Accessed 3 December 2014, DOI: 10.1111/j.1475–4967.2011.00497.x.

Soares, John A., Jr. 'Strategy, Ideology, and Human Rights: Jimmy Carter Confronts the Left in Central America, 1979–1981', *Journal of Cold War Studies* 8, no. 4 (2006): 57–91. Accessed 16 May 2014. EBSCO Host.

Thomson, James A. 'The LRTNF Decision: Evolution of US Theatre Nuclear Policy, 1975–9', *International Affairs* 60, no. 4 (1984): 601–614. Accessed 7 February 2008. www.jstor.org/stable/2620044.

Bibliography 211

Waters, Robert and Daniels, Gordon. 'The World's Longest General Strike: The AFL-CIO, the CIA, and British Guiana', *Diplomatic History* 29, no. 2 (2005): 279–307. Accessed 30 November 2014. DOI: 10.1111/j.1467–7709.2005.00474.x.

Weeks, John. 'Panama: The Roots of Current Political Instability', *Third World Quarterly* 9, no. 3 (1987): 763–787. Accessed 10 September 2012. DOI: 10.1080/0143659870 8420000.

Weeks, John and Zimbalist, Andrew. 'The Failure of Intervention in Panama: Humiliation in the Backyard', *Third World Quarterly* 11, no. 1 (1989): 1–27. Accessed 10 September 2012. DOI: 10.1080/01436598908420137

West, Lois A. 'US Foreign Labor Policy and the Case of Militant Political Unionism in the Philippines', *Labor Studies Journal* 16, no. 4 (1991): 48–75. Accessed 10 November 2014. EBSCO Host.

Whitehead, Laurence. 'Explaining Washington's Central American Policies', *Journal of Latin American Studies* 15, no. 2. (1983): 321–363. Accessed 12 February 2009. DOI: http://dx.doi.org/10.1017/S0022216X00000742.

Academic papers and reports

Barker, Michael J. 'Taking the risk out of civil society: harnessing social movements and regulating revolutions', Refereed paper presented to the Australasian Political Studies Association Conference, University of Newcastle, 2006. Accessed 10 July 2014. www.newcastle.edu.au/Resources/Schools/Newcastle%20Business%20School/APSA/INTLREL/Barker-Michael.pdf.

Melia, Thomas O. 'The Democracy Bureaucracy: The Infrastructure of American Democracy Promotion', Discussion paper prepared for the Princeton Project on National Security Working Group on Global Institutions and Foreign Policy Infrastructure, September, 2005. Accessed 14 September 2012. www.princeton.edu/~ppns/papers/democracy_bureaucracy.pdf.

Theses

Domber, Gregory. 'Supporting the Revolution: America, Democracy and the End of the Cold War in Poland, 1981–1989', PhD dissertation, George Washington University, 2008. Accessed 29 August 2014. Available from http://transatlantic.sais-jhu.edu/ACES/ACES_Working_Papers/Gregory_Domber_Supporting_the_Revolution.pdf.

Index

9/11 attacks 193

AAFLI 58, 172, 173, 175
AALC 58, 101
Abrams, Elliott 61, 75–7, 111
AFL-CIO 16, 83, 107, 129, 130, 131, 135, 140, 141, 143, 144, 145, 155, 156, 157, 158, 159, 160, 161, 164, 165; AID funding 114, 115; CIA 49; Philippines 170, 172; Reagan administration democracy campaign 102–4; role in democracy promotion 58–9; Solidarity 167
Africa 23, 117, 131, 195
Agree, George 33, 81, 85, 105, 114, 128, 144, 145, 154; American Political Foundation 27–8; Bipartisan democracy foundation 82–4, 132–3; global democracy campaign 98–9; government funding 32; Michael Samuels 30; privately-run campaign 106; removed as President of APF 133
AID 57, 58, 140, 141, 159; Democracy Program 129, 131; funding for democracy promotion 84, 101, 114–15; Guatemala 163–4; NAMFREL 175
AIFLD 58–9, 161, 162, 164
Albania 12
Allen, Richard 40, 42, 54, 72, 73, 88, 130; democracy study 104–5
American Friends of Free Speech Abroad 166
American Political Development Foundation 31
American Political Foundation (APF) 23, 26, 30, 40, 41, 81, 85, 87, 91, 92, 93, 101, 107, 133, 159; AID 114–15; democracy promotion study 91, 93, 81, 97, 99, 104–5, 128, 130, 132;

founding 28; funding problems 28; Mark Palmer 82–4; Michael Samuels 32
anti-nuclear protests, Europe 43
Aquino, Benigno 169
Aquino, Corazon 174, 175, 176
Arab Spring Uprisings 195
Arbenz government 58
Argentina 51, 98
Arias, Arnulfo 155
Armacost, Michael 169, 170, 171, 173, 175, 177
Armitage, Richard 169, 171, 173, 174
Asia 117
Asia Foundation 60, 143
Aurora Foundation 167
autonomy/control dilemma (dichotomy) 14, 20, 25, 33, 87

Bailey, Norman 73, 74, 86, 87, 110
Bakshian, Aram 90
Barletta, Nicolas Ardito 155
Barnes, Michael 136, 143
Benin 23
Betancourt Institute 64
Betancourt, Romulo 64
Bishop, Maurice 103, 161
Blair, Dennis 85
Blaize, Herbert 161, 162
Bosch, Juan 17
Bosworth, Stephen 171
Brady, Lawrence 73
Brazil 58
Briggs, Everett 159
Britain 43, 155, 156; *see also* UK
British Atlantic Committee 156
Brock, William: APF 28; bipartisan democracy foundation 84; democracy study 104–5, 130; NED autonomy

152–3, 154; USTR 40; West German model 99
Brodhead, Frank 164
Brown, Hank 144–5, 162
Brown, Irving 48, 49, 58, 156, 157
'Building Freedom' 77, 78
Bukovsky, Vladimir 166
Burnham, James 14
Bureau of Democracy, Conflict and Humanitarian Assistance 8n17, 194
Bureau of Democracy, Human Rights and Labor 8n17, 194
Bureau of East Asian and Pacific Affairs 25
Bureau of Human Rights and Humanitarian Affairs 25, 61–2, 76, 78
Bureau of Inter-American Affairs 136
Bush, George H.W. 170
Bush, George W. 1; administration 4, 61, 193, 195
business community US 57–9

Cambodia 23
Cam Ranh Bay 169
Caribbean 160, 161
Caribbean/Central American Action 164
Carnegie Foundation 22
Carothers, Thomas 192
Carpio, Jorge 163
Carter administration 3, 24–5, 29, 41, 50, 51, 53, 54, 61, 64–5, 76, 85, 137, 141, 157–8, 193
Carter, Jimmy 25, 30, 40, 76, 192
Casey, William J. 40, 42, 45–6, 48, 49, 73, 74, 75, 86, 100, 167, 171, 174, 176
Center for the Democratization of the Soviet Union 166
Central America 52–3, 54, 56, 57, 59, 63, 80, 84–5, 105, 112, 135, 160, 161
Central American democracy institute 63–4, 71, 80, 114–15, 116, 119
Centre for International Private Enterprise (CIPE) 116, 135, 141, 143, 145, 177
Centre for Strategic International Studies 30, 130
'centred' Cold War strategy 40, 45–6, 71, 72, 92
Cerezo, Vinicio 163, 164, 165
CGT 102, 157
Chamber of Commerce, US 58, 143, 144
Childress, Richard 169
Chile 2, 51, 58, 98, 103, 119, 143, 190
China 24
Chomsky, Noam 2

Christian Democratic Party (Italy) 106
Christian Democrats (Guatemala) 163
Christopher, Warren 25
Church Committee 23
CIA 3, 26, 31, 57, 58, 59, 87, 89, 101, 102, 106, 118, 120, 122, 139, 140, 141, 143, 146, 155, 159, 166, 167; Church Committee 23; collapse of state–private network 17–18; Philippines 170, 173, 188; Reagan administration democracy campaign 113; Solidarity 48–9; state–private network 5, 12
Clark Field 168, 171, 176, 177
Clark, William 54, 61, 73, 74, 75, 81, 88, 89, 91, 93, 100, 110, 120, 134
Clinton administration 4, 193
Cold War 4, 5, 7, 10, 13, 15, 23, 40, 57, 102, 118, 137, 141, 156, 166, 187, 191, 194, 196
COMELEC 175
Committee on Overseas Voluntary Activities 19
Committee on the Present Danger (CPD) 42, 109
Committee of Santa Fe 51
Commission on Security and Cooperation in Europe 24, 25
Committee in Support of Solidarity 167
Conference on the Democratization of Communist Countries 107–8, 111, 165, 166
Conference on Free Elections 107, 111–12
Congress 32, 51, 62, 65, 75, 85, 97, 98, 99, 116, 128, 129, 130, 131, 133, 134, 135, 136, 137, 138, 139, 150, 151, 158, 161, 190, 191, 194; criticism of NED 159–60, 167, 168; debate over NED 142–5; El Salvador 54; Grenada 162; Guatemala 164; Philippines 170, 173, 174, 176, 179, 188, 189; Project Democracy 117–21, 122; rise of Human Rights 24
Congressional Democrats 98, 118, 119, 120, 122, 188
Congressional observer mission, Philippines 174
Conry, Barbara 141
containment 11–12, 84, 46, 49, 65, 89, 90, 163
Contras 60, 61, 155
credibility 14, 59, 80, 82, 86, 113, 121, 122, 128, 129, 140, 142, 144, 167, 191
CTP 103
Cuba 16, 161

214 *Index*

CUS 103
CUSG 165

'de-centred' Cold War strategy 40, 45, 46–7, 71–2, 92
decolonisation 14
'democracy bureaucracy' 194
Democracy Program 145, 152, 156, 159; original parameters 129; time constraints 130–1; partisan interests 131–4; interim report to Congress 137–42
democracy promotion 91, 92, 97, 129, 137, 143, 150, 151, 160, 161, 172, 179, 187, 188, 190, 191, 192, 193; as anti-communism 157–9; anti-Soviet strategy 107–11; El Salvador 53–6; and Human Rights 61; initial blueprint for 20–3; NSC/State Department clash 86–7; organisational structure, governmental 112–16; pre-emptive in allied dictatorships 30–2; private sector 1970s 26–8; projected campaign in Soviet bloc and Third World 78–81; Reagan administration vision 100–1; rise of and scholarship 4; towards Soviet bloc 165–8; towards Third World 111–12; USIA/NED conflict 152–3
democracy promoters 6, 32, 33, 40, 41, 49, 51, 56, 59, 61, 64, 65, 81, 82, 91, 97, 128, 130, 134, 135, 137, 144, 154, 188, 191
Democratic Enlargement 193
Democratic National Committee 27
Democratic Peace Theory 193
democratic propaganda 43–5, 47
Democrats 22, 27, 54, 98, 119, 130, 131, 133, 136, 137
Department of Commerce 24, 73–4, 110
Department of Defence 89, 173
Department of the Treasury 24
Derian, Patricia 25
détente 43
DIA 173
Diem, Ngo Dinh 16, 173
Dodd, Christopher 118, 130
Doe, Samuel 119
Dolan, Anthony 90
Domber, Gregory 167
Dominican Republic 17
Douglas, William. A. 26, 31, 33, 64, 81, 85, 88, 128, 129, 135, 163, 168, 170, 172, 192; global democracy campaign

105–6; initial blueprint for democracy promotion 20–2; 'Promoting Democracy' article 56–60

East Germany 12
Eastern Europe 13, 24, 47, 51, 61, 71, 79, 80, 89, 98, 107, 108, 167, 190, 192; *see also* Soviet bloc, Soviet Empire
Egypt 195–6
El Salvador 49, 52–6, 59, 61, 63, 64, 65, 77, 78, 91, 112, 135, 153, 154, 163, 173
Enders, Thomas 52, 54–5, 135
Eisenhower administration 12, 19
Ethiopia 23
European Theatre Nuclear Forces 42

FAO 30
Farfield Foundation 140
Fascell, Dante B. 143, 158; Human Rights foundation 25; Democracy Program 130; interim report 137
France 44, 155, 156–7, 158, 160
Force Ouvriere 102, 156–7, 158
Ford Foundation 22, 24
Frankel, Charles 18
Fraser, Donald: Human Rights foundation 25; International Department for Democratic Party 26; West German Party Foundation 27
Free Europe Committee 108
Free Trade Union Institute (FTUI) 135, 141, 143, 145, 155–7, 158, 161, 164, 175, 177
Freedom House 82, 107, 166, 167
Front National 157
FSLN 29–30, 190; *see also* Sandinistas
Fund for Democracy 115–16

GABRIELA 178
Gairy, Eric 161, 162
Georgia 195
German Marshall Fund 28
Gershman, Carl 157–8, 159, 164
Godson, Joseph 156
Gray, Charles 172
Grenada 103, 111, 161–2, 163, 167, 168, 176, 190
Grenada Civic Awareness Organisation 162
Guatemala 2, 12, 29, 56, 58, 59, 162–5, 167, 168, 176, 190
Guilhot, Nicolas 4
Guyana 58

Haig, Alexander 47, 71, 73, 89, 90, 131, 135, 154, 166, 192; democracy institute for Central America 63–4; democracy promotion memo to Reagan 78–81; economic and political warfare 73–5; El Salvador 52; Poland 48; Project Truth 43–4; views on Soviet Union 46
Haiti 195
Helman, Gerald 115
Helms, Richard 18
Helsinki Accords 24, 25
Helsinki Commission 137
Helsinki Watch 25
Herman, Edward 164
Herrera, Ernesto 175
Holland 43
House Foreign Affairs Committee 54
House Foreign Affairs Subcommittee on International Organisations 26, 118, 137
House of Representatives 136, 143–5, 159, 169
Honduras 57, 105
Hook, Sidney 14
Hoover Institution 166
Hormats, Robert D. 74
Human Rights 3, 26, 27, 28, 31, 41, 47, 50, 53, 54, 65, 137, 141, 157, 173, 191, 192, 193; Carter administration 24–5; El Salvador 53–4; Guatemala 163, 164, 165; ideological warfare 61–3; neoconservatives 50–1; Nicaragua 29–30; Poland 167; positive doctrine 1982 75–8
Hungarian Revolution 12
Huntington, Samuel P. 19, 28
Huks 170

IBM 58
Ikenberry, G. John 2
Ikle, Fred 54
India 91
Interagency Group on Human Rights and Foreign Assistance 25
Inter-American Foundation 60
Inter-American Leadership Development 136
Inter-American Press Association 121
Inter-University Union (UNI) 102, 157, 158, 160
International Department for Democratic Party 26–7
International League for Democracy 21–2, 23

International Political Committee (IPC) 117, 136, 139, 195
Iran 12, 2, 23, 29, 30, 31, 50, 85, 176
IT&T 58
Italian elections 1948 106

Jagan, Cheddi 58
Japan 62
Joint Baltic American National Committee 166
Johnson administration 18

KABATID 178
Kaplan, Philip 175
Kaplan, Robert 170
Kastenmeier, Robert 121
Katzenbach Commission 18, 19
Kemble, Eugenia 131, 158
Kemp, Jack 143–4
Kennan, George 11, 12, 46
Kennedy administration 10, 19, 41, 51, 57
Kennedy, John F. 1, 15
Kennedy, Richard T. 61
Kinzer, Stephen 2
Kirkland, Lane 58, 133, 156, 158
Kirkpatrick Doctrine 50–1, 56, 59, 78, 168, 179
Kirkpatrick, Jeane 50–1, 65, 111–12, 157
Kolko, Gabriel 2
KMU 172, 177

Labour Committee for Transatlantic Understanding 156
Labour Party 43, 156
Lagomarsino, Robert 136, 143
Lake, Anthony 130, 193
Laos 23
Latin America 17, 20, 21, 51, 57, 63, 64, 103, 179, 195
Laurel, Salvador 'Doy' 175
Lefever, Ernest 61
liberal democracy 191, 196
liberalisation 88, 91
'Liberation' 11, 13, 107
Liberia 119
Loiello, John P. 131
Lord, Carnes 47, 87
'low intensity democracies' 6
Lugar, Senator Richard 174, 176

McFarlane, Robert C. 100, 113, 163
Madagascar 23
Madison, Christopher 158

216 *Index*

Magsaysay, Ramon 170
Manatt, Charles: APF 28; bipartisan democracy foundation 84, 130, 132
Marcos dictatorship 173; *see also* Marcos Ferdinand; Marcos government; Marcos regime
Marcos, Ferdinand 168, 169, 170, 171, 172, 173, 174, 175, 176, 177, 178; *see also* Marcos government; Marcos dictatorship; Marcos regime
Marcos government 172; *see also* Marcos Ferdinand; Marcos dictatorship; Marcos Ferdinand; Marcos regime
Marcos regime 169, 170, 171–2, 173, 175, 176, 177; *see also* Marcos dictatorship; Marcos Ferdinand; Marcos government
martial law 72
Mejia, General Oscar 163
Menges, Constantine 161
Meyer, Cord 18
Middle East 4, 61, 193, 195
Middle East Partnership Initiative 194
military aid 51, 53
Modernisation 3, 10, 21, 22, 24, 33, 41, 57, 191, 192; goals, basis and approach 15–16; decline 19–20; weaknesses 16–17
Montt, Efrain Rios 164
Moynihan, Daniel Patrick 27, 50
Mubarak administration/regime 195–6
Muravchik, Joshua 2, 3

Nach, James 171
NAMFREL 170, 173, 175, 176
National Alliance of Russian Solidarists (NTS) 166
National Endowment for Democracy (NED) 4, 5, 7, 116, 122, 129, 130, 131, 132, 133, 134, 136, 138, 139, 140, 141, 150, 151, 156, 157, 159, 160, 179, 187, 188, 189, 190, 191, 192, 195, 196; conflict with USIA 152–4; Congressional debate 142–5; Grenada 161–2; Guatemala 163–5; Philippines 170, 172, 174, 175–7, 178; Soviet bloc 165–8
National Democratic Institute (NDI) 141, 143, 145, 158, 175, 176
National Democratic Front 169
National Guard 30
National Labour Centre (NLC) 103
National Republican Institute (NRI) 141, 143, 145, 154, 158, 161, 162, 175, 176
National Security Council (NSC) 25, 28, 44, 74, 80, 84, 85, 86, 87, 88, 89, 92, 99, 102, 103, 104, 106, 110, 115, 153, 154, 161, 163
National Security Planning Group 47
National Students' Association 18
NATO 13, 42, 44, 74, 79, 102, 118, 156
Nau, Henry 2
New Jewel Movement (NJM) 161, 162
New National Party (NNP) 161, 162
New People's Army (NPA) 169, 170, 171, 172, 173, 174, 177
Newsom, David 98, 99
Nicaragua 23, 29–30, 31, 32, 49, 50, 52, 56, 59, 65, 85, 103, 107, 108, 111, 112, 168, 169, 172, 174, 177, 190, 191
Nigeria 91, 114
Ninkovich, Frank 18
Nixon Administration 20, 23, 154
Nixon, Richard 30
Noriega, Colonel Manuel Antonio 155
NSC 68, 13
NSDD 32, 75, 88, 89–90, 91, 93, 108–11, 117, 163, 165, 166, 171–2
NSSD 11–82, 109

OAS 63–4, 71, 80
Obama administration 4, 193
O'Neill, Thomas 137
ORIT 103

Pakistan 25, 98
Palmer, Mark 81, 82–4, 110, 130, 132
Panama 155, 159, 160
party institutes: conflict over 132–3; comparison between West German and US 133; Central America 135–6; earmarking of funds for 135, 144–5; NED weak point 142
Percy, Charles 121
Perle, Richard 73
Peru 103
Philippines 25, 57, 98, 119, 179, 188; parliamentary elections 1984 170; Presidential elections 174–6; US bases in 168–9, 175; US policy and NED democracy promotion in 168–78
Pierre, Eric 103
Pipes, Richard: CPD 42; NSDD 75, 108–9; propaganda 47; Sakharov Institute 166; Solidarity 75; Soviet bloc 73; views on Soviet Union 45; Westminster Address 90
plausible deniability 13, 14, 80, 82, 86, 113, 167, 191

PRM 28, 24
Podhoretz, Norman 50
Poland 47–9, 55, 57, 71, 76, 78, 79, 80, 85, 102, 108, 158, 165, 166, 188
Polish-American Charitable Foundation 167
Polish United Workers' Party (PZPR) 47
'political warfare' 12, 45
Portugal 26, 30, 31
Portuguese crisis 26
Portuguese Socialist Party 26
Project Democracy 116, 117–21, 122, 128, 129, 130, 134, 136, 137, 138, 139, 140, 141, 143, 145, 146, 156, 158, 160, 166, 169
Project Democracy Working Group 130, 152
Project Truth 43–4, 61, 88, 100, 102, 112, 120, 158
public diplomacy 116
Puddington, Arch 158

Quick Count system 175
Quirino, Elpidio 170

Radio Free Europe (RFE) 30, 47, 107, 154
Radio Liberty 30, 47, 107
Ramparts magazine 17, 18
Rashish, Myer 74
Raymond, Walter 114–15, 120, 152
Reagan administration 3, 6, 59, 64, 73, 92, 98, 150, 151, 154, 155–6, 158, 159, 160, 161, 168, 178, 188, 190, 195; coherent strategy, lack of 40–1; Democracy Program 135–6; democracy promotion, vision of 100–1; El Salvador, initial policy 52–3; Grenada 161–2; Human Rights policy 61–3, 75–8; Philippines 168–77; Project Democracy 116, 117, 121, 128, 130; Solidarity 47–9; Third World, initial policy 50–1
Reagan, Ronald; 33, 40, 43, 45, 52, 97, 104, 110, 111, 129, 139, 141, 163, 193; democracy promotion proposals 81; Human Rights 51; Marcos 171, 174, 176; Poland 48; Westminster Address 91–2, 93
Reaganites 40, 65, 71, 79, 81, 92, 93, 102, 104, 134, 153, 163, 167, 174, 176, 188; 'centred' Cold War strategy 45–6; economic and political warfare proposals 72–5; private model of democracy promotion 85–6; rollback against USSR 89

Regan, Donald 174, 176
Reform the Armed Forces Movement (RAM) 173, 176, 177
Republicans 22, 27, 130, 131, 132, 137
Republican National Committee (RNC) 105
Richards, Richard 105
Richardson, John 107, 154, 165
'regimented democracy' 21, 31
'ringed autonomy' 14, 87
Robinson, William 4
Rockefeller Foundation 22
rollback 88, 89, 109–10
Rostow, Walt 15, 19
Rusk, Dean 19
Russia 195
Ryan David 2

Samuels, Michael 41, 64, 80, 81, 82, 83, 85, 88, 128, 129, 130, 135, 163, 168, 170, 172; government positions 30; pre-emptive democracy promotion in allied dictatorships 30–2; 'Promoting Democracy' article 56–60
Sakharov, Andrei 166
Sakharov Institute 165–6
sanctions 73–4, 109
Sandinistas 29, 30, 52, 56, 103, 112; *see also* FSLN
School for Democracy 116
Schmitz, David 2
Schuette, Keith B. 131, 154
Serbia 195
Shah of Iran 50
Shanker, Albert 131
Shultz 100, 108, 111, 119, 176
Senate 121, 145, 159, 173
Senate Foreign Relations Committee 54, 118, 121, 171
Service d'Action Civique 157
Sigur, Gaston 169
Sinyavsky, Andrei 166
Social Democratic Party (West Germany) 43
Social Democrats USA 157
Socialist Democratic Party (PSD) 163
Solidarity 76, 77, 114, 135, 188, 190, 192; AFL-CIO early support 48; martial law 71; NED funding 167; Reagan 91, 102, 108; rise 47–8
Solarz, Stephen 119, 169, 171
Somoza, Anastasio 29, 30, 50, 52; *see also* Somoza dictatorship; Somoza regime

218 *Index*

Somoza dictatorship 29, 174; *see also* Somoza, Anastasio; Somoza regime
Somoza regime 29, 52, 169, 172; *see also* Somoza, Anastasio; Somoza dictatorship
South Africa 103, 114
South Korea 119
Soviet bloc 25, 51, 61, 62, 65, 71, 72, 78, 79, 82, 85, 89, 91, 92, 93, 102, 104, 112, 114, 135, 160, 179; containment 11; Human Rights 62, 76; NED 165–8; US democratic propaganda 12, 47; *see also* Eastern Europe; Soviet Empire; Soviet Union; USSR
Soviet communism 6, 7, 98, 122, 160
Soviet Empire 89, 91, 100, 161, 165, 188; US democracy promotion strategy 107–11; *see also* Eastern Europe; Soviet bloc; Soviet Union; USSR
Soviet Union 15, 24, 33, 46, 47, 62, 65, 71, 79, 86, 88, 109, 111, 117, 191; US democratic crusade against 91; NED 165–7; *see also* Soviet bloc; Soviet Empire; USSR
Special Planning Group (SPG) 100, 116, 117, 120, 195
Smith, Tony 1–2, 3
State Department 44, 53, 56, 60, 63, 65, 71, 79, 87, 89, 93, 100, 102, 103, 104, 105, 106, 108, 110, 114, 115, 136, 140, 141, 153, 156, 159, 161, 163, 165, 188, 193, 194; APF 81, 82–4; clash with Reaganites over democracy promotion 85–6; conflict over Human Rights 25; 'de-centred' Cold War strategy 40, 45, 46–7; El Salvador 54–5; International Political Committee 117; NSDD 32, 90; Philippines 169, 171, 173, 174, 176, 177; Project Democracy 116; Westminster Address 90, 92
state–private network 5, 10, 26, 31, 57, 101, 113, 121, 122, 128, 139–40, 145, 146, 189; comparison with proposed democracy promotion organisation 59; components and strategic functions 12–13; decline 17–18; tensions with state 13–14
Stearman, William 87
Subic Bay 168, 171, 177

Taffet, Jeffrey 20
Taiwan 119
Third Force 29–30, 173

Third World 4, 6, 10, 12, 19, 24, 33, 49, 61, 65, 71, 80, 85, 89, 90, 91, 100, 102, 104, 107, 114, 118, 135, 140, 145, 191; initial blueprint for democracy promotion in 20–2; projected democracy promotion campaign 56–60; US policy towards 14–17; wave of revolutions 1970s 23, 29
Title IX of the Foreign Assistance Act 26
Torrijos, Omar 155
Trade Union Congress of the Philippines (TUCP) 170, 172, 175, 177, 192
Truman administration 12
Truman, Harry S. 1, 137
Tsongas, Paul 119

UK 154, 155, 160; *see also* Britain
Ukraine 195
Union of the Center (Guatemala) 163
United Fruit 58
Urengoi gas pipeline 73
USIA 100, 118, 120, 140, 141, 144, 156, 157, 160; conflict with NED 152–4; Fund for Democracy 115; Human Rights 62; International Political Committee 117; Project Democracy 116; Project Truth 43–4
USICA 28, 32
USSR 11, 24, 43, 44, 46, 47, 62, 63, 76, 77, 82, 86, 88, 92, 98, 107, 108, 109, 110, 111, 117, 143, 145, 165, 166, 167, 188; *see also* Soviet Union

Vandenburg, Arthur 137
Venezuela 103, 104, 195
Vietnam 16, 18, 19, 21, 23, 145, 169
Vietnam, South 58, 173
Vietnam War 4, 17, 53, 145
Voice of America (VOA) 47, 107

Walesa, Lech 71
Warsaw Pact 12, 48
Weinberger, Caspar 40, 73, 74, 75, 100, 171, 174, 176
Weinstein, Allen 130, 131, 136, 152, 153, 157
West German Party Foundations 26, 27, 59, 83, 99, 100, 101, 133
Western Europe 10, 62, 65, 73, 79, 100, 102, 104, 112, 117, 118, 135, 139, 156, 157, 160–1; US policy towards 41–5; US secondary sanctions 74–5
Westminster Address 84, 91–2

WFTU 135
White House 32, 105, 106, 115
Wick, Charles Z. 43–4, 47, 100, 116, 120–1
Williams, William Appleman 2

Wilson, Woodrow 1
Wolfowitz, Paul 169, 171, 173, 174, 175, 177

Zablocki, Clement 143

eBooks
from Taylor & Francis
Helping you to choose the right eBooks for your Library

Add to your library's digital collection today with Taylor & Francis eBooks. We have over 50,000 eBooks in the Humanities, Social Sciences, Behavioural Sciences, Built Environment and Law, from leading imprints, including Routledge, Focal Press and Psychology Press.

Choose from a range of subject packages or create your own!

Benefits for you
- Free MARC records
- COUNTER-compliant usage statistics
- Flexible purchase and pricing options
- All titles DRM-free.

Benefits for your user
- Off-site, anytime access via Athens or referring URL
- Print or copy pages or chapters
- Full content search
- Bookmark, highlight and annotate text
- Access to thousands of pages of quality research at the click of a button.

Free Trials Available
We offer free trials to qualifying academic, corporate and government customers.

eCollections
Choose from over 30 subject eCollections, including:

Archaeology	Language Learning
Architecture	Law
Asian Studies	Literature
Business & Management	Media & Communication
Classical Studies	Middle East Studies
Construction	Music
Creative & Media Arts	Philosophy
Criminology & Criminal Justice	Planning
Economics	Politics
Education	Psychology & Mental Health
Energy	Religion
Engineering	Security
English Language & Linguistics	Social Work
Environment & Sustainability	Sociology
Geography	Sport
Health Studies	Theatre & Performance
History	Tourism, Hospitality & Events

For more information, pricing enquiries or to order a free trial, please contact your local sales team: www.tandfebooks.com/page/sales

www.tandfebooks.com